Advance Acclaim for

Sexual Dilemmas for the Helping Professional

Revised and Expanded Edition

"From its witty opening—a hypothetical scenario set on two shark-surrounded desert islands—to its culmination in a crisp, pithy summary of the entire book in the form of concrete guidelines for practice, this monograph is a clinical and didactic triumph. It covers an astonishingly broad range of situations and settings with clinical focus and practicality, with candor and directness, and with a fine and refreshing even-handedness in illuminating the psychology of *both* client and professional. Filled with keenly observed clinical vignettes, unusually frank self-revelations, and case examples both poignant and ironic, this book is a gold mine of straightforward advice and vital coping strategies."

—THOMAS G. GUTHEIL, M.D.
Co-Director, Program in Psychiatry and the Law
Massachusetts Mental Health Center
Harvard Medical School
Boston, Massachusetts

"The stature of this pioneering work continues to grow. Synthesizing the perspectives of a seasoned clinician and a veteran social critic, *Sexual Dilemmas* delivers an indispensible overview to both the layperson and the professional. It also fills a longstanding gap in the education of professionals by providing reflection and insight on a crucial moral problem within the professions. A must for the individual and institutional bookshelf."

—PATRICIA M.L. ILLINGWORTH PH.D.
Departments of Philosophy and Medicine
Center for Medicine, Ethics and the Law
McGill University, Montreal

Liberal Arts Fellow in Law and Philosophy
Harvard Law School
Cambridge, Massachusetts

Broad Acclaim for the First Edition

"This is an extraordinary book—well-balanced, fair, informative, well-written and thoughtful. Some will find it provocative and some will take issue with one point or another but it is a book that every therapist, professional and para-professional, and every client or patient should read."—Carol Nadelson, M.D., *Department of Psychiatry, Tufts University School of Medicine, Boston; Past President, American Psychiatric Association*

"A serious and comprehensive analysis of the issues involved in therapists' seducing (and being seduced by) their clients sexually and emotionally. Important and valuable reading for anyone concerned with therapeutic relationships."—Albert Ellis, Ph.D., *President, Institute for Rational-Emotive Therapy, New York*

". . . an impressive volume combining reportage from a wide range of human service occupations . . . Case material of the richest sort extending over the widest field of mental health activity is liberally cited. It is all highly readable and the case selections have been made with precision and thought. . . . a readable and extremely well-organized set of problem-solving exercises . . . It would be difficult to imagine a member of any helping profession for whom this book would be inapplicable. . . . one of those unusual books that can be read not only by trainees and therapists of the widest variety but also with profit by clients and patients."—*SIECUS Report*

". . . a very readable (clear, live, impelling) book. . . . This book should be assigned and discussed early in training programs; it should be readily visible and available in any agency; it should be read carefully by program heads; it should be kept close at hand. This is a rare book: You can read it fast; it is entertaining; it avoids jargon and clears away the cobwebs. It gives the reader what I would call the '3 big W's'—it tells you *what* the problem is, *why* it is, and *what* to do about it."—*American Journal of Family Therapy*

". . . [since] many professionals are still ambivalent about discussing the problem openly, the frank forum given by the authors is appreciated. This book would be equally useful to give to clients who feel they have been sexually exploited by mental health professionals in the past and have difficulty talking about it or knowing what to do legally. . . . It is more than just an intellectual understanding of countertransference. It is a real gut-level issue involving the therapist as a real person with real feelings separate and apart from his or her traditional role. *Sexual Dilemmas* presents us with viable alternatives for dealing more effectively when such an impasse surfaces in our work."—*Psychotherapy Newsletter*

"This book belongs in every agency's library. . . . an honest look at issues which are almost always present but seldom openly addressed in helping institutions. . . . The authors establish clearly written guidelines throughout the book. . . . any helping professional considering a personal relationship with a client or co-worker should read this book."—*Journal of Nervous and Mental Disease*

". . . makes for easy reading by both clinicians and clients. It can also be readily used as a reference tool and would be a good adjunct to a Professional Development course in University training programs. . . . raises many valid points regarding the lack of training and exposure to ethics of many paraprofessionals and professionals."—*Journal of Psychotherapy in Private Practice*

". . . This is a very readable book and is of relevance to anyone concerned with therapeutic relationships. The major importance of this book is that it focuses on an important area which is often denied or ignored. . . . a stimulating and valuable book worth reading."—*Behavioral Psychotherapy*

". . . helps fill the gap between the 'should' and reality. . . . For one's patients or clients or students, for one's colleagues, for oneself, this book is a must in the helping professions."—*International Social Science Review*

". . . This is a book that should be in all our libraries. . . . For the sake of one's clients, one's peers, one's self, read this book!"—*Journal of Nurse-Midwifery*

"A sensitive consideration of sexual issues likely to confront mental health professionals. . . . There is much wisdom in this book, but perhaps its main value is that it gives word to often undiscussed but obviously significant matters."—*Journal of Family Therapy*

". . . both timely and much needed. . . . a valuable resource for all engaged in therapy and helping others."—*Psychiatric Journal of the University of Ottawa*

". . . the issues raised by this book are germane to all helpers, including family therapists. . . . they have performed a valuable service in an interesting manner."—*Journal of Marital and Family Therapy*

". . . a good orientation for untrained or psychologically naive helping professionals. . . . It will also be useful for teachers and others with quasiparental or authoritarian roles vis-a-vis persons with whom they work."—*International Journal of Group Psychotherapy*

". . . The writing style makes for easy reading; the points made are readily comprehended and are associated with circumstances falling within the experience of most counselors."—*Religious Humanism*

". . . a pioneering book. . . . a useful addition to the literature, especially for the training of counselors and paraprofessionals."—*Contemporary Psychiatry*

Sexual Dilemmas for the Helping Professional

Revised and Expanded Edition

Jerry Edelwich, M.S.W. and Archie Brodsky

BRUNNER/MAZEL, Publishers • New York

For information concerning workshops on sexual dilemmas for the helping professional, please contact:

Jerry Edelwich, M.S.W.
61 Sunny Slope Dr.
Middletown, CT 06457
203-347-3836

Library of Congress Cataloging-in-Publication Data

Edelwich, Jerry.
    Sexual dilemmas for the helping professional / Jerry Edelwich and
Archie Brodsky.—Rev. and expanded ed.
        p.   cm.
    Includes bibliographical references and index.
    ISBN 0-87630-627-X (pbk.)—ISBN 0-87630-628-8
    1. Psychotherapists—Sexual behavior.   2. Psychotherapy   patients—
Sexual behavior.   3.Psychotherapist and patient.   I. Brodsky,
Archie.   II. Title.
    [DNLM: 1. Ethics, Professional.   2. Professional-Patient
Relations.   3. Psychotherapy—standards.   4. Sex Behavior.
5. Transfer (Psychology)   WM 62 E21s]
RC480.8.E3 1991
616.89′14—dc20
DNLM/DLC
for Library of Congress   90-15154
                                                                        CIP

The following publishers have generously given permission to use extended quotations from copyrighted works:

Selections from Gutheil, T.G. (1989). Patient-therapist sexual relations, 6(3),4-6. Reprinted with permission from the *Howard Mental Health Letter*, 74 Fenwood Road, Boston, MA 02115.

Selections from Marmor, J. (1972). Sexual acting-out in psychotherapy, 32(1), 3-8. Reprinted with permission from the *American Journal of Psychoanalysis* published by the Association for the Advancement of Psychoanalysis, Inc., 329 East 62nd Street, New York, NY 10021.

Selections from Dahlberg, C.C. (1970). Sexual contact between patient and therapist, 6, 107-124. Reprinted with permission from *Contemporary Psychoanalysis*, 20 West 74th Street, New York, NY 10023.

Published by
BRUNNER/MAZEL, INC.
19 Union Square
New York, New York 10003

MANUFACTURED IN THE UNITED STATES OF AMERICA

Designed by Tere LoPrete

10   9   8   7   6   5   4   3   2   1

For Diana

Contents

Acknowledgments

As we prepare this new edition for press, our sense of continuing indebtedness to those who made the first edition possible is matched only by our gratitude to new and vital contributors. Even as this book has evolved, the influence of Diana Preice, Harold J. Bursztajn, and Lee M. Silverstein remains central. At the same time, our work has been enriched immeasurably by our association with the Program in Psychiatry and the Law, Massachusetts Mental Health Center (Harvard Medical School), codirected by Thomas G. Gutheil and Harold J. Bursztajn. Building upon the legal insights and documentation provided for the first edition by Paul E. Mason, the Program's weekly discussions have exposed us to thoughtful contemporary viewpoints on the clinical, experiential, forensic, and policy dimensions of our chosen theme. Numerous individuals have contributed to this rare creative interchange through their thinking, writing, and research. Among these, we are especially indebted to Thomas G. Gutheil, Larry H. Strasburger, Linda M. Jorgenson, Shannon T. Woolley, Patricia M. L. Illingworth, and Michael L. Commons.

As before, we are pleased to acknowledge the assistance of Stanley Bailis, Geraldine Battistolli, Al Brown, Mallory Crawford, Jean DeFlorio, Donna Dewan, John Elliott, Cheryl Ford, Gail Fuller, Charles Harris, Diane Kiczuk, Joy Kosta, Vivian Kotler, Carolyn LaMarre, Kathy Lieberman, Neil Luberoff, Peg McGuire, Hank Mandell, Stephen Merriman, Amy Meterparel, Shelley Meyers, Steve Mogel, Carol Nadelson, Nelen Noel, Anne Olmstead, Dot Pansius, Donald Pet, Linda Roberts, Ruth Rogers, Stanley Sagov, Mary Ann Scippa, Ed Soter, Joanne Sullivan, Beth Van Gordon, Joanne White,

Dale Wriggins, and Anna Zaremba. A constant source of support has been David Powell of ETP, Inc., Windsor, Connecticut. Thomas Quinn volunteered his thoughts and practical help at a pivotal moment. Our thanks also to Barbara Sanderson of the Minnesota Task Force on Sexual Exploitation by Counselors and Therapists and Gary Schoener of the Walk-In Counseling Center in Minneapolis for the spirit of openness and sharing in which they have conducted their pioneering work.

We extend our appreciation as well to the many people around the country whom we interviewed, clinician and client alike, for their willingness to speak of their experiences in such a sensitive area. Although they must, of course, remain anonymous, those who learn from their testimony will remain indebted to them.

Finally, anyone who finds this book useful will have benefited, as we have, from the confidence that our editors, Susan Barrows (first edition) and Natalie Gilman (second edition), have shown in our work.

J.E.
A.B.

Introduction

In 1880 Dr. Josef Breuer, a Viennese physician and a mentor and colleague of Freud, began treating a young woman identified as Anna O., who exhibited many symptoms of hysteria. The "talking cure," aided by hypnosis which Breuer (1966) and Anna developed, was the beginning of modern psychotherapy. But although the two-year course of treatment was successful for the patient, it was calamitous for the doctor. According to Freud's recollection, Breuer was so interested in the case that his wife became jealous. Since the patient was by then almost fully recovered, Breuer terminated the treatment. Anna reacted by going through an hysterical childbirth, the culmination of a false pregnancy aroused by this unusually close (though entirely proper) doctor-patient relationship. The shocked Breuer, after seeing his patient through this last crisis, hastily left for a vacation with his wife. It was not long before he abandoned the exploration of the unconscious which Freud was to carry on (Jones, 1953).

Breuer is not the only person who has given up the therapeutic endeavor because of an inability to deal with the sexual dynamics that complicate the relationship between therapist and client. Psychologists, psychiatrists, physicians, social workers, teachers, prison personnel, counselors in fields such as substance abuse and child and family services—anyone who ministers to the needs of others is bound to have unsettling experiences with emotional currents that run outside the bounds of professional propriety. These crosscurrents arise from normal, universal human feelings. Nonetheless, if not properly dealt with, they can have such consequences as:

- diversion of time and energy from the professional relationship to the fulfillment of personal needs and desires;
- loss of therapeutic effectiveness and of therapeutic benefits for the client;
- self-doubt, frustration, and reduced job satisfaction for the therapist;
- potentially damaging experiences for the client, ranging from "double messages" to overt exploitation;
- personally or professionally compromising situations for the therapist, resulting in some cases in loss of job, livelihood, and career; civil liability; and/or criminal prosecution;
- additional civil liability for supervisors, consultants, and employing agencies.

From our interviews with people in a wide range of human service occupations and settings (including private practice, state-run facilities, universities, and military installations), it is apparent that most professional and paraprofessional training programs do not adequately prepare students to cope with these issues. It is not surprising that this is true for, say, psychiatric technicians, alcoholism and drug addiction counselors with "street credentials" only, social workers who come into the field with bachelor's degrees in academic subjects, or teachers whose professional training focuses on areas other than the teacher-student relationship. What is surprising is that the uncertainties expressed by these individuals without formal training are echoed by those who have graduate degrees in social work, psychology, or psychiatry. Even psychoanalysts, whose extensive training focuses explicitly on the questions of therapeutic transference and countertransference, do not always find it easy to keep personal feelings out of their professional relationships (Malcolm, 1980a, 1980b).

These issues were brought out into the open by Pope, Keith-Spiegel, and Tabachnick's (1986) survey of 585 psychologists in clinical practice. Among these therapists 87 percent (95 percent of the men, 76 percent of the women) had at times felt sexually attracted to clients, and 63 percent felt guilty, anxious, or confused about the attraction. About half said that their training had left them entirely without guidance in this area, while only 9 percent considered their training or supervision adequate to this challenge. The researchers concluded that "attraction to clients is a prevalent experience among both male and female psychologists. Our data suggest that this widespread phenomenon is one for which graduate training programs and clinical internships leave psychologists almost entirely unprepared" (Pope et al., 1986, p. 155). The same inattention to sexual countertransference feelings during training and supervision has been noted in psychiatry as well (Gartrell, Herman, Olarte, Feldstein, & Localio, 1986; Rieker & Carmen, 1983) and for female psychiatrists and psychologists (Woolley, 1988).

According to our interviewees, some training programs deal with clients' sexual problems, but not with sexual feelings and attitudes on the part of the therapist and the effects these have on treatment. Although trainees may be advised about the impropriety of sexual relationships with clients, they still may not be prepared for the pervasiveness and subtlety of sexual interchanges between therapist and client. Even when a program does attempt to address the issue in all its complexity, the difficulty of communicating about this sensitive subject tends to make the instruction seem abstract and didactic. There is a difference between hearing about seduction in the classroom and being on the receiving end of a series of suggestive gestures and remarks.

The consequences of a repressive, punitive attitude toward normal personal feelings can be disastrous. As Pope et al. (1986, p. 155) caution, "If training programs, by their behavior and example, suggest that the issue of attraction is to be shunned and that feelings of attraction are to be treated as dangerous and antitherapeutic, it is not surprising that individual psychologists tend to experience feelings of attraction with wary suspicion and unsettling discomfort." At the very least, those feelings will not be available as useful barometers for therapeutic exploration. At worst, there is the risk that unexamined feelings may be acted out. In between are a range of avoidance maneuvers therapists use in response to discomfort and fear of punishment (internal or external). Too many therapists take the easier course of "dumping" a client rather than work through disruptive feelings for the benefit of both client and therapist. In contrast, a supportive educational approach trains the therapist to continue therapy rather than break it off.

A social worker recalls his first years on the job:

What I had been taught had little meaning for me as a practicing professional. I had no way to interpret my feelings or guide my behavior. If I felt attracted to a woman client, I would feel guilty, as if there were something wrong with me. And I had no guidelines about when it was appropriate to act on such feelings.

A similar story is told by a psychiatrist in private practice:

> When I began practicing I was aware of my sexual feelings toward patients, but I was not comfortable with them. Although I knew that I wasn't in any danger of acting out these fantasies, I was uneasy at the thought that the patient might become aware of them. I thought I had to guard them, hide them, even if the patient brought up the subject. The only way I was able to learn to share my feelings with patients (when appropriate) was by first sharing them with supervisors.

These individuals overcame their uncertainty and discomfort through experience—some of it supervised experience, some of it simply the accumulation of "hard knocks" on the job. The purpose of this book is to make the learning process quicker, less painful, and more effective by providing a focus for both self-exploration and supervisory intervention. The book is intended to help practicing professionals and trainees, as well as teachers, trainers, supervisors, and administrators bring the issues out into the open and develop appropriate guidelines.

* * *

Whenever two people come into proximity with each other, a greater or lesser degree of sexual energy is generated. As with electromagnetism (a commonly used metaphor for sexuality), the energy may be positive or negative, a matter of attraction or repulsion. It is stronger in some instances than in others, but it is always there. People choose, however, to express it in different ways.

This universal sexual energy is especially apparent in the intimacy of the therapeutic session. In psychoanalytic theory, the sexual feelings that arise in the course of therapy are thought of in terms of *transference* (whereby the patient reacts to the therapist as a surrogate for "significant others" in his or her life) and *countertransference* (whereby the therapist reacts to the patient on the basis of similar associations). Any emotion (including anger or resentment as well as sexual desire) can be transferred from past life situations to the present therapeutic situation. Thus, the entire range of feelings that a therapist and patient can have about each other can be understood as examples of transference.

That is not, however, the only way in which they can be understood. Even among psychoanalysts there is disagreement about what constitutes transference and how pervasive it is (Malcolm, 1980a, 1980b). Some analysts treat everything that happens between analyst and patient as a form of transference. Others insist that the analyst and patient are also two human beings who necessarily have an extra-analytic personal relationship at the same time as they are engaged in the analytic procedure. Indeed, one does not have to resort to the concept of transference to explain the attractions and repulsions that occur in a therapeutic relationship. Nor need one rely on the notion of misuse of transference to hold that acting on such an attraction is unethical and legally actionable as a form of malpractice. As we will show in Chapter 10, this breach of fiduciary responsibility can be understood in more general terms, applicable to those (e.g., behavior therapists) whose theoretical orientation does not encompass transference and countertransference.

Therapy is a place where great hopes are raised—and sometimes dashed. It is a place where people may be thrilled or very disappointed with each other. The atmosphere of therapy lends itself to intense feelings, both good and bad. Here are two people who meet repeatedly, in some cases frequently, to discuss things that people usually talk about only with their most trusted intimates (if at all). They are alone together and may sit close to each other. One of them, the client or patient, tends to be in an emotionally vulnerable position, expressing needs for closeness, caring, nurturance, and love which may be experienced as indistinguishable from sexual desire. Sometimes the therapist also is vulnerable, with unresolved personal problems and discontents that spill over (consciously or otherwise) into the professional hour. Over a period of time these two people develop a dialogue, an intimacy, in which help and support are sought and given. Outside of therapy this kind of intimacy often is associated with sexual intimacy; it is not surprising, then, that people make the same association in therapy. Nonetheless, to act on this association is inappropriate, usually damaging, and always unethical on the part of the therapist.

This book was written primarily for the vast majority of helping professionals who practice therapies in which transference, while sometimes acknowledged, is not deliberately explored. We have chosen not to get involved in theoretical controversies about the origin of sexual and other disruptive personal feelings in client-therapist relationships. Rather, we take the sexual energy between client and counselor to be a "given." Our focus is on how the various manifestations of this energy can be recognized, what kinds of issues it can produce, and what can be done about these when they arise. In the chapters that follow, five major dimensions of sexuality are explored as they affect both counselor and client:

- seduction
- power
- opportunity
- self-interest
- morality

Case studies and narrative accounts illustrate the dynamics by which these themes play themselves out—the overtures, reactions, denials, hidden agendas, and limit-testing that take place in both obvious and subtle ways beneath the surface of the therapeutic exchange.

Like our previous volume, *Burnout: Stages of Disillusionment in the Helping Professions* (Edelwich with Brodsky, 1980), this book offers practical guidance for dealing with problems that might otherwise compromise services to clients. Readers of *Burnout* will be familiar with the approach taken here: to legitimize what are often uncomfortable feelings by reporting the experiences of people who have had similar feelings; to define professional standards and ethics in the relevant areas; and to demonstrate problem-solving techniques. As a helping professional, one will hear things, see things, and feel things that one may never before have heard, seen, or felt. One will be subjected to unanticipated pressures from clients, from fellow staff members, and from within oneself. How does one cope? As with the career crises that constitute job burnout, dealing successfully with the problems presented by one's own sexuality and that of clients involves coming to terms with the disparity between what one expects and what actually happens. Such professional growth is an ongoing process rather than an achieved state. It is a form of on-the-job training that never ends.

There is one way in which our present investigation differed from its predecessor, at least at the outset. With the topic of burnout, we had no difficulty finding interviewees. Anyone and everyone volunteered to vent their disappointments, discontents, and grievances. People wore the designation "burned out" like a badge. When it came to sexuality, however, we found many professionals understandably reluctant to talk about their feelings and experiences, although there were many willing interviewees and a few eager ones who used the interviews therapeutically to reevaluate their handling of past situations. On occasion, the mere mention of the subject brought forth skeptical questions: "Isn't this all just transference?" "Doesn't everybody already know this?" Wouldn't anybody who works with people have been trained to deal with these questions?" (*Should* they have been trained? Yes. *Have* they been trained? No.) These were signs, we believed, that the issues we were exploring were unusually sensitive ones that very much needed to be opened up for discussion.

A decade later, much has changed. The issues are still sensitive ones that trigger feelings of awkwardness and embarrassment, but nearly everyone working in the field knows they cannot be taken for granted. They are professional issues of great weight and immediacy. Faced with the specter of ethics reviews, malpractice litigation, loss of license to practice, and (in some states) criminal prosecution, clinicians know that their reputations, careers, and livelihoods are on the line. Therapists are seeking consultation (as they should) about the slightest hint of a boundary violation, as in these examples:

- "I never saw Ms. A in my office before I started dating her. I met her socially in the first place, and when she asked about going into therapy, I gave her the name of a colleague. Did I do anything wrong? Could she sue me if we break up?"
- "I've gotten several letters from a patient I terminated with several years ago, saying she feels emotionally attached to me and wants to see me again. I replied that I wouldn't reopen therapy, but she keeps writing. Should I return her letters unopened or keep them on file? Should I send her a registered letter or agree to speak with her once on the phone?"

Some have reason to tremble about indiscretions of 20 years ago. Even those who never committed a breach of ethics are worried, as illustrated by this comment by a male psychologist in private practice:

"Hey, I'm 40, never married, politically on the left. I dress informally and have some background in holistic therapies. I'd be a prime candidate to be set up on a charge like that. I have to be extra careful. I couldn't do touch therapies if I wanted to! And I'm glad my office is in a busy part of town, with a waiting room full of other people's patients and a secretary always on duty."

As he speaks he holds out a patient record form with a box labeled (in red letters) "Sex assault allegation precautions." Among other questions, the therapist is asked to note whether the window shades were open and the office door left ajar during the patient's session. "That's how far it's gone," the psychologist says.

With an undetermined number of psychotherapists engaging in sex with clients and an undetermined number of others at risk for being falsely accused of such misconduct, therapists face a real "occupational hazard" (Nelson, 1982, p. C3) for which systematic training is needed. Furthermore, supervisors are being made aware that liability travels up the line of authority, and agency administrators know that the viability of an agency may depend on how adequately the sexual dynamics between clients and clinicians are monitored. Thus, anyone who sees clients in a clinical capacity, anyone who has clinicians working under his or her authority or supervision, anyone responsible for the management of a human services organization needs to have a working mastery of the issues discussed in the following chapters.

* * *

The features of the therapy situation that make it all the more natural to feel intense personal emotions ranging from desire to disgust also make it all the more dangerous—as a rule, prohibitively dangerous—to act upon such feelings. Thus, anyone who works with others in a helping capacity needs to be able to distinguish between normal human feelings and unethical acts. This is true both for feelings of attraction, which may lead to favoritism and failure to confront of (if denied) punitive treatment, and for feelings of dislike or discomfort, which may lead to "benign neglect" or directly prejudicial treatment. In both cases the feeling may be spontaneous, but the act is a choice.

In order to make responsible choices, the helping professional also needs to distinguish clearly between the role of a client and the role of a professional. Some clients can be expected to act deceptively, seductively, or destructively because they have not yet learned how to satisfy their needs through responsible action. To allow one's own behavior to be influenced by emotional reactions to the client's behavior is to make the client's problems one's own and thereby to make one's own problem the client's problem. Those who earn their living as teachers, guides, and models for those in distress have a higher standard of behavior to live up to, regardless of how provocative a client may be. As a psychiatrist told her colleagues at a conference, "It is no more reasonable for the therapist to respond sexually to the seductive behavior than to join a violent patient in smashing windows" (Nelson, 1982, p. C3). Still, if it were always easy to live up to that standard, this book would not be necessary. Although therapists and counselors are assumed to have learned the lessons of responsible and efficacious behavior that they seek to teach their clients, a given individual on a given day may not feel as though that were the case. Helping professionals are also human beings, and human beings do not always feel as strong as they do at their best moments. That is why guidelines are useful.

On the question of sexual relations between client and therapist, the guidelines are clear. Although some doctors have been sleeping with their patients since the days of Hippocrates (and some teachers with their students since the days of Socrates), a consensus has developed within the helping professions (and the courts) that there is no place for sex or other forms of personal intimacy in a professional helping relationship with a vulnerable person. Notwithstanding attempts to justify the practice by evaluating its consequences on a case-by-case basis (Shepard, 1971), it is evident to most practitioners that the emotional security, consistent availability, constructive involvement, and caring "neutrality" offered by the therapeutic relationship are incompatible with, and compromised by, intimate equality and mutual revelation. Yet to answer this question is to raise a number of others. Do the ethical standards by which physicians, psychotherapists, and schoolteachers are bound apply to university professors as well? To trainers and supervisors of clinicians? To other service professionals? Where does the barrier to client-therapist intimacy begin? (That is, what levels of communication and contact are appropriate, and what levels are not?) When does it end? (That is, what restraints on client-therapist contact are called for even after termination of therapy?)

Even a therapist who would never think of having sexual relations with a patient will routinely face challenges and dilemmas of a sexual nature on the job. What does one do if one is attracted to a client? How does one respond to flirtation on the part of a client? To implicit sexual overtures? To explicit offers? What are some of the ways in which one may unintentionally compromise one's relationship with a client by giving "double messages" that encourage the client to seek further intimacy? Is it appropriate to accept an invitation to have lunch with a client? What about dinner? What limits on self-disclosure should one observe when speaking with a client? When is it appropriate to share with a client one's perception of disruptive sexual undercurrents in the therapeutic relationship?

Finally, when is a client no longer a client? Whereas sexual relationships with *current* clients are recognized to be professionally taboo, there is just beginning to be a consensus with regard to *former* clients. Is it a good idea for two people who at one time were client and therapist to become boyfriend and girlfriend? Husband and wife? Is such a shift in roles permissible if preceded by a specified waiting period? Or if it occurs only after the client is reestablished in therapy with another practitioner? Is it appropriate for a therapist and client to terminate therapy so that they can "legitimately" begin a love affair? Most of the people interviewed for this book believe that the issue can be negotiated—that is, that romantic involvements with ex-clients can be justified if one or more of the above criteria are met. We take a different position, one that is supported by a growing number of professional organizations. While recognizing occasional legitimate exceptions and the need to exercise individual judgment in such instances, we believe that for a helping professional to have an intimate personal relationship with a former client not only is unwise, but raises many of the same ethical and legal questions as a liaison with a client currently in therapy.

A therapist who feels an attraction to a client will commonly refer that person to a colleague or to another agency. Usually the therapist does this with the intention not of having a love affair with the client, but of never seeing the client again. In this way (so the reasoning goes), the therapist will not be subject to temptation, and the client will have the benefit of a more "objective" therapist. Therapists even more frequently "refer out" clients whom they dislike or feel they cannot help. The aversion may stem from a "personality clash," a prejudice against a certain category of client (based, for example, on the kind of crime that client may have committed), or a sense of frustration at being unable to treat a certain category of client successfully. An alcoholism specialist may refer a client out when family conflicts emerge as a major issue; a family therapist may do the same in the case of alcoholism. Many therapists refuse as a matter of principle to work with child molesters, wife beaters, or rapists. Some counselors are uncomfortable with homosexuals, some with aggressive men or seductive women, some with people who are inarticulate or who dress in a particular way. And there are some who readily accept a client's insistence that he or she can be helped only by someone of the same sex or race.

Professional training programs typically endorse the practice of making referrals on any of the above grounds. Again we offer a dissenting view. We question whether this practice is really in the interest of the client, the counselor, or the agency. We believe it to be better for all concerned if, wherever possible, one seeks peer or supervisory support in resolving one's own discomfort so as to be able to address the problems of the client. By raising this question we hope to help counselors and their clinical supervisors confront whatever obstacles threaten to sidetrack the counseling relationship.

Other sexual dynamics of concern to helping professionals are those occurring among staff members, such as intra-agency love affairs, gender-based discrimination, and sexual harassment. These "facts of life" are not, of course, confined to the helping professions; they are present wherever people work together. Nevertheless, human services personnel tend to be exposed to an especially intense sexual atmosphere on the job. Stressful working conditions, with staff members spending long hours together at close quarters (sometimes in residential facilities), can contribute to this highly charged atmosphere. The open expression of emotion in therapy sessions, team meetings, and client-staff therapy groups accentuates the vulnerability of staff members to unsolicited approaches and unanticipated feelings of intimacy. In the fishbowl environment of many agencies, client reactions to visible liaisons between staff members may have consequences, therapeutic or personal, for all concerned. Moreover, the staffing patterns of some agencies (where, for example, a male director may lack the educational credentials of some of his female subordinates) create recognizable, even stereotypical sexual interchanges.

Here the issue is not so much one of ethics as of learning to cope with the pressures. No job description or orientation session will prepare a professional woman to cope with having her therapeutic judgments repeatedly challenged or dismissed by a male colleague whose advances she has rejected. How can she tell if the man's behavior represents deliberate retaliation, a defensive reaction to what for him is a painful rebuke, or honestly reasoned professional criticism? Such personal conflicts take on an ethical dimension when they cloud clinical judgment and compromise services to clients. Another ethical dimension comes into play when overt or covert harassment is involved. In the human services as in other fields of employment, women (and, in certain circumstances, men) can expect to be faced with sexually coercive behavior.

Guidelines for dealing with these various sexual dilemmas are developed throughout the book and summarized in the final chapter. To some readers these guidelines, particularly those concerning relationships with ex-clients and routine referrals of disagreeable clients, may seem overly restrictive. Therapists who are accustomed to evaluating any situation in terms of individual psychodynamics may contend that the level of generality at which we address these questions represents an oversimplification of complex questions. Our experience has shown, however, that people working in public and private agencies who face a diverse case load under difficult conditions, often without adequate training or supervision, need some degree of generality, simplicity, and clarity. All of us need some practical and ethical benchmarks for coping with the daily challenges of working with people. Moreover, the viewpoint expressed in this book derives not from psychoanalytic theory, with its emphasis on past determinants of present behavior, but from Reality Therapy (Glasser, 1965) and Rational-Emotive Therapy (Ellis & Harper, 1975). We do not believe there are therapists and clients who are doomed to have personality conflicts or are fated to fall in love. Every act represents a choice, and part of a helping professional's mandate is to transcend personal feelings when making choices that affect a client's well-being.

Still, some of the things said in this book will be controversial, and rightly so. The fact that everyone has the capacity and the responsibility to choose does not mean there is one correct choice for everyone. The prescriptions and proscriptions in these pages are intended to stimulate discussion, not to suppress thought. Out of all the many contexts in which helping professionals work, out of all the cases a therapist comes across in a working lifetime, there will be some to which these guidelines do not apply. And there will be practitioners who, for sound reasons, will take a different point of view on some of the issues covered here. At the same time, personal choices increasingly are being constrained by regulations and laws that do not recognize individual differences.

* * *

Since the first edition of *Sexual Dilemmas for the Helping Professional* was published in 1982, the contours of the subject covered by the book have enlarged significantly. A growing public and professional consciousness of sexual abuses in therapy has been manifested in numerous ways. Civil litigation and complaints to professional regulatory boards have become commonplace. Individuals seeking release from traumatic memories have brought charges against therapists for offenses committed a decade or two earlier, in some cases seeking an extension of the statute of limitations governing malpractice liability. The various helping professions have written into their codes of ethics a proscription against sexual contact with clients. Some of the professions have brought sexual contact with former clients and with trainees or supervisees under closer scrutiny as well. Several states have enacted legislation making it a criminal offense for a therapist to have sexual contact with a client. Consumer self-help groups have formed to support victims of abuse and to bring the issue to public attention.

Although studies of incidence rates (usually by self-reports of questionable validity and representativeness) have yielded findings similar to those in the previous decade, increased attention has been given to male victims, victims of abuse by therapists of the same sex, and child and adolescent victims. At the same time, feminist therapists have argued that sexual abuse in therapy, of which more than 80 percent of victims are female (Gartrell, Herman, Olarte, Feldstein, & Localio, 1986; Gonsiorek, 1989b), must be understood in the context of other forms of sexual abuse of women.

With respect to the sites of abuse, the spotlight has moved outward from the private therapist's office and the chaotic, underfunded public agency to encompass other settings as well. *Holistic health centers* can be expected to have high rates of patient-therapist sexual contact because of their unorthodox ideologies, the social mingling and physical familiarity they encourage (often in out-of-the-way locations), the blurring of the distinction between client and counselor, and the dominant presence of therapy "gurus." Interactions in holistic centers typically involve a lack of clarity of boundaries and a clash of unspoken standards. When a person who feels victimized lodges a complaint, a scandal may follow, with successive waves of revelations of what may have been regarded as common and accepted practice in such a milieu.

Given the nature of their clientele and staff, drug and alcohol rehabilitation centers have always carried a high risk of sexual exploitation. In the 1980s and 1990s, however, the state-run centers featured in many of our illustrative examples have been partially supplanted by *private residential treatment centers* (Peele, 1989). Although these facilities typically have a more professionalized staff, the combination of vulnerable clients and (in some cases) ex-addict counselors in a residential setting is still a volatile one, particularly when the same individuals may be involved in professional counseling and peer support groups (another form of boundary blurring). Administrators of addiction-treatment centers, whether public or private, need to exercise special vigilance over client-staff interactions (for examples of abuses, see Schoener, 1989c, pp. 122, 128).

The recent attention given to sexual abuse by *clergy* and other *pastoral counselors* has lifted the veil of reticence from an age-old tragedy. Given the emerging documentation of such abuse (Fortune, 1989a, 1989b; Minnesota Interfaith Committee on Sexual Exploitation by Clergy, 1989; Rice-Smith, 1990, in preparation; Schoener & Milgrom, 1989c; Woodward & King, 1989), the scope of the problem remains to be defined. What is clear is that this kind of abuse entails a betrayal of trust at least as great as that which results from sexual exploitation by secular counselors.

The past decade has seen the publication of several important books on the subject of client-therapist sex (Burgess & Hartman, 1986; Gabbard, 1989; Pope & Bouhoutsos, 1986; Smith & Bisbing, 1988), a few of which focus on the subjective experiences of the client (Bates & Brodsky, 1988; Plasil, 1985; Walker & Young, 1986) or therapist (Rutter, 1989). Ongoing research, theorizing, and practical clinical and legal investigations are taking place in a number of university and other settings. The Program in Psychiatry and the Law at Massachusetts Mental Health Center (Harvard Medical School) is undertaking an effort to clarify the ethical breaches involved in patient-therapist sexual contact in a way that honors the patient's integrity and autonomy (Gutheil,

1989a, 1989b). The Program is also analyzing the role of the victim's subsequent therapist, with emphasis on the dilemmas of mandatory reporting, informed consent to litigation, double agency, and personal liability (see Chapter 10).

The tone of much of the work in this emerging field has been set by that of the Walk-In Counseling Center in Minneapolis and the Minnesota Task Force on Sexual Exploitation by Counselors and Therapists. (The latter group cosponsored the first national conference on the subject in 1986.) The pioneering clinical experiences and legislative accomplishments of these organizations are exhaustively documented in two indispensable guidebooks (Sanderson, 1989a; Schoener, Milgrom, Gonsiorek, Luepker, & Conroe, 1989) that illuminate all sides of this complex cluster of issues for the practicing clinician, administrator, or researcher. Particularly to be recommended are the sections on treatment of victims and assessment and rehabilitation (where possible) of therapist perpetrators, subjects that are beyond the scope of this book (except in the forensic context explored in Chapter 10).

This revised edition of *Sexual Dilemmas for the Helping Professional* takes account of these various developments, expanding our original discussion as appropriate and referencing many new sources. In this new context, however, the book still keeps its original character and aims to serve the same needs it did in its first edition. A practical guidebook addressing issues too often slighted in professional as well as paraprofessional training, it seeks to help all therapists (from the least to the most sophisticated and well-trained), as well as those who teach, supervise, and manage them, prepare for a complex set of personal, ethical, professional, and legal realities. The purpose of this book will have been served if it helps those who have privileged access to vulnerable human beings keep clearly in view the essential distinction between exercising one's own best judgment and rationalizing unprofessional conduct.

Sexual Dilemmas
for the Helping Professional

Revised and Expanded Edition

1
Troubled Waters

Sidney Simon, the humanistic educator known for his work in values clarification, tells the following story as part of an exercise designed to help one clarify one's values and perceptions concerning sexual choices in a world of conflicting interests and desires (cf. Simon, Howe, & Kirschenbaum, 1972).

The survivors of a shipwreck are marooned on two small, otherwise uninhabited islands separated by a narrow strait. The strait is full of the hungriest, most ferocious sharks imaginable. It is impossible to swim safely from one island to another.

A young couple engaged to be married are lucky enough to survive the wreck, but in the tumult and confusion they are separated. Alice ends up on Island I, Bob on Island II. Alice loves Bob in the old-fashioned way—the kind of love celebrated in romantic songs and poetry. She feels that she cannot stand another day without him. But how can she cross the shark-infested strait?

She goes over to Charlie, another survivor who has landed on Island I. "Charlie," she says, "would you build me a raft so I can get over to the other island and be with Bob?"

Charlie looks her up and down. "Sure, baby, I'll build you a raft, but first you have to go to the sand with me."

"Go to the sand?"

"Well, there are no beds here, so we'll have to do it on the sand."

Alice is outraged. "You disgusting, despicable, obnoxious man. I've never heard anything so reprehensible. I wouldn't go to the sand with you if you were the last man left on the earth."

"Have it your own way," says Charlie, "but if you change your mind, I'm in the Yellow Pages."

Alice paces around. What should she do?

Then she hears banging noises coming from the northern end of the island. She walks in that direction and finds Donald, an industrious-looking fellow who is busy with a construction project. "Donald," she asks, "would you please build me a raft so I can go join. . . ."

He stops her in mid-sentence. "Don't bother me," he says with a dismissive wave of his hand. "I'm not interested in your personal problems. I have no time for such frivolity. I'm busy here building my own raft so I can get off this godforsaken island myself. So why don't you just take an about-face and go down the road."

"But, but, look, excuse me. . . ."

"I'm sorry, I told you I have no time. I'm not interested, so just hit the highway. Take I-95 South and make a left."

But that would bring her back to Charlie. She ponders her alternatives. Is it better to do something or nothing? Does the end justify the means?

To make a long story short, she goes back to see Charlie. Here, so as not to be too graphic, the camera discreetly pans the sky as we report that Charlie does indeed build the raft.

Alice wastes no time in getting across to Island II. "Bob, Bob," she cries out as she runs toward him," oh, honey, am I glad to see you! You don't know what I had to do. . . ."

Bob's expression makes Donald's look warm and inviting by comparison. "I do know what you did," he says in a low but firm voice. "I saw the whole thing, and I don't approve. That's it, Alice. We're finished. I'm through with you. Give me back my ring."

"But I did it for you—for us!"

"You didn't do it for me; you did it for you. I didn't make you do anything. That's it. I'm not going to compromise. It's all over between us. See you around sometime."

Alice walks around on the beach. "Those sharks would be more hospitable than these pigs," she says to herself. Again she is left to ponder her choices, only now she has even fewer and less palatable choices than before.

Suddenly a man comes out from behind the bushes. It is Ernie, who has been observing everything. He runs over to Alice, gushing with emotion. "Alice, I saw what happened, and I don't care. I love you. Will you marry me?"

* * *

What is going on in this story? What aspects of sexuality and sexual relationships do these characters embody? How does their behavior reflect our society's mores and its beliefs about people? Which characters strike us as "good," which ones as "bad"? Do these moral judgments have any validity? Can we think of better ways to cope with the situation depicted?

The answers to these questions lie as much in the way we hear or read the story as in the way it is told. Today, many of us would read the story as sexist—that is, as being based on arbitrary, but nonetheless ingrained assumptions about how men and women differ. On the other hand, the sequence of events narrated here might well have seemed reasonable and even inevitable to readers a generation ago as well as to some readers today. If we accept certain unstated assumptions about how men and women act, the whole story falls into place. If we question those assumptions, many other possibilities open up.

In the first place, why didn't Alice build her own raft? Nothing was said about her being unable to use her arms and legs—or her mind. If she didn't know how to build a raft, she might have asked Charlie to help her build one rather than do it for her. Of course, Charlie might have exacted the same price for the smaller favor as he did for the larger one. Alice might then have gone to Donald and asked him if he would take her over to Island II when he had finished building his own raft. Had he been unwilling to do that, he might have let her watch him build his raft so that she could learn to build one for herself. It is true that Donald didn't simply refuse to build a raft for Alice; he told her to get lost. Would he have responded differently if Alice had merely asked if she could stand around and watch? If she had offered to help *him*? We don't know because she didn't ask or offer. And even if he had still chased her away, couldn't she have found a bush or tree behind which to watch Donald as Ernie would later watch her and Bob?

If Alice was the victim in this story, she had learned to be a victim. She had learned not to be able to build a raft. Her inability to take care of her own needs can be characterized as *learned helplessness* (Seligman, 1975). Learned helplessness can sometimes be an effective way to gain one's ends, as when a woman stands by the highway waving at passing cars instead of changing her flat tire herself, or when a man fidgets with a loose button on his vest until someone takes pity and sews it on for him. And speaking of men, why didn't *Bob* build a raft and go over to Island I to rejoin Alice? Was he helpless, too? Or was it simply not as important to him as it was to her?

All five characters in the story had learned to be the people they were and the men or women they were. Acting according to expectations they had formed about others and that others had formed about them, they exhibited restricted, predictable patterns of behavior. Each of these one-dimensional characters, in playing a stereotyped role, illustrates an aspect of human sexuality.

To begin with Alice, the narrative does not specify that she flashes her eyes and wiggles her hips when she asks Charlie and Donald to build her a raft. Nor does it say that she does not. Her indignant reply to Charlie's proposition, although in part a reaction to his crudeness, suggests that she has no conscious intention of seducing him. Yet a request accompanied by a mere friendly smile from a woman is enough to make many men sense a sexual overture. Throughout the story Alice is the prime object of attention; the energy that is released revolves around her. If only by virtue of the way she is viewed by the male characters, Alice represents *seduction*, defined for our purposes as the use of one's wiles to obtain a desired end. Men and women both engage in seduction—but only on desert islands, of course. Here in the civilized world we helping professionals expect female clients to blink their eyes and shift in their seats; we expect male clients to put their hands on their hips and strike Brando-like poses. But we ourselves would never stoop so low!

Charlie's behavior seems outrageous to most readers, as it does to Alice. Note, though, that Charlie does not pull a gun on Alice and say, "If you don't have sex with me I'm going to blow your brains out." Rather, he operates on the time-honored principle of quid pro quo— something for something. And he does in fact fulfill his end of the bargain. He could, after all, walk off saying, "Take me to the Better Business Bureau. See you in Small Claims Court." By specifying his terms and living up to them, Charlie acts within the requirements of business ethics. Most of us, however strongly motivated to help people, would not go to work if we were not paid. To that extent we are like Charlie. What we find objectionable about him is his extension of business ethics to sexual relationships, which we think of as being governed by mutual affection and desire. By making sex part of a bargain, Charlie engages in an exercise of *power*. What he does overtly often occurs in subtler forms in the various contexts of everyday life, particularly the work environment.

Donald's absorption in productive activity can be seen as an extreme form of task-orientation. He might be a useful person to employ to do certain types of jobs. But his complete indifference to everything going on around him also bespeaks his *self-interest*. Donald evaluates Alice's request strictly in terms of how it affects his interest as he defines it (which differs from the way Charlie defines *his* interest). "What's in it for me?" he asks himself. If there is nothing in it for him, then he doesn't care to get involved. He would rather just keep on "doing his own thing." We are acting like Donald when we don't stop to help someone whose car is stalled at the side of the road.

Bob is perhaps the most unsympathetic character of the lot. In his response to Alice's plight he shows himself to be rigid, narrow-minded, judgmental, unsupportive, unloving. He makes no allowance for extenuating circumstances or for his own role in motivating Alice's actions. In the same extreme, overdrawn way that each of the other characters symbolizes a particular attitude or orientation, Bob stands for *morality*. Many of us would think of him as moralistic rather than moral. We, in his place, would be more understanding. If we didn't like the sight of Alice "going to the sand" with Charlie on the opposite shore, we would just turn the other way and watch the sunset. Or would we? In any case, before we condemn Bob for his intolerance of infidelity, we should consider whether there are not some other issues that we would refuse to negotiate. Almost everyone has had occasion to say, "I don't care what anybody else does; I just won't go along with that." Unfortunately, we tend to label as immoral those who compromise on our high-priority issues, and to label as moralistic those who refuse to make the same compromises we do. We can well imagine situations in which Bob's refusal to compromise his principles, like Donald's concentration and dedication, would be regarded as laudable.

As for Ernie, we may speculate on the sincerity with which he says, "I love you," to a woman he doesn't even know. If Donald is like the person who drives right past someone who is stranded and waving for help, Ernie is like the driver who does stop—if the person at the side of the road looks like a movie idol. Who among us has never felt like picking up an attractive hitchhiker? When we do that, we are, like Ernie, seizing an *opportunity* to take advantage of someone else's vulnerability.

These characters may seem unappealing, but it is less easy to condemn them once we have taken a good look in the mirror. The currents of sexual energy which they dramatize are potentially present, in varying degrees of intensity, whenever a client walks into a helping professional's office. They walk in with the client, and they sit behind the desk with the therapist. Moreover, even after two decades of feminist consciousness-raising, they all too often take the stereotypically sexist forms illustrated in our story.

As helping professionals we cannot eliminate these dynamics. But we can become more conscious of them. We can more readily tell when we are seducing or being seduced, when we are exercising power or being subjected to its exercise, when we or our clients are taking advantage of opportunities or acting out of self-interest. Informed by this awareness, we can make choices about what is moral and what is moralistic and in so doing become better able to teach others to make such choices.

As an aid in this learning process, the chapters that follow will explore the five dimensions of sexuality we have highlighted—seduction, power, opportunity, self-interest, morality—as they apply to interpersonal relationships in the helping professions. The five categories are not mutually exclusive. For example, Charlie's behavior illustrates "opportunity" and "self-interest" as much as it does "power." Similar overlaps inevitably occur in the interview reports and case studies cited throughout this book. Nonetheless, the chapter divisions provide a convenient focus for clarifying the salient issues. In identifying these, our purpose is to get beyond conventional, unthinking habits of response and to consider more useful ways to handle troublesome situations on the job. The solutions that elude us in the heat of day-to-day work may be the very ones that can serve as rafts for negotiating safely the shark-infested waters of client-therapist as well as peer relationships in the human services.

2
Seduction

In our desert island fable, seduction appears in the person of Alice, who unwittingly arouses passions ranging from lust to moral indignation in the men around her. But what if Alice were not the self-respecting woman and devoted fiancée that she has been depicted to be? Let us imagine her instead as a young woman who had been referred to a social worker by her welfare caseworker because of her inability to hold a job. Although there is some suspicion of a drug or alcohol problem, no evidence of substance abuse emerges during her first several visits to the social worker. The woman does, on the other hand, allude to numerous personal problems both in her weekly therapy sessions and in frequent after-hours calls to a crisis line.

The social worker she is seeing is Larry N., who is in his twenties. Larry is intelligent and conscientious, but has been on the job for less than six months. He observes that his client is withdrawn and defensive. As the weeks go by she begins to open up, but when confronted with issues that she does not want to discuss she either retreats to tears and confused utterances or flirts. She begins by moving her eyes and establishing eye contact, then rearranges herself so as to expose more of her breasts or her legs. Thinking that this behavior is deliberate Larry confronts her about it. She denies any conscious intent, explaining that "it just happens" when she feels defensive. She admits that when people have their attention drawn from her face to some other part of her body, they tend to lose track of the conversation and (in Larry's paraphrase) "everything goes to hell in a handbasket."

Larry, worried that he may be losing his objectivity concerning this woman, consults with his supervisor, who advises him to be alert for the escalation of physical overtures into verbal ones. Sure enough, at his next session with this client, she says, "You know, you've really been able to help me a lot in just a short time. Your life seems squared away; you don't have problems like I do. You seem so confident in everything you do." She then tells him that she finds him physically attractive and would like to make love with him.

Lacking any experience in handling such a situation, Larry manages to state feebly that the professional relationship does not allow for what she is suggesting. Neither he nor she pursues the issue any further. But Larry does have some other thoughts about it. "She's God's gift to counselors," he silently exclaims. He runs through his mind the possibility of taking up her offer. "If you want something 'on the side,'" he tells himself, "here's your prime opportunity." But he realizes that if he acted on this fantasy, it could mean the end of his career and possibly the end of his marriage. He goes back to his supervisor, who explores with him his susceptibility to flattery from a client. ("I have to admit," he says in retrospect, "it was a big blowup for my ego.") He and his supervisor also review whether the client has made enough progress with him to justify continuing the therapy. They decide to continue the sessions, but with stricter guidelines, including the elimination of after-hours calls and the insistence on a clear agenda for each session.

This textbook case of seduction in the client-therapist relationship highlights several patterns that will appear frequently in our accounts. First, the client's behavior is not thought out in advance. Rather, it appears as an unconscious mechanism aimed at relieving the pressure of having to deal with difficult personal issues. The client's approach is a characteristic one: "You Tarzan, me Jane." For his part, the therapist is only too happy to imagine himself as Tarzan. There are two people here who are feeling and contributing to the sexual energy being generated.

The magnitude of that energy is considerable. When Larry was interviewed months after this encounter, he still felt uncomfortable about it. As he recounted the incident, he shifted in his chair. So did the interviewer, who sat up, suddenly alert, at the mention of an explicit sexual offer. With so much body language evident upon mere recollection, one can imagine the intensity in the air when it actually happened.

* * *

Alice appears in other guises as well. She shows up at a seminar in a university classroom as an exceptionally beautiful student wearing a see-through blouse. As seen through the eyes of the 35-year-old professor, Richard J., this student comes to the seminar each week with "all but bare breasts." There is no inadvertence about this; it is "a flagrant display, with walk, eye play, and verbal style to go with it." Richard can only guess at her motives, since neither he nor she makes any direct overtures about having an affair. Finding her "an easy woman to look at, but not someone I'd want to spend much time with," he does not divert himself to any great extent with fantasies about her.

To virtually all the other students in the seminar, however, it is an accepted fact that he is having an affair with her. The women come to his office and make lighthearted complaints about what strikes them as an unfair bid for his attention. Although they stop short of direct expressions of jealousy, Richard senses a "Why not me?" attitude in the insinuations that persist despite his frank denials. The men respond differently—that is, with male camaraderie in the office, but with envy and antagonism in the classroom. As Richard sees it, much that happens in this seminar must be understood with reference to this one student's flirtatiousness and to the reactions it arouses. With the participants more or less embarrassed and on edge, intellectual arguments are sharper than they would normally be. "The openness of these dynamics," Richard concludes, "made this one of the most difficult classes I've ever had to teach."

In this seminar, as in the counseling situation described previously, there is an avowed and an unavowed agenda. The avowed agenda is the course material. The unavowed agenda is the drama of what appeared as a public seduction attempt to those who witnessed it. We have seen this drama unfold from the professor's point of view. Richard knows from what other students have told him that the behavior of the student in question has become an object of public scrutiny. It is conceivable, on the other hand, that he is projecting somewhat, in that some of the students' responses may be less intense than he indicates. Nonetheless, as long as he perceives the other students' reactions as he does, the unspoken agenda will obstruct the academic agenda, just as Larry's client's seductiveness obstructed her therapy.

* * *

A classic incarnation of the dynamic of seduction is Dora, one of Freud's (1963) early patients, whose case inspired him to develop the theory of transference and countertransference. Malcolm (1980b) speculates that Freud chose the name Dora for this frustrating patient because he unconsciously associated her with Pandora, mythical source of the box full of evils that plague the world. In what Malcolm (1980b, p. 102) calls "the tense, irritating, subterranean drama" of his relationship with Dora, Freud for the first time faced fully the Pandora's Box of passions from which his teacher Breuer had fled—the passions that the analyst (or other therapist) and patient come to feel toward each other. In Malcolm's words, Freud had

> a profound and skeptical knowledge of himself and of his motives and of the danger of his creation. He knew he was playing with fire, but he had the Promethean audacity to persist in his dangerous game of therapy. (Malcolm, 1980b, p. 108)

Freud's successors are trained to face the occupational hazard of being sexually stimulated by a patient's revelations—and some of them still get in trouble. Moreover, psychoanalysts are far outnumbered by the many kinds of teachers, therapists, and counselors (like Larry N. and, with his greater sophistication, Richard J.) who are not trained to negotiate consciously the "tense, irritating, subterranean dramas" in which they play an unwitting part.

In this chapter and those that follow there are many such dramas, many Doras and Alices. There are male Doras and female Freuds as well as the other way around, for seduction is not the exclusive province of either sex. And there are cases in which Dora and Freud are of the same sex.

Therapeutic and Antitherapeutic Seduction

When we think of seduction in "helping" relationships, we think first of the occasional flagrant instance of deliberate, one-sided exploitation, usually by a male counselor or client. A Manhattan psychiatrist seduces patients with the argument that "You need love and warmth" or "It's good for your therapy." A university professor extorts sex from undergraduates in exchange for the promise of a good grade. A man who has hired a female lawyer to handle a real estate transaction tells her that "I picked you because you're a woman" and insists that she go out with him socially. When she refuses, he is irate, as if dating were one of the normal prerogatives of a client in a business relationship.

These abuses are just the tip of the iceberg. The term "seduction" encompasses a broader range of interactions that occur not only in therapeutic relationships, but in all human relationships. It is of the nature of human interchange that people are drawn into emotional involvements, positive or negative, which support or interfere with the avowed purposes of the individuals involved. One may be seduced into antipathy as well as attraction.

The more subtle as well as universal dimensions of seduction are captured by a psychiatrist's description of the therapeutic encounter as "a sparring match between two people who are perpetually feeling each other out." Seduction, in this larger sense, underlies the other dimensions of sexuality that we have identified. Just as Alice stands at the center of the shipwreck fable in Chapter 1, with each of the other characters defining himself in relation to her, seduction likewise creates the context in which power, opportunity, self-interest, and morality are at stake. It is the motivating force that makes everything else happen. To understand the sexual issues that confront the mental health professional, we must consider the physical, emotional, and psychological aspects of seduction.

Like most other things in life (including drugs, alcohol, food, work, and recreation), seduction, even in the therapeutic setting, is not inherently evil; nor is it inherently good. A female therapist with many years of experience explains how therapy itself involves a form of seduction:

> Therapy is like sex in that a person wants it and is scared of it at the same time. The therapist has to seduce the person into talking about his or her feelings and being open to change. For the person being seduced, both the dangers and the payoffs are the same as with sex. Sometimes the openness, the trust that is elicited, is betrayed. On the other hand, the kind of seduction that I aim for in therapy, which I would call "positive" or "therapeutic," is one that facilitates the client's getting into a better relationship with herself, not with me. I will (in that sense) "seduce," I will manipulate, if the aim is to get people to help themselves.

This apt characterization is applicable to any kind of therapy and any kind of therapist or counselor. Scheflen (1965, p. 257) goes so far as to describe the psychotherapeutic relationship as one of "quasi-courtship":

> I have argued that quasi-courting serves the purpose of clarifying aspects of a relationship that allow favorable states of attentiveness and involvement for specific tasks. If this is so, then quasi-courting is one device used covertly and automatically by patients and therapists to induce rapport and to maintain and regulate their relationship. . . .
>
> The fact is that the patient and the therapist do have certain feelings for each other. These feelings . . . provide an environment for the learning experience which psychotherapy must be if it is to be successful.

In psychoanalysis a more ambitious variation of seduction takes place. There one is seduced into identifying the therapist temporarily with an important person in one's life, so that one can use the relationship with the therapist to discharge as well as gain insight into one's feelings toward this other person. Analytic transference, then, is a special form of therapeutic seduction.

Something analogous to therapeutic seduction occurs in the classroom, as illustrated by the experience of a social scientist with his university students:

> I have found that I can effectively illustrate points about human behavior (socialization, cognitive development, roles, peer pressures, and so forth) by talking about my children. These are among the examples I know best, and I can talk about them with ease, with humor, with feeling, and (it seems) with authenticity. This is not to say that such anecdotes prove anything; my purpose in using them is simply to make my points clear enough to think about critically. To my surprise, though, I have found that they sometimes have a deeper impact. I have been told many times over that one of the most important things I do in my classes is to acknowledge my involvement with my children—the attention I pay to them, the caring I give them. "It was when you spoke about your children that I began to listen to you"—that's the way they put it, "they" being my women students, for no man has ever

said this to me. It seems that when I say something that strikes students as real, it legitimizes the rest of what I have to say, which may be a good deal more abstract.

This example of classroom seduction differs from that which centered around the see-through blouse in that here the students' personal engagement with the teacher supports rather than disrupts the teaching of the course material. Here there is no conflict between the avowed and unavowed agendas. The "subterranean drama" is in harmony with the task at hand. The same criterion applies in a therapeutic situation. Do the personal feelings that arise between client and therapist serve the purpose of therapy, or do they undermine it?

In *Games Analysts Play*, Shepard & Lee (1970, p. 37) remind us that "game playing" is not a corruption of life, but a fact of life:

> . . . the play and interplay of human relationship belongs, in both figurative and literal senses, to a "living" theater. We are not acting. We are being.

They caution against "the unconscious belief . . . that even though games are the breathing machinery of the common man, there are others belonging to some superhuman tribe who are above being drawn in or affected." Their conclusion is worth keeping in mind when looking at seductive situations, impulses, and acts in the therapeutic context:

> The question now is to differentiate those games which are the essence of life from those which are intellectually and emotionally constructed for the purpose of delusion—a delusion both for those who are playing and for those who are being played upon. (Shepard & Lee, 1970, p. 38)

Our focus will be on the seductive games that represent a delusion for the client or counselor or both—and what one can do about them.

How Clients Seduce

A 40-year-old male psychologist with considerable experience in practice and in teaching, as well as what is called worldly experience, speaks confidently of his ability to discern a seduction attempt before it goes too far:

> I can spot a seduction right away. It's like knowing in a second that a person is schizophrenic. I believe that I'm right virtually all the time, and yet it's really hard to describe what I'm picking up because it's so intuitive. It may be a look, a smile, eye contact, voice patterns, gestures. Whatever it is, if I see it quickly enough, I can often head it off at the pass. The same is true with students as with therapy patients. There have been students that I've dated some time after I've had them in class, but the cues were there from the first lecture.

For those who are not as experienced or as observant as this man, here is a breakdown of some forms of seductive behavior and signs of seductive intent:

Fantasy. Fantasy is where it all begins—and usually ends. On the one hand, fantasy is a component of seduction, courtship, and sexual relationships. On the other hand, the fantasies that are never acted upon far outnumber those that are. What matters in practice is the relationship between fantasy and action.

In itself, a sexual fantasy is a normal and very common human experience. Fantasies need not conform to any ideology or ethic. In the realm of fantasy one need not be and almost surely will not be strictly monogamous, heterosexual, or professionally proper. There is no reason, for instance, for a high school teacher to have to feel guilty about having sexual fantasies about a student half his age. Therapists and clients routinely fantasize about each other. Such fantasies become a problem only when they are acted upon.

In itself, a fantasy is a private matter. It is only when a fantasy leads to a form of action (such as talking about it) that it becomes known to anyone other than the person having the fantasy. Richard J., the professor in the vignette earlier in this chapter, was careful to specify that he could not attribute thoughts, desires, or motives to the student who appeared to be "coming on" to him. He knew that he was not having fantasies about her, but he did not know whether she was having fantasies about him. A young woman who counseled prison inmates was informed by her supervisor that "there are a lot of people here who are more intimate with you in their thoughts than they ought to be." It is not surprising that men confined to the male world of a prison (including guards as well as inmates) would have fantasies about one of the few women they could even look at. But how could the woman's supervisor know what these men were doing "in their thoughts"? If, on the other hand, they revealed their interest in her by talking or otherwise doing something about it, then they were not just having fantasies.

Preference for therapists of one sex or the other. One way in which one acts out the tendency to confuse professional with personal relationships is by choosing (in situations where choice is possible) a therapist of the sex to which one is attracted. An example is the man who said to his lawyer, "I picked you because you're a woman." One woman who frankly described herself as a seductive person ("that's my role in life"), having noted that she had been propositioned by more than one therapist, remarked, "I don't know if I choose males or if it's just their availability." Given the preponderance of women in the helping professions (other than psychiatrists), it is likely that her preference for males had something to do with it. Even in a correctional or treatment facility where clients are assigned to counselors, they may find ways to express their preferences, as when a young woman who directed a therapeutic community for drug abusers found that male residents were coming to talk to her rather than to their male therapists.

Edited self-presentation. Gender influences not only whom one chooses to talk to, but also what one chooses to say. Students of clinical psychology are taught the story of the schizophrenic patient who sat in a room throwing his feces at the walls. When a woman came into the room, he immediately stopped this behavior. Questioned, he replied, "I wouldn't want it said that I don't know how to behave in the presence of a lady." This is only an extreme illustration of a kind of "observer effect" that occurs in many therapeutic situations, such as this case reported by a female caseworker at an alcoholism rehabilitation center:

A male client in the course of several interviews portrayed himself as a warm, caring person in his relationship with his girlfriend. Meanwhile, he admitted to a male counselor that he actually abused his girlfriend. It was only when I compared notes with this other counselor that I found out how unreal a picture of himself the client had given me. His purpose in doing so became clear shortly thereafter when he began to focus his romantic interest on me.

This client's edited self-presentation was designed to make him more attractive to the counselor. It served his personal agenda, but was detrimental to his therapy.

Voyeurism. A client may express an interest in a therapist's personal life that goes far beyond normal curiosity. In the small world in which many "recipients of services" live (especially those in prisons and residential treatment facilities), a young, attractive person who also is a significant figure in a client's daily life can easily become an object of obsessive interest. "Are you married?" or "Do you have a lover?" is often the opening gambit in a chain of inquiries that leads to a sexual offer. Sometimes the client seeks information not from the therapist directly, but from other therapists or fellow clients or residents. Such grapevine gossip is likely to be aroused when the counselor appears to be sexually involved with another client or (as is more frequently the case) another staff member. When the actual or suspected lover is a visible presence in the agency, the client, student, or patient is more susceptible to imagining himself or herself (however unrealistically) as a disappointed rival. The students who came to Richard J.'s office to elicit information about his relationship with a member of the seminar radiated the insecurity that tends to be aroused by the suspicion of an in-house love affair.

Extracurricular contacts. A good sign of a client's interest in the person as opposed to the professional persona of someone in a helping role is the initiation of unnecessarily frequent contacts in the form of office visits and phone calls. When someone repeatedly finds pretexts to see a teacher, physician, or therapist at close quarters, it is usually in the service of a not very well-hidden agenda. A medical school professor recalled this instance:

A student in one of my classes whom I had advised on a particular matter called me again to inquire about a detail that could easily have been worked out with my secretary. No sooner did I put down the phone than the thought flashed through my head: "She's tipped her hand. I've got her." One phone call, innocent-sounding but out of context, as good as put her in my bed. And no sooner did I have that thought than I felt guilty about thinking of a student in such exploitive terms.

As one gains experience in one's field, one becomes better able to judge intuitively when someone has set out on this path to vulnerability. "I know it when it happens" is the way one experienced therapist put it.

Verbal exhibitionism. Clients sometimes attempt to create a sexual bond with a counselor by recounting their sexual exploits in graphic physical detail. Aside from being a good way to get through a therapeutic hour without any serious self-examination, this behavior enables the client to gauge (and perhaps arouse) the therapist's interest in the activities described. The client can then conclude, "And you're the kind of man/woman I like to do these things with." Both male and female therapists report that this approach is typical of homosexual clients. Something of its flavor comes through in the following account: "One client of mine could pour it on for an hour, telling me everything she did with her latest partner. She seemed to be getting kicks out of it, as if she enjoyed watching a straight person react." Indeed, straight therapists often *do* react, not by accepting the sexual proposition, but by being distracted by the storytelling, since homosexual practices still have shock value when revealed to the uninitiated.

Body language. The escalation to outright seduction begins with physical cues, which may progress from the visual to the tactile. Larry N.'s client began (just one session before she propositioned him) by making eye contact and striking revealing poses. Clothing is a tipoff; both women and men (especially homosexual men) will come in with tight pants (such as designer jeans) and V-neck blouses or unbuttoned shirts. Patients in a physician's office have additional opportunities to reveal themselves physically, as one physician's commentary suggests:

I may notice that a patient is slow getting dressed after an examination; she may want to undress even though all she has is a cold; she may present the same breast lump for examination on every visit. Sometimes, just when I'm about to leave, the patient will bring up a new issue that requires my sitting down and engaging with her again and may even require her getting undressed again.

Clients flirt by touching their own bodies, as by stroking their legs. More intimate gestures involve physical contact with the therapist—bumping knees, touching hands, sitting on his lap. A college teacher describes a typical form of undergraduate flirtation: "This coed would come up in the morning and rest her big breasts on my chest—she'd practically drop them on me." Such advances are an intermediate step between see-through blouses or "making eyes" and a direct offer.

Spoken invitations. Another route from suggestion to proposition is by way of verbal overtures. Larry N.'s client took this route when she complimented him first on his enviable position in life, then on his skill as a therapist, and finally on his physical attractiveness. These three "pitches" are commonly observed stages in an escalating verbal seduction: "You've got it made." "You've been so helpful to me." "You're my kind of man/woman." Another approach is to probe for any personal dissatisfactions the therapist may have. A vignette that features this among other seductive techniques is contributed by Marty P., a relatively inexperienced therapist in the field of substance abuse:

A 19-year-old woman was referred to me for an alcohol problem which she denied. After going through the usual defenses—tears, avoidance, anger—she started working the sexual angle. She was fantastically good-looking, with long blond hair, green eyes, super-clear complexion, and nice proportions with clothes to advertise them. Frankly, it was difficult to keep my mind on therapy. When she made her move, she started by asking me to join her for lunch. When I told her I was going to meet my wife, she asked me if I was happily married. I told her I was. Then she rubbed my lower leg and said, "How happy? I can make you happier." You think I didn't have fantasies about her after that?

Once the overtures and advances reach this point, it is but a short step to a direct solicitation like "Why don't you and I go out and have some fun together?" or even "I'd like to make love with you."

Styles of seduction. There is more than one way of seducing. Traditionally, there are two ways—what a woman does and what a man does. These contrasting styles persist in the behavior of those who are served by the helping professions, although the stereotyped gender roles do not always hold. This is how these styles of seduction are seen by two female therapists:

- "Some female clients strike me as not being aware of the way they pull their skirts up, strike sexually inviting poses, and so forth. The men seem to be more consciously flirtatious. With them something more explicit happens as they seek to establish their maleness. One man, by way of making a point in conversation, took hold of my ankles as if to pull me off the couch. It fit into the joke he was telling, but there was also a suggestion of caveman sexuality."

- "I have two very different types of women clients. Some present themselves as weak and vulnerable. They revert to what we think of as feminine ploys—they cry, bat their eyelashes, talk in girlish voices—to get across the message, 'I need someone stronger to depend on.' On the other hand, there are active lesbians who act just as men would, trying to seduce me by opening doors, pulling out chairs, giving inappropriate compliments."

Presenting a mirror image of the world that created them, clients either exhibit the "learned helplessness" discussed in Chapter 1 (in connection with Alice) or try to play upon that helplessness in others. Both of the therapists quoted here identify the "learned helplessness" role with women. One associates the "macho" role with men, the other with homosexual women. The association of these "passive" and "active" roles with gender is breaking down and will break down further. Whether the roles themselves will become less distinct is not so clear.

Why Clients Seduce

In psychoanalysis the tendency for the patient to focus obsessively on the analyst as a person is labeled a "transference neurosis" brought on by the association of the analyst with the patient's prior love objects. How does this concept translate into the full range of therapy and other "helping" situations where (as is not always the case in analysis) the patient or client tends to be at a disadvantage in age, education, economic status, and success in coping with life? What makes people act seductively toward their therapists even in relationships where the analytic procedure is not employed and the depth and intensity of the analytic relationship are not achieved? The list that follows includes those motivations that have appeared frequently in our observations and interviews. It is not an exhaustive list, nor are the items mutually exclusive. Often it is difficult to disentangle one motive from another. Indeed, the behavior under consideration appears more often than not to be overdetermined (cf. Shochet, Levin, Lowen, & Lisansky, 1976).

To gratify sexual desire. Given that sexual energy can exist between any two people, a true sexual attraction occasionally arises between therapist and client. People do, after all, "turn each other on." Nonetheless, those who are the objects of clients' attentions tend not to attach much weight to this motive. In the words of Hollender and Shevitz (1978, p. 776), "The main issue is not the nature of the patient's provocativeness but what is being sought: almost never a sexual relationship and almost always special attention or nurturance." A male university professor says, "Am I going to kid myself that these students are falling in love with someone 30 years older than they are? I know what they're in it for." A colleague concurs, though with a different emphasis: "When I ask myself whether there is anything about me that would make a young woman look twice at me if she saw me walking down the street, I have to answer, 'Probably not.' It's the exposure over time, the way I present myself in my role, that makes the difference."

Still, uncomplicated sexual interest cannot be dismissed as a consideration. A therapist at a university mental health center observes, "It's hard to say when someone is using seduction to avoid treatment issues and when someone is just interested in having a sexual relationship." If it is difficult for a professionally trained observer to make this distinction, it must be doubly difficult for the client to do so.

To divert attention from treatment issues. Larry N.'s client, who initially was not making progress in therapy and was not familiar with what therapy was all about, resorted to seduction as a reaction to stress. As far as both she and Larry could tell, she did not do it with any ulterior motive, but in reaction to being confronted with questions she was not accustomed to asking herself. Similarly, the young woman who propositioned Marty P. had gone through a list of defenses ("tears, avoidance, anger") before turning to seduction. Twice she had tried to walk out of the office, only to be restrained by the threat of sanctions. She was trapped. When one is caught in a psychological trap, it is primarily one's own attention that one seeks to divert from therapy by putting up a sexual smokescreen. At the same time, to the extent that this move is successful, the therapist's attention is diverted as well. If the client and therapist spend their hour together focusing on the client's most recent sexual exploits, the therapist's love life, or the attraction that exists between the two of them, they will not be focusing on the client's problems. When the client's avoidance strategy (conscious or unconscious) is thus served, the purpose of therapy is compromised.

Sometimes the diversion of the therapist's attention is part of the client's purpose rather than simply a side effect of the client's discomfort and anxiety. The more this is true, the more calculated the diversionary strategy tends to be, as in this account by a female therapist at a psychiatric halfway house for young adults:

> I called a male resident into the office to reprimand him for not doing a required chore in the house. Before I knew it he was changing the subject to "You have really nice eyes" and "You have such a calming effect on me when you talk." It wasn't until about 15 minutes later that I realized he had gotten me off the track. I wasn't at all flattered. I regarded his behavior as manipulative. He was trying to be a ladies' man, as when he pulled out a chair for me. Not only weren't we dealing with his problem, but the problem was becoming mine, namely. "Oh, how can someone as

nice as you, someone with such a lovely smile, be saying these things?"

At this level of calculation, the sabotaging of therapy becomes outright manipulation.

To bribe or manipulate. Seduction may be attempted in the expectation of a quid pro quo. There are numerous variations on this manipulative theme. The bribe may be explicit or implicit. The payoff may be sex itself or simply the flattery that goes into the seduction attempt. The client may propose a clearcut "contract" with the therapist or just act in such a way as to induce the therapist to go along with what he or she wants.

A typical form of bribery is the "maybe someday" approach. Here the client hints that sex may be in the offing in return for the therapist's granting a dispensation or "looking the other way." The client is saying, in effect, "If you play ball with me, I'll play ball with you. If you say what I want you to say, like telling me that I'll be able to drink safely again, maybe you and I can get it together some time." Often, however, the client tries to obtain the *quid* for a lesser *quo*. Then the implicit message goes: "If you treat me right and don't give me a hard time, I'll go on being as nice and agreeable and complimentary to you as I am now." Such antitherapeutic bargains are commonly struck without the slightest reference to sex. Even so, sexual imagery and sexual "come-on" may be used to spice up the package. A client presents himself as attractive and friendly; he builds up a good-humored rapport with his counselor. Then, when an unpleasant requirement comes up, he draws upon his accumulated goodwill. "Come on, Mary," he coaxes, "you can let it go for a couple of days."

In return for flattery, in return for sex or the promise of sex, the client may want the therapist to avoid confronting difficult issues, to overlook violations of legal requirements or therapeutic agreements, or to give the authorities (e.g., the court, an employer) a false report on the client's status or progress. The list of possible payoffs is endless. Whatever is at stake, though, the client is drawing the therapist into an antitherapeutic alliance.

To establish an unholy alliance in conjoint therapy. Seductive manipulation on the part of the client aims to undermine therapeutic objectivity. One context in which such manipulation occurs deserves special mention. In marital or family therapy, one partner may use seduction to gain the allegiance of the therapist against the spouse or other family members. Typically, this is done by male clients in couple therapy with a female clinician. In an attempt to bring the therapist into collusion with himself, the man employs the usual techniques of seduction— smiles, winks, a pleasant manner—along with others tailored to the conjoint situation. He may turn his back on his wife and shower the therapist with attention. Or he may denigrate his wife while flattering the therapist. One man, speaking of the fact that he had been more sexually experienced than his wife prior to their marriage, implied that the therapist, too, was experienced. "The hidden agenda," concluded the therapist, "was for me to take the husband's part and gang up on the wife."

Another side of the story is filled in by a woman, herself a counselor with an associate's degree, who entered into couple therapy with her boyfriend:

> The therapist was an older man, and I just happen to be attracted to older men. I saw him as suave, worldly. I found myself trying to enlist his support by sitting in a certain way, looking at him in a certain way, smiling a lot—all the tricks. It sounds foolish, I know, but I wanted him to think I really liked him. I felt funny getting into that position after being a counselor. But he did take my side on the big issue between me and my boyfriend.

Perhaps the therapist took her side because of her seductive mannerisms; perhaps he did so because he really agreed with her. She will never know the answer, which is a measure of what she lost by playing the seduction game.

To compromise the therapist's position. If a client succeeds in seducing a therapist, the power relationship between them changes. Now they are, in one respect, equals. Indeed (although the emotional vulnerability of the client in this situation tends to be great), a client in a manipulative frame of mind can even be said to have the upper hand. A probation officer who is having an affair with a parolee is not about to send that person back to jail for a violation of probation. When a therapist has a secret lover in a therapy group, it is difficult to avoid giving that person special treatment, whether gentle or (by overcompensation) harsh. There is always the risk that the lover will respond to confrontation with the retort, "You didn't mind my behavior last night!" Again the purpose is manipulation, but the method is different. Instead of bribery, it is blackmail.

To gain status among one's peers. Another motivation for seducing a person in a position of authority is to be able to talk about it afterward. This is a major payoff for college students in the absence of some of the more dire concerns of therapy clients. It also figures in the establishment of a pecking order in prisons and residential treatment facilities, where inmates feel such strong pressure to maintain an image among their peers that they sometimes boast about imaginary affairs (with, unfortunately, real people). Although there is no intention here to compromise the teacher or therapist through such public revelation, that may nonetheless be the outcome.

To gain strength through bonding with a stronger person. One of Albert Ellis's "common irrational ideas at the basis of emotional disturbances" is "the idea that one should be dependent on others and needs someone stronger than oneself on whom to rely" (cf. Ellis & Harper, 1975). Therapy clients, students, prisoners, and those who are on the caseloads of various public agencies (welfare, family services, probation, etc.) are by definition in a dependent position. Although some of these individuals live highly developed lives in certain areas, as a rule they have not progressed very far along the hierarchies of needs laid out by Maslow (1954) and Glasser (1976). They are dealing with basic survival issues. In that condition, they are susceptible to the appeal of magical solutions. Many seduction attempts begin with the thought (consciously articulated or otherwise): "If only this strong, successful person were taking care of me all the time instead of just an hour a week, my life might be okay."

Therapists and teachers often are well aware of the talismanic power which, for their clients and students, resides in their persons. But there are about as many interpretations of the nature of this power as there are helping professionals. A social worker who takes a Freudian approach hypothesizes that seductive clients believe that they can be healed through bonding with the therapist:

A female client believes that a male therapist can heal her by his thrusting. It's a visual, physical image—that the sperm will actually heal her. With a female therapist it's a combination of strength and mothering. The client wants to be nourished by sucking on her tit.

A psychologist speaks of "power bonding," by which the client "takes on the controlling force of a deified figure." A teacher evokes the transfer of knowledge, credibility, self-assurance, mastery, all of which the student can partake of by becoming an object of the teacher's personal attention.

These explanations, although highly imagistic and therefore hard to verify, do seem to point to an important dimension of sexuality from the point of view of a dependent person. Indeed, the fact that numerous individuals give similar (though differently worded) accounts of such sexual bonding suggests that the concept has some validity. It does not, however, invalidate the more straightforward motivations we have cited, ranging from self-interested manipulativeness to sexual attraction. For the client, it is not a matter of sexual desire *versus* the transmission of strength. Even if one chooses to be sexually involved with someone because of the potency of his or her role rather than personal attractiveness, the desire for this bonding still is experienced as sexual.

To gain attention and gratification through the use of accustomed strategies. All of the above explanations can be summed up in one sentence: Clients (especially in agencies and institutions to which they are referred by the criminal-justice system) are seductive *because they are clients*. The manipulation of dependency, the corrupt bargains, the deviousness, the sexist caricatures, the learned helplessness, the diversion of attention—these are the ways in which some of the people who require the services of helping professionals have learned to get along in life. When the effects of low self-esteem and lack of opportunity are added to the sexist upbringing that everyone in our society has, there emerges a patterned way of attracting attention and getting what one wants. The pattern then carries over from the outside world to the therapeutic or counseling relationship, as in this account by a woman who counsels prison inmates:

A lot of male inmates think that because I'm a woman they can play games instead of dealing with me seriously. One of them would always call me "Sugar." Instead of answering my questions he'd say, "You're a woman—how can I tell you *that?*" or "I'll tell you when I see you out on the street, but not in here. We'll have to get together some other time." I replied, "My name is Gail, not Sugar. In no way will I see you outside of this place. The problem we're dealing with is here and now, so you can play games or do something to help yourself. If you have trouble dealing with me as a woman, then skip the woman and deal with me as a member of the staff." With this man it worked out well. We got down to some issues, and he did get out of prison. Later I got a letter from him where he went into his feelings, but went back to calling me "Sugar" and talking about seeing me out on the street.

Gail dealt with this man appropriately, but she couldn't expect her impact to last. She couldn't expect to reverse 20 or 30 years of conditioning in a brief therapeutic alliance.

Seductive behavior is to be expected from clients. It should not be seen as being directed at the therapist personally, or as cause to respond in anything other than a professional way. A therapist's job is not to pass judgment, but to help clients find better ways to satisfy their needs. Since a client's behavior in therapy reflects inadequate coping strategies learned elsewhere in life, sexual overtures toward the therapist can be explored therapeutically to shed light on the client's characteristic responses outside of therapy.

From the Clinician's Viewpoint

Clients who act seductively sometimes do so in the belief that a therapist is encouraging them to be seductive—or indeed, that it is the therapist who is being seductive. Clients may draw such conclusions even in cases where the therapist is acting in a professionally appropriate manner. In other cases the therapist actually is being seductive. Finally, there is that vast middle ground where unintended ambiguities of communication on the part of the therapist activate the highly charged sensibility of the client.

We will not consider in any detail here either the sexual exploitation of clients by therapists or appropriate versus inappropriate responses to client seductiveness, since these subjects are treated extensively in the next four chapters. The discussion that follows is intended merely to give some of the flavor of client-therapist sexual dynamics as seen from the therapist's side of the fence. The issue here is not so much how therapists seduce as how they are seduced into seducing, as much by their own impulses as by clients' behavior. Therapists do many sexually provocative things that are not ill-intended, but rather are a product of normal human feelings together with insufficient training and experience. Such behavior, although more or less innocent, is also more or less damaging to the client, the therapist, and the objectives of therapy. These, then, are some of the ways in which therapists, wittingly or not, play the game of seduction.

Attraction to clients. When asked, "Are you ever attracted to a client?" therapists at all levels of training and experience give answers like the following:

"Hell, yes!"
"If I told you no, I'd be a liar."
"Men my age either have sexual fantasies about 20-year-old women or lie about it."

Similar sentiments were expressed in some of the vignettes earlier in this chapter. The feelings they represent are normal and legitimate, as in the case of this 45-year-old female therapist:

A very attractive man, well-educated and well-spoken, came to the clinic. There was no seductive behavior on his part, but I remember saying to myself, "If I were younger, if he were single, watch out!" But I knew that that had no part in the professional relationship; it was just what I was thinking.

This is honest and shows a trained consciousness. The problem arises when one either acts directly on such feelings or, by allowing too much of one's energy to be drawn off by them, "gets sloppy" on the job.

Wishful thinking and self-seduction. A man who specializes in therapy with fellow homosexuals finds that, "When I get a client who is young, boyish-looking, hairless, I do feel an attraction. My mind even starts to wander." The attraction he feels is legitimate; the fact that his mind wanders represents a reduction of his effectiveness as a therapist. When Marty P. confessed that "it was difficult to keep my mind on therapy" when confronted with a beautiful, provocatively dressed 19-year-old woman, he was admitting that at those moments he was not doing the job he was hired to do for his client. The fact that Marty recalled the details of this woman's appearance down to her green eyes says something about where his focus was during their sessions together. Counselors who lack formal training are more likely to dwell on the details of their clients' seductive behavior. A professional social worker or psychologist is less likely to be impressed by (and to talk about) the large breasts, the skin-tight outfit, the cigarette case left behind in the office, and so forth.

There is a thin line between being drawn in by a client's seductive appearance or behavior and drawing oneself into a vulnerable position with a little self-indulgence. When a high school teacher says that he "finds" himself wandering down to the gym to watch the girls or boys exercise in their scanty uniforms, he is not fully acknowledging that he is choosing to go down there. Many counselors prefer not to have a desk between them and their clients, but when one says, "I sit face to face, almost knee to knee, because that's the only way I can get to a client," he would appear to be letting his own need for the reassurance of intimacy put both the client and himself in a vulnerable position.

Ambiguous communications. "I like you" can convey either personal affection or sexual desire. It can be said in one or the other way, and it can be heard (especially through the sensitive ears of clients) in one or the other way. Although it is appropriate to express warmth toward a client, a therapist needs to be careful about the matter of expression, both verbal and nonverbal. There is a big difference between "You are an attractive person" and "I'm attracted to you."

Because clients tend to overinterpret nuance and detail, clarity of communication on the part of a therapist is essential. The therapist who sits too close to a client is giving a mixed message, whether out of unawareness or unexamined needs of his own. So is the therapist who answers a client's questions about her personal life instead of keeping the focus on the client's therapy. So is the therapist who allows "my natural, energetic physical friendliness" unrestrained expression in therapy situations. Another mixed message is the therapist's counterpart of a client's seductive bribe, in which the therapist leaves open the possibility of a personal reward for achieving a therapeutic goal, as if to say, "Well, not now, but maybe somewhere down the road, if you get your act together—you know, if you stop drinking. . . ."

Voyeurism. When a therapist complained to her supervisor about clients who gave elaborate accounts of their sexual activities, her supervisor said, "Perhaps there is a part of you that wants to listen to that." Judging from our interviews, there are many in every branch of the helping professions who are susceptible to this impulse, so much so that they may actively elicit sexual information from their clients. Lawyers in divorce cases have been observed to inquire more deeply than necessary into their clients' sex lives. A priest questions a woman about whether she really is pregnant by the man she plans to marry. A high school counselor takes an undue interest in what the students do after school, and they make up stories to please him. Male ex-addict counselors in a therapeutic community closely question young female residents about their sex lives. And if there are homosexual clients who are only too ready to be graphic about their sexual practices, there is also the "straight" therapist who asks, "What did you do next? And what did you do then? Did you enjoy it? Are there any things you won't do?"

What all of these individuals have in common is not evil intent, but insufficient training, which in this case has clearly detrimental effects on therapy. All too often, clients can sense the difference between appropriate and inappropriate questions. Some clients find this kind of voyeurism alienating and distressing; because of it they may leave therapy. Others manipulate it. Many an intake counselor has stopped taking notes and settled back in his seat while a client brought forth stimulating but irrelevant revelations.

Overidentification. This large issue is at the root of a great many difficulties in therapy (Edelwich and Brodsky, 1980). Its effects will be felt in numerous situations described in this book. Overidentification with a client's feelings (as in "When I was young there was no one there to help me") may lead a therapist to be unwilling to confront a seductive client and become too receptive (emotionally if not sexually) to the client's appeals. If there are unresolved issues in a therapist's own life, the therapist may establish too close or too distant a relationship with a client who presents similar issues. For example, a woman came to a male psychologist to deal with sexual issues. The psychologist, who was then getting divorced, was attracted to the woman—a fact which he recorded in his notes but did not discuss with a supervisor or colleague. The woman felt that she did not benefit from therapy with this man, who in retrospect realized that he was trying so hard not to seduce her that he blocked out what she had to say.

Who Seduces Whom?

The elementary observation that seduction is a two-way street has become hotly controversial, in that it carries overtones of "victim-blaming" and diffusion of moral responsibility. Schoener (1989e, p. 45) states categorically, "There are no data in the literature to show that any client characteristic predicts sexual involvement with a therapist" (cf. Luepker, 1989). Other observers, however, have questioned the validity and the usefulness of treating the patient as a "blank page" on which the therapist's depravity is etched. Clements (1987) questions whether "victim-playing" may not be as large a trap both for feminists and for psychiatry as victim-blaming. Gutheil (1989a), using a descriptive sample of patients from litigation and forensic consultations, identifies borderline personality disorder as a primary factor putting a patient at risk for abuse by a therapist. Analyzing the dynamics of the "patient-therapist dyad," he explains how the patient's rage, neediness, dependency, boundary confusion, manipulativeness, and/or entitlement can act upon an inexperienced, inadequately trained, emotionally vulnerable, or careless therapist. This, in different language, is what we have been talking about in this chapter. Gutheil's article has provoked indignant reactions, such as the charge that "many courageous women who have been abused by therapists, women who are struggling with shame and guilt and who are just now beginning to find a way to voice their complaints, will be further victimized and silenced" by such pejorative diagnostic labeling (Jordan, Kaplan, Miller, Stiver, & Surrey, 1990, p. 129).

For the therapist who treats victims of sexual abuse in therapy, the task of disentangling long-term personality characteristics, the effects of prior life experiences (including childhood sexual abuse), and the effects of the recent traumatic stress of patient-therapist sex is a complex one (Thompson, Benoist, Percy, & Stefanson, 1989). In part, the conflict that has erupted in the professional literature has arisen from looking at different populations. Overrepresented in Gutheil's (1989a) sample is the type of personality most likely to be involved in litigation, especially in the very small percentage of accusations of sexual abuse in therapy that prove false. Schoener (1989e), on the other hand, has viewed a larger sample of victims seeking therapeutic or other assistance at the Walk-In Counseling Center in Minneapolis.

There are deeper philosophical and practical disagreements as well. Feminist therapists seem concerned that any acknowledgment of the complexity of patient-therapist interactions in this area will contribute to perpetuating abuses tacitly condoned by a male-dominated, self-protective profession in a cultural context that sanctions widespread victimization of women. In contrast, Gutheil (1989a, p. 597) asserts that to discuss the matter in its true complexity (besides being a fundamental intellectual obligation) has a necessary educational function: "to alert clinicians to a potential pitfall in order to prevent its occurrence." He emphasizes that "To study the patient-therapist dyad in clinical terms is not the same as indicting the patient (blaming the victim) for some malfeasance, nor is it the same as explaining away, exonerating, or excusing the therapist's behavior." In Mogul's (1989, p. 1356) words, clinicians "have a professional obligation to know how to treat these patients in order to prevent their victimization by us." This is the approach taken in this book.

To illustrate how victimization can coexist with mutual causation, the following story told by a 30-year-old woman opens a window into the complex dynamics of seduction, as well as into the invalidation and withdrawal of support that a person can experience when a therapist crosses the boundary of ethical practice:

> Several years ago I went to a therapist who had opened a therapy center with his wife. I think they both had master's degrees, but I'm not sure. At the first session I spoke about how I was seeing several men at the time and how much I enjoyed the freedom I was feeling from that. Then at the end I told him that I couldn't afford to pay his full fee. He told me that he found me attractive, and I felt complimented. Explaining that he and his wife had an "open" relationship, he asked me if I wanted to have an affair with him. We batted it around for a while, until at one point I said, "Well, either we play and I don't pay, or I pay and we don't play."

After we joked about it I elected to pay, and we agreed on a lower fee.

Afterward I looked at what had happened with a kind of double vision. Maybe he had made an advance to show me that I wasn't being entirely honest about my life. Maybe he really was coming on—and if so, then I felt he couldn't be helpful to me. I recall saying to a co-worker, "Gee, here I go to this guy for help, and he propositions me. What's wrong with me?" I continued to see this man for individual and group therapy for a while and then dropped out, all the while wondering about the fact that someone I went to for help interpreted me in the same way everyone else always had.

Even considering only the one side of this tragicomic tale that we get here, it is difficult to untangle all of its elements. There is the client's suggestiveness during the session (along with the possibility that she chose this therapist with some knowledge of his reputation), but there is also a heavy burden of self-recrimination that she has carried as a result of the therapist's behavior toward her. When so much therapy and counseling are concerned with raising self-esteem, it is particularly unfortunate when the actions of a helping professional lead a person to ask, "What's wrong with me?"

3
Power

A psychiatrist quoted in the previous chapter characterized the therapeutic encounter as "a sparring match between two people who are perpetually feeling each other out." What are some of the dimensions of this power struggle? One side of it is personified by Charlie in our opening story, who extorts sex as a quid pro quo for building Alice a raft. Charlie embodies the age-old battle between men and women to gain the upper hand, with sex as both a token and a prize. In the situations examined in this book, the war between the genders goes on in the context of a struggle for power between client and therapist. Here, too, each side has its weapons. The client's power—be it the power to attract or the power to coerce—is personal and physical. The therapist's power is personal, social, and institutional; it is the power to observe, to know, to teach, to judge, to open and close doors.

Client Power

The term "client," as used here, covers a wide range of people and situations. At one extreme, there is the parolee who comes to the probation office with the aim of getting out as quickly and painlessly as possible. If the parolee is not able to tell the probation officer what the officer wants to hear, he or she may start taking risks, whether through seduction, an appeal for sympathy, or a show of bravado. This stark example of desperate evasiveness is not so far removed as it would seem from what goes on in other therapeutic and "helping" milieux. People in therapy, however seriously motivated to change, put up conscious and unconscious resistances. Students typically feel considerable anxiety about how much they have to learn and how they will measure up when tested. A normally self-confident person who becomes a medical patient tends to experience pain, fear, and embarrassment in this weakened state (Bursztajn, Feinbloom, Hamm, & Brodsky, 1990). All of these people have a need for reassurance. One way they seek to get it is by exploiting what power they have in a situation of relative powerlessness.

Power after the fact. A person who has been a client in a therapeutic relationship can influence the therapist's reputation, at least among a limited number of people. In most cases, about all the client can do is to say, "He didn't do a damn thing for me," to whoever will listen. Vindictive clients can make false accusations of impropriety, but this power to do harm is circumscribed by the greater credibility that the therapist generally enjoys. If, however, the therapeutic relationship escalates into personal intimacy, then the client's power to divulge damaging information becomes something to be reckoned with. Thus, as noted in Chapter 2, students who have affairs with professors are likely to tell their friends about it afterward. A sexual relationship with a client compromises a therapist's ability to confront, a caseworker's or probation officer's capacity to maintain discipline and enforce the law.

Power before the fact. Instances of a client's gaining the upper hand by seducing a helping professional are infrequent as well as relatively straightforward. More subtle as well as more common are the exercises of power that occur before a sexual relationship ever comes about. These gambits on the client's part may be part of an attempted seduction or an alternative strategy for gaining the client's ends. Like the seductive techniques described in the previous chapter, they represent a form of limit-testing as well as a continuation of the (usually dysfunctional) methods of coping that the client has learned in the outside world.

Seduction on the part of a man or a woman can be a power play, an acting-out of deep-seated conflicts in the therapeutic arena. A more direct expression of the need to assert power is through a threatening display of physical strength. The low self-esteem of the woman who doesn't trust people enough to seek their regard except as a sex object is mirrored by the low self-esteem of the man who compulsively presents himself as strong, daring, and virile. Physical intimidation (especially in its more benign forms) may be combined with sexual suggestiveness or a sexual invitation. An example from an account given earlier is the "caveman sexuality" of the male client who momentarily grabbed a female therapist's ankles "as if to pull me off the couch." Although this man was not acting violently, he evoked the symbolism of violence to convey a message: "Whatever else you and I are, we are also a man and woman together in this room. Just in case you've forgotten, you may be the therapist, but I'm bigger and stronger than you are."

Young men with a history of violent behavior, such as those who have been members of street gangs, pose a threat of violence to the individuals, male as well as female, who work with them. Indeed, the risk of outright violence is probably greater for males; since violence-prone male patients often are more threatened by other men than by women and may be guided by an internalized prohibition against striking a woman. But for the growing numbers of female clinicians and social workers, correctional officers, attorneys, counselors, and probation officers who work with these young men before, during, and after their incarceration, the threatened assault has an explicit or implicit sexual component. A 40-year-old social worker who meets her prospective clients in a place called "the lockup" (a small windowless room in a court building where men who have been arrested the previous night await initial disposition of their cases) describes the dread she feels there:

> I don't want to go in there, even though I'm always accompanied by a male public defender or sheriff; *they* don't even want to go in there. When I go there I can expect to be greeted by catcalls and shouts of "Hey, Babe." They didn't tell me about this in social work school.

Such limit-testing by clients often presents the clinician with tests of strength and will, as in this account by a female counselor in a male prison:

> At one point I confronted two inmates for being late for group meeting. They had their hands on their hips and were smiling defiantly; it was obvious that they didn't take me seriously. Partly it was because I was program director only temporarily and didn't

have much real influence. Partly it was because of my kidding manner, which makes it hard to tell when I'm serious. And partly it was because they were so big and I was so small. I had to look *up* at them to tell them off. They projected a macho air, like "You don't let a little woman tell you what the score is."

I kept my cool, but I could feel my nostrils flare and the muscles in my face tense up. Later I confronted these same individuals again, and this time we had a serious argument. They listened to me when they saw that I was no longer kidding.

Provocative behavior can, of course, go much further than this. It can turn into a threat of imminent violence, as in the following account by Gloria G., who in her mid-twenties worked as a housemother at what she called a "glorified reform school" for males aged 12 to 16. Originally responsible for 80 adolescent residents, Gloria prevailed upon the administration to hire another woman to take over half of this large caseload. The other woman, however, turned out to be (as both Gloria and the residents described her) a "tease" whose manner provoked and frustrated the adolescents in her care. Gloria, fearful of violent reprisals either on the job or in the apartment she shared with the other woman, questioned her about what she was doing. The woman laughed it off, saying, "You're just a prude. These kids need a lot of love," despite warnings from male staff members that "You can't do that with these kids."

At this facility, all staff members, male and female, were white. Although the residents constituted a racially mixed group, those involved in the incident in question were black. As Gloria tells it,

I was alone with eight boys in one of my cottages when 12 more came over from one of the other housemother's cottages. They had refused to go to the gym with her. Before I knew it they all formed a circle around me and were saying things like, "There's 20 of us and one of you. We want control of the cottage now." I couldn't get to the phone to get help from others on the staff. The circle closed in on me. Fists were flying, though none hit me. I heard remarks like "We'll get you" and "You won't be able to scream." Amidst all the pushing and shoving, somebody would occasionally bump into me and touch me and then fall back into the crowd so that I couldn't see who had done it.

I was afraid—yes, afraid of being raped—but I couldn't let on that I was scared or I would have lost control of the situation. Inwardly I was sweating it out; outwardly I acted forcefully. I did what I knew from experience would have an impact on the eight kids I worked with regularly, in the hope that the other 12 would get the message. I physically pushed my way out of the circle, which gave me a feeling of having regained control and made the point that I still had authority as a staff person. I said that everyone who didn't belong in the cottage had five minutes to get out of there. If they left, they wouldn't get into any trouble, and they could come back another day. If they didn't leave, there would be consequences—I wasn't sure exactly what. Just then most of them had vacation time coming up which they didn't want to lose, so they dispersed, although two or three continued to "mouth off" for a while.

Even then I wasn't out of danger. There was no guarantee that they wouldn't come back that day, and I had four hours to go before another staff member came on for the evening. I called the gym and related what had happened to the one male staff member who was on the grounds at the time. He did what he could, which was to call back every 15 or 20 minutes to see if I was okay. After a while the kids took the phone off the wall while I wasn't looking. Again I was isolated, but their threatening behavior was not repeated.

Gloria was subjected to an overt form of threat of sexual aggression that is often implicit in the behavior of men toward women, both in the client-clinician relationship discussed here and in the harassment of one staff member by another (Chapter 9). The fear she felt and the danger to which she was exposed are among the "givens" of the job situation for many women working in correctional facilities, drug abuse treatment centers, psychiatric hospitals, and even the public schools. In this instance, Gloria believes that she was forced to run unnecessary risks because of irresponsible management:

Had the kids known in advance that I could call someone to back me up, they wouldn't have pulled what they did. In fact, they knew that I could *not* count on any backup. When I raised this issue quite heatedly the next day at a meeting with the administration and social work staff, they told me, in effect, "Boys will be boys. We expect them to act that way; that's why they're here." I said, "Yes, but then we're not helping them. We're feeding into the behavior by letting them get away with it." I insisted that I have another person working with me, but they said it wasn't feasible. They knew what the situation was, but they didn't care to do anything about it. They also delayed a few months before they fired the woman whose mishandling of these adolescents had contributed to blowing their fuse. The administration acted only after the kids came and ripped up the apartment I shared with her and vandalized her car. They painted "Bitch" all over it and poured sand and sugar down the gas tank.

The "backup" Gloria demanded was, in her words, "support from other staff members and the administration at those moments when I needed it, after which they could tell me privately if they disagreed with my handling of a situation." Unable to obtain this support, she left the agency and took a job at a psychiatric halfway house for young adults.

Guidelines for dealing with the tendency of clients to express power needs in the form of sexually provocative behavior or sexual violence can be distilled from the accounts of therapists experienced in this area. A female psychologist in private practice stresses the need to acknowledge the client's human worth at a level distinct from the behavior in question:

When a client, say, touches me in an inappropriate way, I acknowledge the behavior in the spirit of "Okay, so you needed to do this; now let's get past it." I respond to the need underneath the bravado by giving the client the feedback he's looking for (i.e., letting him know he *is* attractive) while conveying that he doesn't need to act out sexually to obtain warmth and caring from me. Those things are there for him without his having to manipulate them out of me. Conversely, however attractive he is and however intimidating he may think he is, I make clear that I am not an automaton whose buttons can be pushed. It is as if I'm saying, "You don't have power over me. I have power over myself—and you can, too." In this way I give him a model of what it's like not to be under the sway of one's own impulses or someone else's actions.

In dealing with potentially violent clients (most often, but by no means exclusively, in situations where the client is male and the clinician female), it is prudent to observe the following precautions:

1. Do not assume lightly that a client will not be assaultive. Evaluate on the basis of all relevant and available information: current behavior (affect, manner, speech, gestures), clinical history, criminal record, character of prior relationships with women, and so on. Juveniles who have any propensity toward violence should be regarded as likely to assault if they have reason to believe they can get away with it.
2. Do not overestimate the value of professional training (one's own or someone else's) in enabling a clinician to predict or prevent violent behavior. Social workers and counselors sometimes "refer up" potentially violent clients to psychiatrists, whose only advantage in dealing with such clients is that they can prescribe pacifying drugs. Professional training may enable a clinician to make better probability estimates concerning violent behavior, but so does experience (irrespective of credentials). And probability estimates, useful as they are, do not remove all risk.
3. Whenever there is judged to be a significant risk of assault, it is advisable to see the client conjointly with a co-worker.

Of course, what seems to be the wisest course of action may not always be possible. As in Gloria's case, budgetary limitations or administrative indifference may necessitate one's seeing clients alone when considerations of personal safety would dictate having a co-worker present. One must then make a value judgment about how much risk one will accept in preference to seeking other employment (Edelwich with Brodsky, 1980).

Clinician Power

Although instances of "client power" may be dramatic and have serious consequences, the power that resides in the client-clinician relationship is mainly on the other side. As our society is constructed, the brute physical power of the client usually is not equal to the institutionally buttressed power of the clinician. Therapists, counselors, teachers, and others in "helping" roles often forget just how important they are to the people they serve, in how many places they touch their lives, in how many ways they influence their fortunes.

Sources of power. A major aspect of the clinician's power is symbolized by the fact that it is he or she who reads the client's file, not the client who reads the clinician's file. The saying "knowledge is power" is particularly apt when applied to the privileged information revealed in therapy. This knowledge confers upon the clinician not only an intangible personal advantage in the relationship with the client, but a practical kind of leverage as well. For the therapist not only reads the client's file, but also adds to it, and what is added may have a lot to do with whether the client is discharged from a psychiatric hospital, gets a job, or goes to prison. Power, then, lies in both the possession and communication of confidential information.

In this power lies the potential for abuse. A therapist who represents the local sheriff's office in dealing with youths charged with criminal offenses comments,

> It would be easy for me to say to someone I'm working with, "If you don't do whatever I want you to do, I'll tell the probation office that you're being uncooperative." I don't do that, but I could. The very fact that I'm a deputy sheriff (which almost all my clients seem to know, even though I don't tell them unless it's relevant) gives me a certain power to keep people in line. I don't know if that's good or bad—personally, I'd rather my clients didn't know me that way.

Client and clinician have the power to communicate damaging information about each other, but the clinician's power is greater to the extent that the clinician has more credibility. A psychologist employed by a health maintenance organization puts this proposition in stark terms:

> If I wanted to have an affair with a patient, I wouldn't go out with her publicly where I might be seen with her. I'd do it right here in the office. If she accused me of anything I'd deny it. It would be her word against mine. And since she's the one with a problem, her word would be the one in question. Every therapist is on his

own once he closes the office door. And someone who gains a reputation as a "good therapist" within the organization isn't going to be questioned.

It is because of this assumed credibility of the therapist about what happens "behind closed doors" that we recommend that a client who is sexually abused by a therapist document the abuse publicly so that others who have had similar experiences can come forward. (Chapter 10 discusses both the risks of reporting and steps being taken to encourage reporting and to support those who report.) It is easier for a therapist to refute one client's testimony than that of several clients who have had no prior knowledge of one another. In the first successful lawsuit ever brought by a patient against a psychiatrist for inducing her to have sex with him on the grounds that it was therapeutic, the psychiatrist tried to discredit the patient's story as a paranoid delusion. His credibility was broken down by the testimony of other women that he had behaved similarly toward them (Freeman & Roy, 1976).

A clinician's power over a client does not stem only from what the clinician knows about the client and what the clinician can say about the client in a court hearing or on a confidential report. A different type of power emanates from the clinician's very being, as perceived by the client. To someone who is unhappy or in trouble, the helping professional sitting across the desk appears as a strong, successful person, as one who (having made good use of experience) "has it made," and as a repository of the "answers" that will bring fulfillment. Seen in that light, the clinician has a wide-ranging power of influence, both by precept and by example. A thoughtful analysis of some components of this personal magnetism is given by Alan L., who teaches psychology at a university. Although Alan is talking about his students, he might just as well be referring to clinical patients, for his discussion of the subtle power struggle between student and teacher is (in most essential respects) applicable to the therapeutic relationship as well.

A teacher's power in relation to students is great, but it is easy to misunderstand what the power is. It isn't a matter of extorting sex for grades, which is rarely done and is even less frequently successful. A teacher who tried that would be too vulnerable. There are, on the other hand, two less tangible sources of power that are not less real for the fact that they exist chiefly in the student's mind.

The first is the power to occupy a person's attention—visual, aural, intellectual attention—over an extended period of time. As a teacher one is in a position to make a sustained presentation of self in an area where one appears competent, insightful, self-assured. In effect if not in intention, one is misrepresenting one's greatest strengths as an index to one's whole being. One is giving the impression that one is what, on broader exposure, one would turn out not in fact to be. It is unfair to exploit such a false impression.

Second, a teacher who is impressive in the classroom and conveys an image (accurate or otherwise) of achievement can confer a sense of high personal value on particular students simply by paying attention to them. To do so on some basis other than a student's academic capabilities (such as sexual attraction) is unwise insofar as it is misleading. This second form of power, like the first, is rooted in appearances—in what may be inaccurate perceptions of the teacher or of the teacher's judgments about the student. The student, therefore, is in a position to be harmed if the teacher presumes on these impressions.

Having delineated the bases of a teacher's power, Alan L. goes on to describe the power struggle between the student's wiles (at various levels of seduction) and the teacher's ethics:

When a student calls or comes to your office more often than would normally be expected, it means that he or she wants something more from you. But for many students that "something" not only is not sexual, but may be very mundane. The student may simply see you as being able to supply a bibliography, to clarify points in the lecture notes, or to give answers to questions that it would take a lot more time to find on one's own.

The pursuit becomes more serious, more directed, when the student (if she is a woman) not only invents a person in your image who has something for her, but also makes a decision that there is something about her that you ought to know so that you can be of additional value to her. As I intuit it, she says to herself, "This man is smart, insightful, expert, gentle, tolerant (or whatever), but all those qualities are of little use to me because they are not being applied to me." The next step—when it may begin to be sexual—is when she decides, "I want them to be applied to me." Then she's hooked. She'll do whatever she has to (which may not be in bed) to get you to pay attention to what is important about and to her.

In order to do that she'll have made an emotional commitment. I don't know how well she knows that, but I know it. When someone has told you what she needs to have you know about her, her body language is a language of pain, a language of capitulation. The head is bowed; the back of the neck is literally exposed. You can hear the pain in the voice and see the pain in the eyes. Partly, this pain is rooted in anxiety about disclosing what has been carefully guarded till now, something that is seen as bad or weak, something that may cause rejection. Partly, too, this pain is about not having you. The "having" is not always sexual or sexually meant, but it is an intense form of emotional possession that feels very like the kind that goes with valuable sexual intimacy. (I've felt a similar intensity of possession on the part of young men who have made an intellectual "father" of me.)

Then you make up your mind what to do about it. As a rule (by which I mean I make it a rule for myself) I try to forestall the intimate revelation, to head it off before it bonds the student to me. I do this not so much for the student's sake, but because I know I don't have the emotional energy to sustain the needs that follow. When I've let it get past that point, I've obligated myself to pay an enormous price. It's taking on a moral burden, and I tell you I don't like it.

As Alan indicates, a teacher's or clinician's power can be used for good or for ill. The following sections pinpoint some of its uses and abuses.

Legitimate uses of power. In Chapter 2 it was suggested that there is a kind of seduction that can be called therapeutic. It occurs when the client is seduced not into having sex with the therapist, but into doing what (in keeping with the goals of therapy) is in the client's own interest. The same principle holds for the exploitation of "clinician power." It is entirely appropriate for Alan L. to use his charisma as a professor to inspire students to learn. A therapist can use the same kind of leverage to elicit constructive behavior and encourage openness to growth.

An inexperienced social worker in a women's prison found herself the object of complimentary attentions from lesbian inmates. It troubled her that her response to this behavior was a manipulative one—"like 'handling' men who flirt in an office situation where you don't want to antagonize anyone." Recognizing that the women who opened doors and pulled out chairs for her were leaders among the inmates, she cultivated them by replying graciously to their overtures. "No matter what my personal feelings," she told her supervisor, "I refrain from throwing their compliments back in their faces and threatening them with disciplinary reports." When she succeeded in winning over these inmates "to my side," the prison was kept neater and there was less violence and drug use.

Still, her misgivings about what she was doing led her to consult with her supervisor. He told her, "I think that what you're doing is appropriate. One of the tools in a helping professional's repertoire is to know when to be seductive, when to be manipulative. If you can use those skills to get the client to behave in a more acceptable manner, to get things done, to stick to a program of self-development, then there's nothing wrong with doing so. But you have to check yourself periodically; always ask yourself whether you're doing it in the client's interest or your own."

"It's a relief to hear that," said the social worker. "I thought I was doing something reprehensible."

It is important, however, to distinguish between legitimate manipulations of the power inherent in the clinician's personal presence and any appearance of potential availability for a sexual or otherwise inappropriately personal relationship. To seduce a client into experiencing the natural consequences of responsible behavior by interposing the immediate reward of pleasing the clinician is acceptable therapeutic technique. To indulge a client in the wish that good behavior will earn a sexual reward is to compromise the clinician's power and ultimately disillusion the client.

Illegitimate uses of power. The most obvious abuse of the clinician's power is the exploitation of clients for sexual gratification. Furthermore, the unequal power relationship is so strongly present in the dealings between client and clinician that, as a rule, even a sexual relationship with a former client is to be regarded as exploitative on the part of the therapist. (This issue will be discussed fully in Chapter 5.) The illegitimate use of the clinician's power is not, however, limited to taking outright sexual advantage of a client. Such cases are simply the most visible manifestations of a broader pattern of ethically questionable behavior.

A form of therapeutic seduction which, while not physical, is self-aggrandizing for the clinician and harmful to the client is the "power seduction" described here by a female psychologist whose experience ranges from private practice to directing social service programs:

> The "power seduction" that some therapists get off on is not something I ever read about in a textbook; rather, I experienced it myself when I was in therapy. With some therapists I felt, "That person really heard me. I'm glad I opened up." With others I had the same "not nice feeling" I used to get as a teenager after parking with some guy that I didn't care about and who didn't care about me. I felt that I had been manipulated into doing something I didn't really want to do—in the one case, a sexual performance; in the other, a client performance.
>
> To bring a woman to orgiastic tears is not that different from bringing her to orgasm. The "Don Juan therapist," like the Don Juan lover, has techniques for giving the appearance of caring. The client responds to the techniques by opening up, giving trust, sharing feelings. So what does the therapist do next? Some cold, rejecting thing that tells the client how shallow the show of caring was. For the therapist it's an ego-trip: "Look how powerful I am! I can make somebody cry." But for the client it's the same kind of betrayal as when someone says, "I love you; come sleep with me," and then leaves you hanging.

When power seduction is carried on continuously with the same client, it can be used to create and maintain an unhealthy dependency on the therapist. In the words of the same psychologist,

> I've seen therapists keep up a "love fantasy" that has the client coming in for years. These therapists deny responsibility by calling it transference, but I can see that they are actively seducing people into the office if not into bed. Look, there are techniques for

making clients fall in love with you; I could do it myself if I wanted to. The trouble is that it's not in the client's interest. It fixates the client's development in a state of dependency long after the dependency has ceased to be therapeutically useful.

In addition to the capacity to inspire emotional attachments, therapists are sometimes also tempted to presume upon the aura of omniscience which is another source of their power. People tend to assume that helping professionals have all the answers. Helping professionals who encourage this belief or act as if they themselves subscribe to it may be acting from unexpressed, unexamined power needs. In a case in point, a woman who was repeatedly beaten by her alcoholic husband, was referred to a legal aid attorney, who obtained a court order barring the husband from having any contact with his wife. Shortly thereafter the husband was committed to a veterans' hospital for treatment of his alcoholism. After a brief period of detoxification, he began therapy with an inexperienced social worker at the hospital. Within a month the social worker had prevailed upon the man's wife to take him back on the grounds that he "needed her" to complete his therapy, which the social worker thought was going well. The wife, who had suffered such severe concussions from the beatings that she had difficulty remembering her telephone number, asked the attorney to have the protection order rescinded. Advised by psychiatrists that the man was potentially homicidal, the attorney could do little but have the woman sign a waiver absolving her of responsibility for the consequences of rescinding the order. The beatings then resumed.

The attorney's response to this sequence of events was one of "personal and professional outrage." The social worker had achieved the success of a "reconciliation" on paper by giving advice that placed the client's life in jeopardy. In this case the social worker may have been so carried away by the novice's grandiose dreams of being a miracle worker (Edelwich with Brodsky, 1980) that she was blinded to the obvious realities of the situation. It isn't only novices, however, who give their need for power precedence over the welfare of clients.

Therapeutic interpretation (even when it does not entail directive advice) can be damaging when wielded as a weapon. A social worker recalls a "power-driven" colleague who led groups in which she sat as a trainee:

An example of this man's arrogance that still pains me occurred in the case of a college undergraduate who had been raped at knife-point while waiting for a bus. He told her—and the group— that the reason she (like all rape victims, he said) felt so devastated was that inwardly she had wanted to be raped. I suggested that whatever guilt she felt may well have come not from having desired the assault, but from a concern that she might inadvertently have done something to provoke it. Other women in the group who had had similar experiences backed me up. Later the social worker was irate with me for contradicting him in the group, but I felt I had to say something right then and there to counteract the guilt he was laying on the woman.

Here the male social worker disseminated to the group a speculative interpretation of the rape victim's motivations. He presented it not as a hypothesis tentatively offered for discussion, but as the authoritative pronouncement of a professional expert. He cast himself in this light without regard for the consequences that the rape and its "therapeutic" sequel might have for the woman, such as lifelong guilt, self-doubt, and impaired sexual response. The power of a therapist to harm as well as heal, especially when interpreting sensitive sexual material, still tends to be underestimated. The kind of insensitive and uninformed approach illustrated here too often goes unchallenged, especially when the therapist is male and has professional credentials.

Further observations about the same social worker by his former trainee suggest that he was conscious of when his power was nearly absolute and when it was limited by the presence of a qualified observer.

It's hard to catch someone like that because he's smart enough not to pull the same stuff when he can be held accountable. Having sat in on as many training groups as I did, I saw that this man never submitted a tape of a session for supervisory evaluation if he had done anything out of line on the tape, even if there was something very good on another part of the tape. He submitted only the innocuous tapes. Similarly, he did therapy differently—he was more restrained—if there was a colleague in the room observing. But if the observer was a trainee like myself, he did whatever he pleased.

Although I object to a lot that he did, I can understand his consciousness of being observed. It's something you can't help but be aware of. When I've been under observation I've at times tried to ignore the presence of the observer, but I can't fool myself; I know the person's sitting there. I've sometimes changed what I was doing to please a supervisor who was right there watching. Generally I've been more hesitant to take risks and try new techniques while being observed.

One might apply the Heisenberg Uncertainty Principle (from physics) to therapy by saying that the presence of an observer inevitably changes a therapeutic relationship between two individuals (Bursztajn et al., 1990). To generalize from the above account, it appears that observation can inhibit both legitimate creative innovation and therapeutic license. Therapists in private practice, as in any setting where observation and supervision are lacking, are least subject to the controls that limit abuses of power in therapy.

The following case resembles those discussed under "Sexual Harassment" in Chapter 9, since it concerns the assumption of power by one staff member over another. It is included here because, as in the previous example, the power assumed (and abused) was that of interpretation and diagnosis. The story is told by Phyllis D., a nurse who learned that a resident psychiatrist was speaking about her as if she were one of his patients.

At my first hospital job the doctors and nurses would sometimes hang out after work at a place across the street. One afternoon I was propositioned by a resident in psychiatry with whom I had spoken a few times there. I told him I wasn't interested. I was taken aback when he then informed me that I had a severe sexual hangup. He said I should go into therapy—not with *him*, of course; that wouldn't be proper. No, I should have therapy with someone else so that I could go to bed with him! I ignored him until a couple of male psychiatric technicians came to me and said, "Do you know you're being talked about?" It turned out that the resident was spreading this story about my so-called sexual hangup, saying things like, "It's really too bad—such a lovely girl . . ."

I was really upset. It was clear to me that I simply wasn't attracted to this guy. I had no personal relationship with him, and to me he looked like a hairy ape! Yet I began to have doubts. "Maybe he's right," I thought. After all, he was a psychiatrist, so he would know. I had to defend myself by saying, "Wait, do I have to have a hangup not to desire a man who's fat and hairy?"

If he could do this to me, I wondered, what was he doing to his clients?

The question is very much in point. That this man could play upon his psychiatric knowledge to create confusion and conflict for a fellow professional (albeit a young, inexperienced one) says something about the potency of the image of expertise that helping professionals have in sexual matters. The word "hangup" is, of course, too imprecise to be part of the vocabulary of any discipline. Yet when it is uttered with professional authority, its very vagueness can help create or exacerbate problems for the naive hearer—problems such as guilt, self-fulfilling prophecies of sexual inadequacy, or coercion into sexual experiences that the person does not want, does not need, and cannot afford emotionally and psychologically.

Phyllis eventually resolved the matter in a way that we recommend in Chapter 9:

> Not really knowing how to proceed, I reported the incident to my nursing supervisor. I also confided in about 10 other women with whom I worked, and one or two revealed that the same thing had happened to them. The male technicians who had told me the story told me that they were sufficiently concerned about what was going on to back me up at a hearing if that became necessary. Meanwhile, though, my complaint got passed through channels, and the resident was instructed by his supervisor to let people know that what he had said about me had been merely an expression of his own pique at my rejection of him. He was told that he would face disciplinary action if any further incidents occurred.

Since Phyllis was a staff member rather than a patient, the improper conduct at issue was not the sexual offer, but the context of intimidation in which it occurred and the slander that followed. The remedy, though, would be the same in either case. Phyllis acted correctly in taking the matter to her supervisor. Not every employer, however, can be counted on to follow up as satisfactorily as did the administration of this hospital.

Phyllis therefore revealed the embarrassing episode to her co-workers and sought corroborative testimony in the event that she had to document a formal complaint. A generation ago the burden of proof would have been entirely on Phyllis. There are still places and circumstances where one can get away with what the resident did to her, and there are people who will do this sort of thing as long as they can get away with it. Increasingly, though, there are remedies for clients and staff members who are subjected to abuses of professional or institutional power.

4
Opportunity

In Chapter 1 the symbol of opportunity is the sinister figure of Ernie lurking behind a bush. Out he pops when least expected, proclaiming love to a woman who, given the choices open to her, just might want to believe him. If we imagine the island in our fable as the Garden of Eden and Ernie as a snake, we get a sense of the role played by opportunity in the sexual dynamics of therapeutic relationships. Opportunity is the snake in the grass that can waylay the therapeutic relationship at an unguarded moment. Yet usually there is no human snake, no Ernie consciously intent upon exploiting Alice's vulnerability. Often it is both the client and clinician who bite into the apple of opportunity—opportunity that arises from the special vulnerability of people in certain situations as well as from a human vulnerability that is universal.

The case study that follows has Ernie popping out from behind bushes all over the place, even though all of the principals are intelligent, morally conscious human beings. The case concerns Ellen A., a health insurance administrator in her late twenties, and a male psychiatrist whom she has been seeing for a year and a half. Throughout her adult life Ellen has suffered from periods of depression connected with fluctuations in her weight, which tends toward the obese. During one such period, her close friends Lionel and Norma W., a psychiatrist and a clinical psychologist, suggested that she see Dr. M., a colleague of theirs who specialized in clinical pharmacology. Ellen began weekly sessions with Dr. M., during which various antidepressant drugs were tried until satisfactory results were achieved with lithium. As her condition improved, Ellen saw Dr. M. less often—first monthly, eventually once every three months. At this stage Dr. M. referred Ellen to a female therapist whom she has continued to see on a weekly basis for in-depth psychotherapy. She also takes a laboratory test twice a month to regulate the amount of lithium in her bloodstream. The results are sent to Dr. M., who relays them to Ellen by telephone.

In the early weeks of her therapy with Dr. M., Ellen, unhappy and sometimes agitated, spoke openly and fully as one would in insight therapy. This unedited communication was helpful to Dr. M. in making a diagnosis and establishing a baseline for measuring Ellen's later progress; it was also something Ellen very much needed at the time. Dr. M. provided a safe atmosphere in which she could reveal herself and seek comfort. She was as yet too distressed to take note of the fact that Dr. M. was a tall, well-tanned man in his late thirties with impressively sculptured features. As she regained her equilibrium, she found herself describing him to others as handsome and sexy, but she did not fantasize about him until about six months after she began the lithium treatments. As she recalls it, "One spring day I was driving down the street when suddenly I had the most vivid erotic fantasy about Dr. M. I was excited that it had happened, not because it was about him particularly, but because it meant that I was getting healthy again if I had enough extra emotional energy to be attracted to a man."

Ellen continued to have fantasies about Dr. M. and occasionally dreamed about him. Lionel and Norma, who saw her often, remarked to each other that the therapist they had recommended had come to have a prominent place in Ellen's thoughts. One evening while they were visiting Ellen, Dr. M. telephoned her at 10:45 P.M. to give her the results of her lithium test. Ellen greeted him warmly and chatted with him for about twenty minutes. Lionel and Norma were surprised and disturbed. For a therapist to call a patient at that hour, except in an emergency, seemed inappropriate to them. Later they confronted Ellen with their concern that Dr. M. was "feeding" her fantasies about him by calling her late at night. They suggested that she ask him whether such calls were part of his usual professional routine. Ellen reacted with discomfort and irritation, as if her friends were bent on spoiling a perfectly innocent good time. At first she didn't see what all the fuss was about. But Lionel and Norma have been unwilling to let the matter drop, and Ellen has continued to explore it with them, though not with Dr. M.

In Ellen's view, there is nothing improper or even remarkable about the late-night calls she gets from her therapist, which, she believes, came about as a convenient way for two busy people with irregular schedules to make contact. Although she does not recall exactly how the pattern was established, she thinks that Dr. M. must have called her one evening and asked, "Is this too late to call you?" and that she replied that it was not. Since then he has often called after 10 P.M. She concedes that the calls do feed her fantasies about him. When he calls she is usually alone, sometimes in bed. She finds it comforting to hear from him so close to the end of the day.

Yet there is nothing sexually suggestive or overly personal about the conversations themselves. Dr. M. calls only when he has a lab report to convey. That formality disposed of, he asks Ellen how she is doing, and she speaks to him much as she would during a therapy session (although the telephone time is not billed). She may also ask him about his research, and they speak about their shared professional interests and contacts. The same mutuality characterizes their meetings in Dr. M.'s office. Although Ellen believes that her fantasies about Dr. M. have not interfered with her ability to communicate with him openly as a therapist (except about the fantasies themselves), psychotherapy is no longer the focus of their relationship since he referred her to the woman therapist. Usually she requires only about half of their scheduled thirty minutes to deal with therapeutic issues. The rest of the time they spend chatting. At the end of one session, she recalls, Dr. M. remarked "It's been very nice talking to you; too bad it has to end. One of these times we'll have to schedule more time."

It is this personal rapport, this informal quality of their relationship, that Ellen fears she might lose if she questioned Dr. M. about the appropriateness of his late calls. She admits that fears of rejection as well as embarrassment have kept her from telling him about the aura of nocturnal fantasy that has come to surround her end of the phone conversations. She is frankly reluctant to lose either her fantasies or the reality of "our enjoyment of each other's company."

At the same time, she questions the need to raise the issue with him in view of the absence of any impropriety on his side or any confusion on hers about what their relationship is. Dr. M., while sharing his intellectual concerns with her, has not revealed to her any personal information about himself except incidental details such as where he goes on vacation. (For guidelines on self-disclosure see Chapter 6.) Ellen still does not know whether or not he is married. ("I'm afraid to find out!") She understands clearly that the sexual fantasies in which she has indulged are nothing more than that. She sees no danger that she would try to act them out. Although she has had "stray thoughts" about having a sexual relationship with Dr. M. once she is no longer in therapy with him, she has never contemplated terminating their professional relationship for that purpose.

After Lionel and Norma brought up the issue of the late calls, Ellen sought the advice of her primary therapist. The therapist confirmed that Ellen had told her, too, that she did not mind being called late at night. The therapist thought it perfectly healthy for Ellen to have fantasies about Dr. M., but found it unusual for a therapist to be calling a patient consistently at such a late hour. Ellen summarizes her own view of the situation in these sour words: "It was fine for me and for him until someone said it wasn't."

In response, Lionel explains why he intervened:

> If Ellen is now able to see her fantasy about her therapist for what it is, I feel that Norma's and my reminders helped her achieve that clarity. We were telling her to check herself before she got too far into the fantasy to be able to distinguish it from reality. It was clear to us that for her the lithium levels were not what the calls were about; they were a pretext for something else. I don't know why Dr. M. didn't see this, too. The communication of lab results was a quick, impersonal, routine matter; there was no emergency. If he couldn't handle it within normal business hours, it could have been done through a secretary or by mail.
>
> I don't call my patients in the evening (except in special circumstances) because I believe that the conventions that define those hours as private time should be respected by helping professionals. A clinician who is too busy to call patients during the day should restructure his or her schedule to include a call hour. I can see answering messages at 8 or 9 P.M. if one's office hours end at that time, but even then I'd hesitate because of the implications of calling in the evening.
>
> There are, in addition, special features of the psychotherapeutic situation that should have argued against making these calls. Therapy concerns itself with people's sense of themselves, their presentation to others, their manifest and less manifest motivations. Since these areas are not satisfactorily worked out for the patient (that's why the patient is in therapy), it is impor-

tant for the therapist to be a model of clarity, of appropriateness, of awareness of where one stands emotionally. In Ellen's
case there was already ambiguity about who her primary therapist was and whether she was getting drug therapy or insight
therapy from Dr. M. Instead of clarifying his role, he opened
up further ambiguity.

Here was a patient with a history of obesity, low self-esteem,
and difficulty in establishing sexual relationships. When this issue
arose she was not involved in a sexual relationship and had not
been since she began treatment with Dr. M. For this woman to
be seeing a young, attractive, successful male therapist was a
set-up for transference issues of the kind that should be systematically examined in a safe therapeutic milieu, that is, in the office.
By letting these issues cross over into an undefined extra-hours
relationship—especially when therapy sessions were not scheduled so as to allow time to work them out in depth—was to risk
making a mess that would have to be cleaned up later. This is not
to say that the results necessarily would have been catastrophic.
Indeed, if the situation had blown up, Dr. M. might have been
able to make some therapeutic use of it. But we don't take such
risks knowingly. Doctors always use antiseptic when doing minor
surgery despite the fact that most people wouldn't be infected
even without antiseptic. In the same way, Dr. M. didn't take precautions against what *might* happen.

It would be better for Ellen to put the energy she's invested
in this fantasy into finding a real lover. Even aside from the sexual
implications, the symbolism of the late-night calls raises questions
of dependency. I believe that a therapist should, whenever possible, help people learn to solve their own problems. I don't think
Dr. M.'s actions in this instance have been having that effect. He
is a skilled, sensitive psychopharmacologist who is aware of the
principles I am invoking. It seems a striking lapse of
consciousness—one that would call for peer review—that he
didn't see what my wife and I immediately perceived to be
bizarre. If Ellen were my patient rather than my friend, I would
raise the issue with him myself. I would still like to speak with
him about it as a colleague, but I think it would be better coming
from Ellen than from me. With Ellen, Norma and I recognized
that we risked making the problem worse when we spoke to her.

But we felt that we knew her well enough and would remain available to her to support her in working out the issue. I think that the results thus far have confirmed us in that judgment.

Perhaps the only thing that can be said with confidence about this case is that the issue is not one of impropriety, but of therapeutic error. As to the latter, it is unlikely that peer review, which Lionel rightly says would be useful, would yield a unanimous conclusion. In Dr. M.'s defense it can be said that Ellen has never given him reason to suspect that she has been making so much of their contacts, since her behavior toward him is always appropriate. On the other hand, a therapist is expected to take into account other levels of response that may not be apparent in a person's conscious self-presentation. As Ellen herself concedes, "I can keep it within bounds; others perhaps could not." Dr. M. might ask himself how he could tell, in the kind of attenuated relationship he has had with Ellen, whether the patient was losing perspective.

If Dr. M. has failed to entertain doubts that normally would occur to a therapist, what may have motivated this lapse? He is not taking advantage of the situation to gain anything for himself—except the enjoyment of his friendly exchanges with Ellen. Has this mild pleasure (in the context of some difficulty in his own life) seduced him into therapeutic inattention? It seems more likely that he regards his conversations with Ellen as themselves therapeutic. One of the things that a therapist can be is simply a paid friend. When he made the remark Ellen reported—"It's been very nice talking to you; too bad it has to end"—Dr. M. may have wanted to contribute to building up Ellen's self-esteem by showing that he genuinely valued her company. Such therapeutic gestures would not seem to require coordination with Ellen's primary therapist. However, Dr. M. would be in error for failing to consult the primary therapist if he were going so far as to encourage in Ellen a degree of sexual interest in himself to lift her out of a preoccupation with her lack of sexual fulfillment.

Lionel and Norma also have made a therapeutic input without speaking with Ellen's primary therapist. Lacking any therapeutic mandate for advising Ellen, they have appealed to a different mandate, that of friendship. In making (imposing?) the judgment that Ellen "should" find a lover rather than divert herself with fantasies about Dr. M., they would appear to be insufficiently empathic insofar as they are not taking into account the realities to which Ellen has chosen at present to accommodate herself. They are on firmer ground in critiquing Dr. M. for doing what they believe to be detrimental to her development. In communicating their observations to Ellen, they have willingly taken the risk of damaging Dr. M.'s credibility with her. Dr. M., on the other hand, has made himself vulnerable to this disruption of his relationship with a patient by sanctioning an innocent irregularity of procedure in that relationship. In more than one sense he has created opportunity, and opportunity can be the breeding ground of abuses.

This case, where no such abuses have occurred, shows how qualified, well-intentioned people can align themselves on opposite sides of the thin line that separates what is appropriate from what is inappropriate in a therapeutic relationship. Helping professionals need to alert themselves to the tiny cracks in established routine—and in self-control—that can let out a flood of consciously or unconsciously self-serving behavior.

Vulnerability

Alice was susceptible to Charlie's power play and Ernie's opportunistic pitch because she was in a vulnerable position. She was marooned on an island and was separated from and then jilted by her lover. She had few options. The same is true for clients who are marooned on an island of inadequate or dysfunctional learning. People who have not learned how to make use of constructive options are vulnerable to the appeal of shortcuts to security and fulfillment. These shortcuts include substance abuse and crime; they also include manipulating the therapeutic situation or yielding to the abuse of power by a professional. The professional, too, is vulnerable. Clinicians put on their pants the same way clients do. They have good days and bad days, strengths and limitations, areas of satisfaction and areas of discontent. Many clinicians are clients in therapy themselves. Their vulnerability—the vulnerability that exists on both sides of the relationship—is the source of opportunity.

Vulnerability of the client. The vulnerability of the client has been thoroughly documented in the previous two chapters. The clinician's power is the client's vulnerability. Each facet of that power, when looked at from the "down" side of the coin, becomes a reason for the client to seduce or be seduced. The scope of the client's vulnerability to the clinician's influence is captured in these remarks by a male therapist who specializes in treating fellow homosexual alcoholics:

> I am in a position to play around with my clients (if I wanted to) for the same reasons that I once was putty in the hands of my own therapist. I'm their kind of person in two ways, and on top of that I have the serenity that they're seeking. They depend on me to tell them how I got sober, especially in gay circumstances.

One must pay heed to a person who, if only by having traversed the same journey in life, holds the keys to the doors one wants opened for oneself.

An added dimension of vulnerability comes into play in coerced situations—that is, where the clinician can impose sanctions having consequences for the client's life (as with psychiatric evaluation hearings, welfare eligibility checks, or counseling given on the job, in the military services, and in probation offices) or actually controls the client's current life space (as in prisons and mental institutions). Clients who are kept physically isolated from and out of communication with the outside world are most vulnerable. On top of this, the medications routinely used to sedate patients in psychiatric hospitals leave those patients, particularly women, more vulnerable to sexual abuse than they would be when alert. Severe mental disorder itself may make patients indifferent to abuse or unable to resist or to report it.

Vulnerability of the clinician. The vulnerability of the clinician is a more subtle affair. Its nature is summed up by a psychiatrist who has been practicing long enough to observe his own professional development and that of others in the field:

> People often come into the helping professions to help themselves; when their needs are filled, they can begin to give to others. You might say that they come in holding out an empty cup. At that point they can't be expected to give to others what they don't have themselves. The cup is filled as they mature on the job.

Larry N., the social worker in Chapter 2 who was besieged by a seductive client, acknowledged that his cup was not full when he said, "I have to admit it was a big blowup for my ego."

The empty or partially filled cup stands for a range of unsatisfied needs, personal as well as professional (Chodoff, 1968; Dahlberg, 1970; Marmor, 1976). Obviously, the lack of a fulfilling intimate relationship in one's own life makes one more susceptible to inappropriate intimacies with clients. A clinician who, when "between lovers" or experiencing strains in married life, acts differently with clients, even in seemingly harmless ways (e.g., having lunch with them, giving them a ride home from A.A. meetings), is showing the effects of a depleted cup. In addition to this and other sources of personal discontent, there are the motivations referred to in the psychiatrist's statement that "people often come into the helping professions to help themselves." In *Burnout* (Edelwich with Brodsky, 1980) we analyze two such motivations—the desire to cope with one's own personal issues more knowledgeably and the desire to exert control over others. The former may lead to overidentification and an overly close emotional involvement with clients. The latter, dangerous enough in a purely therapeutic context, may occasion extraprofessional demonstrations of personal power.

A nurse who has seen more than one of her colleagues marry an alcoholic or drug-addicted client concludes, "We don't look for strong people." In such cases (at least when seen as a pattern, for there undoubtedly are exceptions) the desire to care and to serve—along with the need to control—reflects a deeper personal agenda carried over into the arena of professional "helping" (Shochet et al., 1976). People who do not have this agenda would generally agree with the 30-year-old school psychologist who says, "I am not easily attracted to someone who needs help. I look for a man who has a sense of competence about him."

The difference between building a relationship on one's own and another's strengths and keeping someone in a state of dependency to satisfy one's own need for intimacy is what social psychologist Stanton Peele (with Archie Brodsky) explores in *Love and Addiction*. After showing that a clinging love relationship based on mutual weakness and fear can be psychologically equivalent to a drug addiction, Peele questions the validity of "labeling as 'one-sided' an addictive relationship that lasts any length of time," even if one partner appears stronger than the other. "An (interpersonal) addict demands so much from a partner that only a person who, at bottom, seeks the same reassurance the addict wants will conveniently meet these demands" (p. 112). This analysis points to an emotional vulnerability that may find tempting opportunities for personal gratification in the job of helping more obviously vulnerable people.

Even when no personal agenda of this sort is brought to the job, the frustrations of the job itself can lead to vulnerability. All of the many dissatisfactions that contribute to burnout among helping professionals can leave a person open to extracurricular need fulfillment on the job. Since these problems (in different forms) have been shown to affect individuals irrespective of age, educational attainment, length of experience, and occupational status level, anyone working in the human services is potentially vulnerable (Edelwich with Brodsky, 1980). (There are differences, however, in the levels of consciousness people can bring to bear on the impulses arising from their vulnerability.) The risks are highest with relatively untrained, inexperienced staff members. A counselor at a drug treatment center who is underpaid and overworked, whose training consists largely of "street credentials," who is regularly overruled by his superiors, who sees cynical indifference and recidivism among his clients, and who is subjected to innuendoes about his own "quasi-patient" status may well seek solace from the female addicts he serves.

Other hazards of professional life afflict people who bear little resemblance to the insecure novice or the paraprofessional counselor. Anything that isolates the clinician from normal social outlets—long hours (including weekends) on the job, geographical remoteness, live-in responsibilities at a residential center—increases vulnerability. Private practice is sometimes experienced as a form of physical and social isolation that makes the therapist more vulnerable both to seduction and to assault, especially when one sees clients at odd hours or in an office at home. Disillusionment with one's position, career, or accomplishments is another predisposing factor. A middle-aged professor feels his cup of well-being emptying out as he realizes that he will never write the Great American Novel or be called to Washington as a foreign policy advisor. He looks for something to take the place of his disappointed ambitions. Vulnerable himself, he turns to vulnerable students who see him as omniscient.

Different clinicians are vulnerable in different ways, and some common types of vulnerability are highlighted in Schoener and Gonsiorek's (1989) six categories of sexually exploitive therapists, which are based on over 1,000 cases seen at the Walk-In Counseling Center in Minneapolis:

- *Uninformed/Naive.* This individual, typically a paraprofessional or lacking any credentials, is unaware of professional boundaries, ethics, and responsibilities. In some cases this deficiency can be remedied with proper training, but in other cases it reflects an underlying absence of social judgment.
- *Healthy/Situational Breakdown.* This is a person who yields to temptation under the stress of circumstances— usually a one-time offender who is genuinely remorseful.
- *Severely Neurotic and/or Socially Isolated.* This clinician suffers from longstanding personal problems, a lack of emotional fulfill-ment, and a corresponding overinvestment in work. Sexual involvements with clients grow out of an overly intense involve-ment in therapeutic interchanges.
- *Impulsive or Compulsive Character Disorder.* This is a chroni-cally rapacious person who may sexually harass staff members and others as well as clients. Carelessness and poor judgment may lead to rapid detection.
- *Sociopathic or Narcissistic Character Disorder.* This self-centered, systematic exploiter also engages in multiple abuses, but in a more deliberate, cunning way, using tactics of conceal-ment and intimidation to avoid accountability.
- *Psychotic or Borderline Personality.* This is a seriously disturbed person whose orientation to reality is questionable. Sometimes this type is readily detected on the basis of bizarre thinking or behavior. However, some of these individuals accumulate consid-erable power and many victims by gathering therapy cults around themselves.

Schoener and Gonsiorek and their colleagues find this scheme useful in assessing the abusing clinician's potential to be rehabilitated and to resume professional work. Gutheil (1989b) adds two types that apply specifically to the relatively small number of female therapists who become sexually involved with clients:

> . . . the therapist with histrionic (hysterical) character traits who is emotionally flooded and succumbs to sexual feelings for a male patient; and the lesbian therapist whose nurturant feelings toward a female patient lose their boundaries and turn into a maternal relationship which then becomes more sexual. (p. 4)

These suggested classifications of therapists, while by no means definitive, put in a clearer light the contrasting images of the rapacious predator with a long string of victims and the well-intentioned therapist in a midlife crisis whose defenses are overwhelmed by a seductive patient or by feelings of romantic love. Most clinicians who become sexually involved with clients—the ones who do it once—probably come closer to the latter image. However, the predators (impulsive/compulsive, sociopathic/narcissistic, or psychotic/borderline) make up for their relatively small numbers by the number of people they victimize. In the case of the clinician who is lonely, unfulfilled, under stress, or personally or professionally insecure, the clinician's vulnerability is the client's opportunity. In the case of the amoral or emotionally disturbed clinician, the client's vulnerability is the clinician's opportunity.

In this book, which is intended for clinicians' training or self-study, we are primarily concerned with sexual liaisons that develop out of mutual vulnerability rather than systematic exploitation. Most of our illustrative examples, which reflect the types of dilemmas readers will face in their work, involve unplanned situations. Ellen's unacknowledged flirtation with Dr. M. is a case in point. Few people come to a new job or begin a career in the human services with the intention of seducing clients. Typically, the client and clinician half-consciously exploit each other's vulnerability (Chodoff, 1968). A young female social worker who has difficulty attracting men makes friends with a male inmate in the prison where she works; as soon as he is released to a halfway house, she becomes romantically involved with him. Residents in a detention center for female adolescents engage in overt seduction with insufficiently trained male staff members who (in the words of a consulting psychologist) "given their status, are only too happy to play the game back." It is on situations like these that the guidelines developed in this book can be brought to bear.

Opportunity for the Client

Part of the opportunity that a clinical situation offers the client is simply the chance to meet an attractive person at close quarters, often repeatedly. With all the emphasis given to transference and countertransference, the worker in the field may need to be reminded that attractions between client and clinician sometimes arise from nothing more than normal impulses and normal responses to stimulation. In the words of a psychiatric social worker, aged 30:

> If a young male patient invites me out, as happens occasionally, I find myself feeling guilty and asking, "Did I do something to encourage this?" After one such incident my supervisor reminded me that I am, after all, an attractive woman of about the same age as some of these men. It's hardly surprising that they would feel an attraction in the hospital just as they would anywhere else. There's no need to overanalyze my own feelings, either, when I'm faced with young, attractive male patients lying in bed without much clothing on.

The feelings described here are normal and are not cause for self-questioning. They can, however, be the ground out of which other opportunities grow.

Opportunity permitted by the clinician. The question, "Did I do something to encourage this?" does not always get such a reassuring answer as the social worker got from her supervisor. Sometimes, usually unwittingly, one does do something to encourage a client's hopes, if only by not doing enough to discourage them. In the case of Ellen A. and Dr. M., the psychiatrist helped create a psychological atmosphere that encouraged his client to have intense fantasies about him. Given a client more disposed to act on fantasies and/or a therapist with more insistent personal needs, an atmosphere may be created that permits the client to go beyond fantasy. Clinicians who say, "It's all I can do to restrain my natural friendliness" or "Clients misinterpret the fact that I'm a very physically expressive person" are, in effect, acknowledging that they place themselves in compromising situations with clients. In many cases it is the clinician's "unfilled cup" that opens up opportunity for clients.

To take an example, a woman in her early thirties who counsels alcoholics (without having had formal training in counseling methods) recounts her first experience of mutual attraction with a client:

> The client was a bisexual woman a few years older than myself. We developed such a strong rapport that she began to do volunteer work for me. I gave her extra attention because I liked her

mind, but I can see that she may have drawn other conclusions. Finally, when she called me every day while I was out sick, I decided that it had gone beyond a counselor-client relationship. I also saw that it was taking a lot of energy from me. So when I came back to work, I terminated some aspects of the relationship to reduce her dependency on me. It was then that she came forward with a frank admission of sexual interest. We talked the whole thing out in conjoint sessions with a lesbian therapist whom I called in. This was my first exposure personally to the issue of bisexuality, and I spent a lot of time afterward examining what it might mean for me to have a sexual relationship with a woman (even though I was not about to have one with a client). Eventually I decided against it. Meanwhile, the client ran away from her sessions with me as she had run away from other issues in her life. I refused to chase after her as others had because I thought it would not be good for her therapeutically. I terminated my professional involvement with her. We're still in contact, though. At first, we arranged to keep in touch through letters, but now she drops by unannounced both at my office and at home.

This story is full of unintended ironies, beginning with the straight-faced discovery that daily calls to the counselor's sickbed meant that "it had gone beyond a counselor-client relationship." The counselor acted correctly in enlisting a colleague for conjoint sessions. Nonetheless, in letting the situation get so far out of hand she showed herself unable (through lack of experience and training) to separate her personal feelings from the demands of the professional situation. If her relationship with this client "was taking a lot of energy from me" (perhaps even contributing to her illness), then she was involved to an extent that was good neither for her, since she was making the client's problems her own, nor for the client, to whom she could not offer strength, safety, clarity of roles, and disinterested support. Although she understood and heeded the ethical injunction against sexual relations with a client, she allowed the client's overtures to divert her into a lengthy reexamination of her own sexual orientation. If she was so impressionable afterward, might she not have unconsciously displayed the same extraprofessional curiosity, the same wavering of purpose earlier, while the client was becoming attracted to her? The denouement, in which she passively accepts her ex-client's continued impositions on her life, shows the same irresolution. Having failed to come to terms with her own sexuality, she has let this personal agenda affect her presentation of herself to clients.

The woman who has contributed the following account is 10 years older and has an M.S.W. degree, but she, too, creates a psychological atmosphere permitting clients to transgress the boundaries of the therapeutic relationship. When clients ask for money for lunch or for bus fare, she "lends" it to them. "I can't say no," she says. "I guess I'm a patsy to help people." Usually it goes no further than this, since she does say no to requests for larger sums. With one young male borrower, however, the following sequence of events occurred:

> It seems that this man has had a crush on me from the time when he was on my caseload to the present. He had only a ninth- or tenth-grade education, so one day he announced that he was going to get his high school equivalency degree. It was because of my support, he told me, that he was going to make something of himself. After that he kept calling me at my office (I wouldn't give out my number at home) and telling me how well he was doing on the tests. What was I going to do—discourage him?
>
> Once when he called and asked how I was doing, I foolishly told him that it was my birthday. That day he showed up at my office with a dozen long-stemmed roses. I don't know where he got the money for them. What was I going to do—throw the roses back at him? Not thank him? It was awkward. I told him, "This was very nice of you," and walked him out the door. I made the whole thing as brief and professional as I could. Afterward I was teased about it in the office.
>
> He's no longer my client, but he still calls me two or three times a week. But you know, in a few months he'll have his equivalency degree.

Was the social worker's encouragement helpful to this client, as she would have us believe? Depending on the circumstances, it may indeed be therapeutic to be friendly to clients, to respond graciously to seductive overtures, and even to employ seductive mannerisms oneself, provided that two conditions hold: (1) that such techniques be used strategically in the client's interest, that is, with the sole aim of encouraging appropriate behavior and personal growth, rather than as a reflection of the clinician's personal or professional insecurities; (2) that there not be the slightest hint that a personal relationship with the clinician could be waiting at the end of the rainbow. In this case the social worker's behavior toward the client has had the effect of encouraging appropriate behavior (studying for the degree) as well as inappropriate behavior (the frequent calls and the gift of roses). Although the story she tells is not one of improper conduct on her part, it was surely unwise (as she admits) to tell a client who had a "crush" on her that it was her birthday. A helping professional who would do this on top of lending money might well be giving unintended double messages. Clients sense whether a therapist can be transgressed upon. For this social worker, the costs of being perceived as permissive have included frequent interruptions for phone calls, personal uneasiness, and loss of credibility with her co-workers ("teasing"). Her client may suffer disillusionment, alienation, and some degree of psychological disorientation if he really expects a sexual reward when he finishes his schooling. He may, of course, be aware that he is operating on a level of fantasy (like a schoolboy with a crush on a teacher) and may adjust quite easily to the reality that awaits him. But such rationality cannot be expected or demanded of people with whom one is dealing because they have had emotional problems or have been in trouble with the law.

Opportunity to impose upon a clinician's personal life. The very fact that one is a helping professional may cause one to be subjected to requests for help outside of professional hours and away from the relatively safe office setting. To be asked to provide medical treatment, psychotherapy, or legal advice gratis can itself be burdensome. In addition, unofficial clients (like official ones) may use the intimate revelations opened up by the "helping" relationship as a springboard for further impositions. An Army sergeant in his thirties who had recently cross-trained into counseling learned about this hazard in the following way:

A woman whose husband was stationed in Southeast Asia moved with her children from civilian to military housing and ended up in the house next door to mine. The day she arrived she saw me with my tool box and asked, "Would you give me a hand hooking up my washer and dryer?" The next thing I knew she had me upstairs putting a crib together. She drew me in before I knew what was up. She was in her early twenties, attractive, with long black hair, and she had this thing about not wearing a bra, which made me uncomfortable. She found out that I worked at the counseling center when my beeper went off and I had to go and use the phone. Immediately she gave me her whole rundown on depression and tranquilizer use and her fear that her husband would abuse their children. "Oh no," I thought, "not more work when I'm off duty!" Meanwhile she got closer to me and started making points by grabbing my arm. I clenched up, took my tools, and went home. I told her that she should get help at the counseling center. After that I kept an arm's length relationship with her, just loaning her my tools. When she came to the counseling center she came directly to me, but I referred her to one of my associates because I was uncomfortable counseling someone so close to home.

The words this man uses to tell his story suggest that he is more comfortable working with his tool box than with complex human problems. However, the discomfort he expresses is felt by clinicians at all levels of training and experience. Psychologists and psychiatrists also can be caught off guard away from the office.

Having sexual benefits drop into one's lap in this manner might appear to be an opportunity for the clinician. More often than not, though, it is experienced (as in this instance) as an unwanted opportunity, one offered at the wrong time and place. The impulse to refer such cases, with all their allure, to a colleague is a common one. Since the ethics of "referring out" difficult cases will be discussed extensively in later chapters, it should be noted that the referral in this case was appropriate. The counselor acted in keeping with established ethical and therapeutic principles in declining to undertake a clinical relationship with someone he knew as a neighbor.

A double-edged opportunity. For some clients the subtler breaches of clinical propriety thus far discussed lead to a "greater" opportunity—that of acting out sexually with a willing clinician. A sexual liaison with one's therapist may provide temporary gratification (a "high") and diversion from the troubling business of therapy. Nonetheless, it is the unanimous testimony of the helping professionals interviewed for this book—therapists and clinicians of many kinds—that such an affair ultimately harms the client and is therefore an outright breach of trust on the clinician's part. One type of harm it does is cited by (among others) a psychiatrist who speaks of her experiences at a university mental health clinic: "I have seen students who were seduced by their therapists either refuse to go back into treatment or delay doing so until they were almost beyond help." This also happened in the case of Julie Roy, as told in the book *Betrayal* (Freeman & Roy, 1976). However the client may feel at the time of the sexual involvement, the uneasiness that almost invariably follows not only removes the therapist/lover as a source of support in the future, but also makes it more difficult for the client to trust any therapist. Several of our interviewees mentioned suicides in which seduction by a therapist was a probable contributing factor. Chapter 5 contains further discussion and documentation of what should already be evident—that having sex with a therapist or other professional "helper" is not a positive opportunity for the client, and that it is the clinician whose self-interest is being served.

Opportunity for the Clinician

For the clinician as for the client, some kinds of opportunity are altogether normal. One is the opportunity to be liked and appreciated. A young psychologist explains the dynamics he has experienced with patients in mental hospitals:

We should always keep in mind that all of us, even those who are impeccable in our ethics, are working for ourselves as well as for our patients. We want to get some goodies out of what we're doing. It's nice to be kind and warm and human and supportive and to get paid for it besides—and it's even nicer to be liked for it, too. For some people the hospital or therapist's office is the only place where they can be treated kindly without paying a price for it, so they repay it in the regard they show us. In my first few years on the job I would keep coming back to female patients whose transference took the form of adoration of me. It's hard not to give extra attention to someone who idealizes you.

Another legitimate form of opportunity is the therapeutic breakthrough. Like seduction and power, opportunity can be used therapeutically. An experienced therapist is alert to the fortuitous circumstance, the unexpected revelation, the catalytic intervention that can move a therapeutic interchange off center after weeks without progress. A social worker describes two such opportunities in her treatment of a prostitute whose troubles with the law were compounded by the physical abuse she suffered at the hands of her boyfriend, who was also her pimp:

> The first time she was in my office I left my pocketbook in there with her when I went out to the bathroom. I often did this without thinking; there was never much money in the bag, and occasionally I learned something from the way the client reacted. This time when I came back into the room the woman was in tears because I had trusted her as no one ever had before. That got our relationship off to a good start. For a while, though, we didn't get very far because she didn't have the habits of expression needed to tell me what was bothering her. She had been sexually violated by her father, but she couldn't talk about her anger; she just cried. Finally I said, "We really have to break out of this," and suggested that we take a walk outside. We continued to talk outdoors when suddenly she picked up a big stick and started whacking the bushes. She got some nice scratches, broke the stick, damaged the bushes, and let out wild screams. That changed her way of dealing with her anger. In small but noticeable ways she became more assertive, cried less, talked back to her boyfriend, and seemed to feel less guilty about the incest with her father.

Especially when working with sexual issues, a therapist should be aware that important facts (let alone subtleties of interpretation) about a client's life may emerge only when one is well into a course of therapy with the client. People have many secrets, and the sudden revelation of one of those secrets should be treated as a therapeutic opportunity, although catharsis alone does not guarantee rapid behavioral change. The social worker in this case, rather than expecting the prostitute to break off with the pimp, was rightly encouraged by smaller signs of her growing independence.

This is one kind of opportunity that comes out of the intimacy of the therapeutic relationship. It is mentioned here to contrast it with the antitherapeutic opportunity that Larry N. (in Chapter 2) had in mind when he silently exclaimed, "You're God's gift to therapists"—the opportunity to satisfy one's own needs or desires at the expense of vulnerable clients. Such opportunities can arise in a variety of clinical settings.

Paraprofessionals. Opportunity is greatest when both the client and clinician are vulnerable. This occurs most dramatically when men with little training in clinical procedures are placed in positions of authority over women, as in therapeutic communities for drug abusers. In one such facility the director found female residents objecting to having to see the female therapists to whom they were assigned, preferring instead to spend unscheduled hours telling male therapists about their sexual escapades. Although the therapists (i.e., ex-addict counselors) did not have sexual relations with the residents, they did ask voyeuristic questions to elicit titillating confessions. The residents, whose seductive techniques were relatively ineffective with their female therapists, appeared to enjoy having vicarious relationships with the male staff members. The director moved to correct the situation by establishing guidelines specifying not only sexual relations, but also "inappropriate sexual conversation or formation of relationships with residents" as grounds for probation after the first incident and dismissal after the second.

This scenario could have been anticipated, given the vulnerability of the residents and therapists to mutual exploitation. Consider a male counselor at a drug and alcohol rehabilitation center who has a recent history of substance abuse, a criminal record, a lack of professional training, insufficient standing in society to get a decent job elsewhere, and unresolved issues concerning women. He can be expected to see in his female addict clients an opportunity for self-gratification. Given sufficient stress on the job, he may use his position to exploit women just as he previously used his access to drugs or liquor to gain sexual benefits.

A textbook case is that of Walter E., who went from the street to prison to Daytop Village to a state civil service job as a drug counselor. Troubled by the "quasi-patient" stigma, his powerlessness within the agency, recidivism among clients ("It was like losing a friend"), the realization that he was making therapeutic errors, and the lack of opportunity for career advancement, he turned to alcohol and marijuana for the solace he had once obtained from heroin. He drank not only with friends on the counseling staff, but also with a female client with whom he became sexually involved. On a particularly frustrating day he got drunk and ran off with the woman, leaving the counseling center unattended and thereby losing his job.

At a drug rehab agency in another state, according to a female social worker who served as a part-time case monitor, male staff members subjected female residents to verbal abuse that was, if anything, worse than sexual abuse. Instead of propositioning the residents, they called them "whores" and "dope fiends" and made remarks like "I'd rather f— a pig than one of you." Moreover, they did this self-righteously because confrontative and directive verbalization was part of the concept of the program. In reality, insofar as such techniques have therapeutic value in exposing irrational thinking and self-indulgent emotional reactions, they should be able to be applied to men and women alike. To attack women for their sexuality cannot be justified as therapeutic. As the case monitor put it, "Nothing so damning could be said to a man as what was said to these young women. They felt bad enough about themselves already. Why further undermine their self-esteem?" The distorted concept of therapy that went unchallenged at this facility gave male staff members the opportunity to exercise their self-interest (i.e., gratify their egos) by denigrating women in the guise of doing their job. Where else would they have the chance to do this? It was a disturbing example of how, in inadequately supervised facilities, female clients can become receptacles for the unexamined attitudes about women held by male staff members.

Those who continue to advocate the "patient-counselor" system of providing therapeutic services sometimes claim that paraprofessional counselors "don't know any better" than to engage in the abuses described here. A male counselor is not likely to be unaware that he is doing something wrong when he seduces or demeans a woman. Indeed, he may be capable of considerable self-restraint when necessary to avoid detection. The effect of his lack of formal training is not to render him oblivious to the destructiveness of his actions, but to allow him a grey area of rationalization, both to himself and to a supervisor who is willing to make excuses for him. Better training and supervision would at least put him on notice that more is expected of him.

At the opposite extreme from the apologists for "quasi-patient" counselors are the elitists who believe that psychiatric training or its equivalent is indispensable for a therapist. The fact is that most of the people doing therapy or counseling do not have such training. State governments and other agencies put people out on the front lines as inexpensively as possible. Once someone has an office as a therapist, clients come in (often under the compulsion of law) and bare their souls without stopping to check credentials. Society has made the judgment that it is better to have people receive this sort of therapy than no therapy at all.

Given that relatively untrained therapists are going to be out in the field, they should at least have adequate supervision. This "should," too, must be qualified by the recognition of limitations (of funds and availability of trained personnel) that too often prevent practitioners from getting the supervision they need. It is evident from the case examples reported here that a lack of adequate supervision has its costs as well.

The case examples in this section thus far have involved male therapists and female clients, which is where the most flagrant abuses by paraprofessional counselors occur. There are analogous cases involving female counselors and male clients, but these tend to have a different character. The women usually are not former clients themselves. Rather, they are college graduates (in the social sciences or humanities) who lack formal training in clinical skills, although they may simultaneously be taking a graduate degree in a related field. Increasing numbers of these women have been working with male prison inmates and parolees in jobs formerly reserved for men. For those who do not feel personally fulfilled, being in close proximity to (and in a position of power over) disadvantaged men offers an opportunity for immediate gratification that may be difficult to resist. At a regional conference of probation officers in 1980, one of the major concerns cited was the increasing incidence of liaisons between female probation officers and male clients or ex-clients.

Trainees. There are many kinds of paraprofessionals besides drug and alcohol rehabilitation counselors. Some occupy paraprofessional positions only temporarily, such as mental health technicians who are studying for a master's degree in clinical psychology. In one psychiatric hospital they are known as "young hotdogs"—men with B.A. degrees in psychology who provide much of the direct therapeutic contact patients receive. According to a senior colleague, these trainees "are trying to be therapists by engaging in frank 'man-to-man' talk with patients in groups." Too often this means probing into the masturbatory habits of a male patient at the patient's first session with a group of clinicians in the hospital. "Clinically what is most relevant is the quality of the person's fantasies," says the senior psychologist, "but the technicians tend to go for storytelling for its own sake. They seem to have no idea that they're speaking with a human being who feels shame." Lacking the experience and/or supervision that would help them understand the consequences of their actions, the "hotdogs" reactivate painful experiences for the patient without making the commitment to follow through and help the patient pick up the pieces. This provocative behavior, intentional or otherwise, can have damaging iatrogenic consequences. Inappropriate as it would be to blame the trainees for their lack of experience or to blame the hospital for not having the resources to set up an ideal training milieu, the consequences must still be reckoned with.

At the same time, we should not place too much emphasis on the mental health aides' paraprofessional status or lack of training and experience. The same psychologist, observing that "it is not always so easy to tell when you're asking questions for the patient's benefit and when you're doing it for yourself," reports that he has seen "an astounding amount of voyeuristic, clinically unjustified questioning on the part of everyone from mental health workers to psychiatrists."

Professionals. Although clinicians with professional credentials presumably have been trained in the ethics of the helping relationship, those who are not under direct supervision have an opportunity to abuse that relationship by virtue of their lack of accountability. This is especially true of those in private practice. In *Betrayal* (Freeman & Roy, 1976) the psychiatrists who served as expert witnesses testified unanimously that to have sex with a client in the guise of therapy was a breach of ethics, but they had no way of disciplining a colleague who engaged in this practice except by refraining from referring patients to him. There are now a number of mechanisms for bringing the isolated practitioner into a community of fellow professionals. These include continuing education, peer review, membership in state psychiatric societies, and voluntary professional accountability groups. Teaching is another way of maintaining contact with peers. As one psychiatrist put it, "It's not good when you have no one to talk to about clinical problems. After all, it can't be that you don't have any."

Professionals occasionally suffer lapses of judgment when opportunity is combined with a kind of professional *hubris*, a feeling that "my station in life entitles me to do whatever I want with the assurance that my good motives will be understood." A well-publicized instance occurred in Brooklyn on the night before Thanksgiving in 1980, when Elisia Fominas, 24, came before Judge Alan Friess on charges that she and her husband had killed their three-year-old daughter. When Fominas told the judge that she had come to New York voluntarily to answer the charges and had no place to stay except prison, the judge released her without bail, took her to his home to spend the night, and (until overruled by his girlfriend) invited her to stay for Thanksgiving dinner. According to Fominas, "The judge went in and slept with his girlfriend, and I slept in another bedroom . . . There were no improprieties." This story was corroborated by Friess' girlfriend, an assistant police commissioner, who testified that she had spent the night in fear of the accused murderess. The media gleefully sensationalized the story. "They took an act of kindness and turned it into something to be ashamed of," commented Fominas, who had been sent back to prison on $100,000 bail by another judge the following day. Judge Friess was cleared of judicial misconduct by the Chief Judge of the Brooklyn Criminal Court, but was later censured (after a hearing which he had requested) by the State Commission on Judicial Conduct. The commission declared that Friess had "exhibited extraordinarily poor judgment and a serious misunderstanding of the role of a judge in our legal system." Friess later resigned from the bench when it became clear that he would not be reappointed when his term expired.

Hospital personnel. A hospital can be a palace of opportunity for those who have access to its resources. Among the opportunities available in the hospital milieu are the drugs commonly abused by doctors and nurses, the doctor-nurse liaisons discussed in Chapter 9, and the vulnerability of patients. Medical and surgical patients are made vulnerable by their weakened condition and semiclothed state. Psychiatric patients are made more vulnerable by their impaired judgment and the drugs used to treat them. The accounts that follow indicate a widespread pattern of abuse of patients by staff members in psychiatric hospitals and other facilities. Each of these narratives, like others in this book, should be understood to represent the uncorrected perspective of one witness. The witnesses, however, are responsible observers, psychologists and social workers with at least several years of clinical experience.

- "In state mental hospitals I have observed abuse of female patients by male staff members that bordered on rape. I have treated two individuals born to women who have been raped while incarcerated in state hospitals. It was not in a state hospital, though, but in a private upper-middle-class community hospital where I worked that a 19-year-old woman, hospitalized for the first time for sociopathy and depression and medicated to the point of grogginess for a week, was taken to a bathroom and used sexually by a man on the maintenance staff."

- "One woman I treated had had documented affairs with two clinical directors in the three halfway houses she had lived in. One of the directors had denied it, and, as usual, his word was accepted in preference to that of the patient, who was 'gaslighted' (i.e., made to feel that she was crazy when she was telling the truth). Then it came out that the director had done the same thing with several other patients. He was fired, but that didn't undo the harm done the patient."

- "A young male patient living in a community residence, who was diagnosed as a borderline personality with sexual identity problems, told me that a male residential director, who was frankly gay, had seduced him into his bed. According to the patient (I could not verify his story), he had slept with the director and had engaged in some petting, though not intercourse, with him. The patient was titillated, but probably suffered harm. I left that job soon afterward, so I could not follow up on the case."

- "A 30-year-old retarded man who was unable to differentiate sexual objects spent a year in a state hospital, where the staff tried to teach him what was appropriate sexually and what was not. During that year a female staff member had sex with him almost every night until they were discovered by another resident. The hospital administration did not document that she was fired for this reason, since to do so would be to admit that she had been doing it for a year under their noses. Instead, they paid her to be quiet by discharging her with severance pay and benefits. It was blackmail. Thus it was never entered into the medical record that the patient had suffered this abuse. The effect on the patient was devastating. Subsequently he was turned down by a residential program because of his continued inability to differentiate appropriate from inappropriate sexual objects."

Two points about these stories are worth noting. First, the abusers were both men and women, both heterosexuals and homosexuals. Second, in at least two cases the effects of the abuses were exacerbated, and efforts to ameliorate the damage frustrated, by institutional politics.

A Culture of Opportunity

In today's society the opportunities for client-therapist liaisons have increased to the point where such relationships have become a highly visible issue. The growth in opportunity is compounded by several factors. One is the trend toward greater sexual freedom throughout society. Another is the patient-to-counselor career path, which has put vulnerable people in the hands of those who are developmentally just one step (in some cases one day) ahead of them.

Finally, the number of people doing therapy continues to grow, along with the number of different therapies they practice. Many of the new therapies are offbeat and informal, without the rules, standards, boundaries, and procedures for training and supervision maintained by the established therapeutic disciplines. While some of the therapists in *The Love Treatment* (Shepard, 1971) can be said to be exploiting the patients with whom they have sexual relations, others seem never to have learned a distinction between practicing therapy and, say, helping a friend. At the extreme, unconventional therapies can take the form of the therapy cults described by Schoener and Milgrom (1989b).

Friends and relatives commonly help each other in situations where the self-interest of all concerned is at stake. When these sources of support are insufficient, a person may turn to a therapist, who offers a special kind of help in which his or her self-interest is (except in certain limited senses) defined out of existence. Given the opportunity offered by the many less than rigorous conceptions of therapy that have gained currency, however, therapists do not always see it as their professional obligation to suppress their self-interest in the interest of the patient.

5
Self-interest

Opportunities are always present, but to act in one's own interest is a choice. If opportunity is represented by Ernie lurking behind the bushes observing Alice's plight, self-interest comes into play when Ernie jumps out to make his pitch. In our analysis of the story in Chapter 1, self-interest was typified by Donald, with his "don't bother me—I'm doing my own thing" mentality. But there are as many varieties of self-interest as there are characters in the story, including Alice herself. For some clinicians, self-interest is tied up with keeping a secure job or living up to the ethical standards of the profession. Others, like Charlie, serve their self-interest by exploiting opportunity and power for immediate gain.

Self-interest takes various forms for clients as well as for clinicians. Although the client's best interest is usually served by dedication to the therapeutic effort, clients are where they are because they tend to interpret their self-interest inappropriately. The female client who plays up to a male therapist to induce him to submit favorable reports to her supervisor at work, the male prison inmate who sends "fan mail" to a female corrections officer to enlist her support for his efforts to win release, the patient who tries to seduce physicians in order to "cut them down to size"—such instances of client self-interest have been presented in Chapter 2, where the many motivations for seductive behavior are analyzed. These motivations are summed up by psychiatrist Bernard Shochet:

> It is my feeling that seductive behavior does not apply solely to
> sexual enticement but to any kind of behavior, conscious or uncon-

scious, designed to mislead and manipulate . . . and to promote the giving of something that the seductive person desires but thinks will not be easily or readily forthcoming. (Shochet et al., 1976, p. 90)

For the clinician, self-interest may take the form of legitimate pride in a therapeutic success, as with the social worker in Chapter 4 who achieved some significant breakthroughs in treating a prostitute who was a victim of abuse. Less legitimate is the generalization of such successes to an image of infallible expertise in an area whose mysteries will never be fully unlocked, that is, the understanding and prediction of human behavior. Helping professionals may find it in their interest (narrowly defined) to promote this flattering image and thereby increase the deference they receive from clients as well as from the courts and other social institutions. Along with the economic and political benefits it confers, the image of omniscience makes it easier for a few practitioners to engage in another form of self-interest which will be the primary focus of this chapter—the sexual exploitation of clients and former clients.

Ethical Implications of Sexual Acting Out with Clients

A college professor, Alan L., says of a hypothetical colleague,

A teacher who claims, "This kid needs me; the way she'll get me is sexually; it will be good for her; she'll learn something from it; I can help her, etc.," is a person I fundamentally don't trust, even though he may very occasionally be right. Although it would be dogmatic to preclude the possibility of benefit to the student in specific instances (and I have seen at least one beautiful marriage develop out of a professor-student courtship), we need to avoid carefully the suggestion that there is a sufficient likelihood of benefit in a given instance to override the ethical objections to exploiting a teacher's power through a sexual relationship with a student. It's self-indulgent reasoning.

In the more fully revealing relationships of medicine and psychotherapy, even the tiny area of negotiability allowed for in Alan's comments is ruled out by professional consensus. Not that rationalizations similar to the ones he mentions are not offered. A 1973 survey of physicians (including psychiatrists) yielded responses such as the following to a question about the potential usefulness of erotic contact with patients in treatment:

"improve sexual maladjustments"
"helps patients' recognition of their sexual status"
"especially in the depressed, middle-aged female who feels undesirable"
"disclosing areas of sexual blocking"
"for specific sexual problems [by being a normal partner]"
"to demonstrate that there is no physical cause for absence of libido"
"to relieve frustration in a widow or divorcee who hasn't yet reengaged in dating"
"in mature patients flowing with nonconflicted [love] feelings"
"in healthy patients by mutual consent making the therapy go faster, deeper, and increases dreams" (Kardener, Fuller, & Mensh, 1973, p. 1079)

Although many of our interviewees attempted to justify having sexual relations with former clients (as discussed later in this chapter), none tried to rationalize sexual contact with current clients. Indeed, several adeptly refuted some of the more common justifications. A female psychiatrist remarked, "It's easy for people not to be aware of how their own needs are interjected into a situation. We can invoke all kinds of reasons about falling in love, but I think we all know about that." A male psychiatrist had this reply for those who say that patients "need love" or "shouldn't have to take another rejection":

Feelings of rejection can be discussed and worked through in therapy. The proper business of therapy is to help the patient find words for feelings and enter into a dialogue so as to reach greater self-understanding and self-acceptance. The claim that this can be achieved through physical intimacy with the therapist can be seen as a rationalization on the therapist's part.

A justification our interviewees have occasionally offered for relationships with ex-clients sheds light on the confusion that permits some practitioners to indulge in sex with present clients. This justification stems from the observation that therapeutic relationships and intimate personal relationships have many of the same features. In the words of a female counselor, "I've had relationships with men where I've played the role of a counselor." A male psychologist asserts, "Any relationship between two people entails manipulation and exploitation. You take advantage of the fact that someone loves you." These statements are in themselves accurate, but their application to clinical ethics is strained and ultimately invalid. Our quotations from Shepard and Lee's (1970) book *Games Analysts Play* in Chapter 2 are intended to be taken descriptively, not prescriptively. The fact that the complex dynamics of human relationships do not cease to operate behind the clinician's door does not give the clinician license to abandon the therapeutic purpose and the constraints necessary to achieve it. Marmor (1972) makes this point clear in discussing the implications of the "parent-child" dynamics of therapy:

> *It is precisely because this kind of unconscious relationship exists between patient and therapist that an erotic exchange between them cannot be ethically or psychotherapeutically justified.* Since when is it necessary for a parent to have sexual intercourse with his children in order to enable them to achieve sexual and emotional maturity? Such behavior between a therapist and patient has all the elements of incest at an unconscious psychodynamic level, and represents an equivalent dereliction of moral responsibility. (p. 6)

Further discussion of the incest parallel can be found in Luepker (1989). As explained in Chapter 10, however, it is not necessary to view the patient as the equivalent of a dependent child or to adhere to a psychodynamic, transference-based model of therapy in order to find a therapist's sexual involvement with patients unethical and legally actionable.

Although the psychiatric and psychoanalytic professions have been slow to acknowledge the problem of sexual abuse of clients (there was very little on the subject in the professional literature before 1970), the past two decades have seen the publication of several clear statements delineating the nature and scope of professional responsibility toward clients and the antitherapeutic consequences of sexual acting out in therapy. The following passages are representative:

- The essential foundation on which the patient-therapist relationship rests in psychotherapy is that of a *basic trust*. On the implicit and explicit assumption that this trust will not be betrayed, the patient is encouraged to set aside her customary psychological defenses and open herself completely to the presumably benign and therapeutic influence of the therapist's professional skill. The ethical psychotherapist cannot and must not exploit the positive transference that develops under such circumstances. (Marmor, 1972, p. 6)

- In an exactly parallel way [to incest] the physician, as a source of healing, support, and succor, becomes lost to his patient when he changes roles and becomes a lover. It is psychologically a frighteningly high price the patient must pay, since good lovers are much easier to find than good caretakers. While the physician, like the good parent, may reassuringly acknowledge the desirability of his patient, it is his responsibility to help guide his patients' growth and development so that they may achieve meaningful and appropriate gratifications in their lives without sacrificing his availability as caretaker. (Kardener, 1974, p. 1135)

- It boils down to the question: Who is the therapy for? From his work the therapist may get the ancillary satisfactions of earning a living, doing a good job, helping, and sometimes learning. These must be enough. The patient comes because he needs help—an admission of weakness. He is encouraged at times to be weak. This implies that the therapist is strong enough, at least, not to take advantage of his patient's weakness. Irrationality is encouraged only because the therapist is the temporary repository of rationality. Anything less is exploitation. It really isn't fair play. (Dahlberg, 1970, p. 121)

Those who claim that sex with patients can be therapeutic are obliged to treat it like any other therapeutic tool. That is, they must present their findings to peer review meetings and professional journals, indicating the conditions under which they have applied "the love treatment" and the results obtained (Marmor, 1972). In the words of a psychiatrist interviewed for this book, "A professional is a person who is committed to sharing perspectives with others." Another inconsistency in the apologists' position is exposed with pointed irony by Marmor (1976), as well as by Silverstein (1977) in the following passage from *Consider the Alternative:*

> If someone claims that sex is just one more "technique of involvement," I reply that I'll believe him (it's usually "him") when I see him apply that technique with young and old, attractive and unattractive, male and female alike. (p. 61)

These published statements, together with the American Psychiatric Association's official declaration in 1973 that it is unethical and impermissible under any circumstances for a psychiatrist to have sexual relations with a patient, have unquestionably raised awareness of this issue among helping professionals generally. This growing awareness is reflected in the level of understanding shown by virtually all of our respondents. In this book, therefore, emphasis has been placed on more subtle questions than the evident self-interest of the clinician who takes sexual advantage of clients.

Countervailing Self-interest: What Does One Stand to Lose?

The fact that most helping professionals do not exploit clients sexually is attributable to other factors besides ethical awareness. If self-interest leads some individuals to go ahead, it gives other individuals reasons to hold back. Among these reasons are the following:

Limitations of time and energy. One check on sexual rapaciousness comes from the limits on human stamina, which are not only physical. In the words of a university professor,

> Anyone who has had a sexual liaison that is more than anonymous—indeed, anyone who has any imagination—would have to realize that after the bed comes a great deal more. When

you involve yourself sexually, you can be sure that more will be asked of you emotionally and intellectually. How many lovers can you take on at that level? You have to become more discriminating.

The professor adds that both parties to a potential love affair usually have this awareness to a greater or lesser degree. "It isn't as if every student who has a crush on me tries to follow through on it," he says. "They know what they're doing." This, too, acts as a restraint on acting out. It should, however, be clear by now that students and clients cannot be counted on to know what they are doing—even if they often do.

Loss of interest. Although the professor's words take for granted a level of concern about personal commitments that not everyone shares, he cites a less rarefied motivation as well when he remarks, "Besides, it gets boring." This can happen not only in a succession of sexual adventures, but also in a relationship that grows out of the circumstantial infatuations of therapy, counseling, or teaching. "When a student who is 17 or 18 marries a professor who is, say, 25 to 35," observes another university teacher, "after a year or so the halo effect can fizzle." Sometimes the demystification brought on by familiarity takes effect much sooner—only here it is the clinician who is disillusioned. Psychotherapists find that clients who initially appear attractive can lose their sex appeal after a period of therapeutic self-revelation. Clinicians who have seen these dynamics play themselves out from beginning to end are less likely to act unrealistically on the basis of "love at first sight."

Loss of job or career. By far the most effective sanction against impropriety on the job is the risk of losing the job and perhaps compromising oneself so badly as to be unable to find other employment in the same field. How formidable this sanction is depends, of course, on how much one has to lose. Suppose that (as happened in an actual case) the counselor coordinator in a drug treatment facility (a 25-year-old former resident) makes the clinical diagnosis that an 18-year-old female resident is a "tease" and tells her, "Your learning experience this week is to go to bed with the counselor coordinator." If this abuse comes to light, he will lose his job, but it isn't a high-level job, and he didn't go through years of schooling to get it. He can't be disbarred; he can't be stripped of his license to practice. There is a considerable gulf between this man and one who, having worked for years to earn a doctorate and a high-paying job, says, "I have lustful feelings, too, but when I get attracted to a student or client I don't have any debates with myself about it. It's not negotiable. I have too much to lose."

There are several reasons why professionals get in trouble less often than paraprofessionals for acting out sexually with clients. A professional is more likely to have internalized ethical standards that preclude such behavior. Greater discretion in carrying out liaisons may be another factor. It should be recognized, however, that a professional not only enjoys satisfactions in life that make illicit affairs less tempting, but also recognizes that the basis of those satisfactions would be threatened by the exposure of improper conduct. The higher one rises on the occupational ladder, the greater the risk becomes. For example, a department chairperson has more to lose than a tenured faculty member, who has more to lose than a non-tenured faculty member, who has more to lose than a part-time lecturer.

Naturally, the likelihood of exposure varies with the setting. It is greater in geographically isolated facilities or ingrown communities where people make it their business to be aware of one another's behavior. One may think twice about the risk of being seen with a client on a military base, as opposed to, say, New York City. A university campus can also be a relatively isolated community. As one professor puts it, "The main payoff for the student in seducing you may be to boast about it, which eventually will land you in the soup." For such a sanction to be effective, however, there must be a firm ethical consensus on the campus concerning sexual involvements between professors and students.

Disruption of marriage and family. Although married and unmarried clinicians generally differ little in their ethics, they do differ in their behavior. For one thing, married clinicians are not as vulnerable to certain levels of interest (beyond the purely sexual and manipulative) that an unmarried clinician may arouse in a client. They also have more to lose. Just how much is enumerated by one who clearly has contemplated his options.

When you're married you have one more person to get pissed off at you if you get caught. At the very least, you have to be more circumspect. You have more lies to tell, more trails to cover, more arrangements to make—and don't forget to keep your checkbook in order.

Furthermore, a person who has children has more to lose by risking his or her job and earning capacity. In this case the career and family sanctions reinforce each other.

Legal liability. In the case of the drug counselor who had little to lose but a dead-end job when he instructed a young resident to have sex with him as a "learning experience," it is pertinent to ask whether the woman he victimized can sue him or whether the state can even charge him with a felony. The same questions arise with psychiatrists and other professional helpers. These rapidly growing areas of jurisprudence will be discussed in Chapter 10.

Rates of Incidence

Given the self-interest that both incites and restrains, how many people actually take up the sexual opportunities that are offered to almost every professional helper? Those among our informants who venture an estimate agree unanimously that "It's a few people doing it a lot rather than a lot of people doing it a little." To override all of the obstacles to sexual acting out with clients (except as a very occasional lapse) that have been cited here, one would have to be (in varying degrees) compulsively dedicated to sexual fulfillment, exempt from the physical, social, and economic limitations under which human beings normally operate, indifferent to both professional ethics and the ethics of personal relationships, and heedless of the consequences for the client and oneself. Given these restrictions, any profession can be expected to have a few, but not more than a few, rapacious people. For example, the testimony of several women reported in the book *Betrayal* (Freeman & Roy, 1976) indicates that the psychiatrist who was being sued had sexually exploited a number of clients.

The reluctance (prior to 1970) of the professions concerned to address publicly the problem of sexual abuse of clients has added to the difficulties of data collection on such a sensitive subject. Interest in the question grew after Masters and Johnson (1970) reported instances of sexual relations between patients and helping professionals of every conceivable discipline, including lawyers and theologians. A decade later Karasu (1980, p. 1508) found that "sexual activities (including sexual intercourse and various forms of erotic contact between therapist and patient) have been increasingly reported in the literature; they have involved clinicians at all levels of training, from psychiatric resident to training analyst."

In the first large-scale systematic study in the area, Kardener et al. (1973) investigated the frequency of such conduct among one professional group—physicians. An anonymous questionnaire survey was sent to 1,000 male physicians divided equally among the specialties of general practice, internal medicine, surgery, obstetrics-gynecology, and psychiatry. The results must be interpreted cautiously, since only 46 percent of the physicians responded and the accuracy and honesty of the self-reports of those who did respond are difficult to assess. On the basis of responses to several questions, the authors estimate that 5 to 13 percent of the total sample engaged in some kind of erotic behavior (defined as behavior primarily intended to arouse or satisfy sexual desire) with patients, while 5 to 7.2 percent engaged in sexual intercourse specifically. Although the distribution of responses by specialty was not statistically significant, the percentage admitting these practices was highest among obstetrician-gynecologists and general practitioners, lowest among psychiatrists. One of the researchers speculates that the effects of the social isolation of the private psychiatrist's office and the emotional intimacy of the psychotherapeutic relationship are outweighed by other factors:

> In fact, the smaller number of patients seen by a psychiatrist, the fact that he generally does not perform a physical examination, and his deeper involvement with the patient-as-person with specific concern for emotional well-being may serve as factors that militate against erotic involvement. (Kardener, 1974, p. 1135)

The data support our consensus observation that only a few practitioners exploit clients sexually. Still, the researchers express concern over the fact that 19 percent of the physicians surveyed, including 20 percent of the psychiatrists, and (in another study) 25 percent of a group of first-year medical students believed that sexual contact with patients might be beneficial in the right circumstances. Some of the supposed benefits cited by these respondents are listed earlier in this chapter. Although the percentage of psychiatrists accepting such rationalizations might be lower now that the American Psychiatric Association has insisted on a higher ethical standard, the researchers' concluding remarks are still apt:

> These figures delineate a core of both physicians-in-training and physicians-in-practice, separated by years of age and years of medical practice experience, who are seriously asking, "Why not?" It is a question deserving of an answer and represents an important challenge to medical teachers engaged in sex education. (Kardener et al., 1973, pp. 1080-1081)

These words, published in 1973, were echoed in 1981 by several speakers at a symposium on "Sexual Behavior Between Psychiatrist and Patient" at the annual meeting of the Canadian Psychiatric Association ("MD condemns sex with patients," 1981). The challenge to teachers in medicine, psychiatry, and other helping professions is ongoing.

Subsequent studies have confirmed and extended as well as qualified Kardener et al.'s (1973) findings. In a further analysis of their own data, Kardener, Fuller, and Mensh (1976) found that male physicians who believed in and practiced nonerotic physical contact with patients were more likely to engage in erotic contact as well. This relationship did not hold true in Perry's (1976) survey of 500 female physicians (which had a 33 percent response rate). Comparing her data with those reported by Kardener et al. (1973), Perry found that more female than male physicians believed in and practiced nonerotic touching, but that far fewer females engaged in erotic contact with patients. Only one female physician reported having had erotic contact with a patient; none reported intercourse with a patient.

A nationwide survey of 500 male and 500 female licensed Ph.D. psychologists by Holroyd and Brodsky (1977), which had a higher response rate (70 percent) than the two surveys of physicians, yielded results remarkably consistent with those earlier studies. Among male psychologists, 10.9 percent reported erotic contact with patients, while intercourse was acknowledged by 5.5 percent. The rates for female psychologists were 1.9 percent (erotic contact) and 0.6 percent (intercourse). Thus, according to these studies, there are no significant differences between physicians (including psychiatrists) and psychologists in the incidence of sexual acting out with patients, but there are significant differences between male and female practitioners. In a statistical confirmation of the general impression that "it's a few people doing it a lot," 80 percent of the psychologists who had had intercourse with patients had done so with more than one patient. (Butler [1975] obtained a comparable figure of 75 percent in response to the same question.) Among Holroyd and Brodsky's respondents an additional 2.6 percent of the males and 0.3 percent of the females reported having had intercourse with former patients within three months after termination of therapy—a finding which raises ethical questions to be addressed in the last section of this chapter.

The patterns discovered in these initial studies have continued to emerge in research conducted in the 1980s, including the California State Psychological Association Task Force on Sexual Intimacy survey of psychologists concerning patients' reports of liaisons with previous therapists (Bouhoutsos, Holroyd, Lerman, Forer, & Greenberg, 1983); Gartrell et al.'s (1986) nationwide survey of psychiatrists; Pope et al.'s (1986, 1987) studies of the feelings, behavior, and ethical beliefs of psychologists; and the Wisconsin Psychological Association Task Force survey of psychotherapists in that state (Kuchan, 1989). (The findings of these and other studies of incidence rates are summarized in Schoener, 1989e, pp. 24–45.) Pope (1988), tabulating the self-reported incidence rates of sexual involvement with clients in a number of major studies over the previous decade and a half, came up with aggregate averages (unadjusted for sample size) of 8.3 percent for male therapists and 1.7 percent for female therapists. A nationwide study of social workers (Gechtman & Bouhoutsos, 1985) yielded considerably lower figures, which may have been a function of the institutional settings in which social workers function or of the self-selection of men for that profession (Gechtman, 1989).

In the most prominent recent study, Gartrell et al.'s (1986) survey of 1,423 psychiatrists, 7.1 percent of the men and 3.1 percent of the women who answered the question acknowledged sexual contact with their own patients. One-third of the offenders—all of them male—were repeat offenders, each reporting involvement with 2 to 12 patients. A majority of the offenders "acknowledged that they engaged in sexual contact with patients for their own sexual or emotional gratification" (p. 1129). At the same time, contrary to all evidence, they "believed that patients with whom they were involved had predomi-

nantly positive feelings about the sexual contact" (p. 1129). Such rationalizations aside, the abusing therapists' admission of self-interested
motives bolsters Butler's (1975) findings, as summarized by Holroyd and
Brodsky (1977):

> 90% of the therapists said they were vulnerable, needy, or lonely
> at the time the relationship began; 55% admitted they were fright-
> ened by intimacy; 70% said they maintained a dominant position
> in the relationship; and 60% saw themselves in a fatherly role with
> the patient. (p. 848)

Although 95 percent of these therapists reported feeling conflict, fear
and guilt, only 40 percent sought professional consultation. A comparable percentage sought consultation in the Gartrell et al. (1986) study.
Predictably, these included 50 percent of one-time offenders, but only
22 percent of repeat offenders—figures that lend color to the impression of an amoral or pathological basis for multiple offenses.

In this study 88 percent of the contacts occurred between male psychiatrists and female patients, 7.6 percent between male psychiatrists
and male patients, 3.5 percent between female psychiatrists and male
patients, and 1.4 percent between female psychiatrists and female
patients. Among over 1,000 cases of sexual exploitation by psychotherapists handled by the Walk-In Counseling Center of Minneapolis, Gonsiorek (1989b) gives the following approximate breakdown by gender:
80 percent male therapist-female client, 5 percent male therapist-male
client, 2 percent female therapist-male client, and 13 percent female
therapist-female client. The larger percentage of female-female relationships in the Minnesota sample may be a function of the fact that
fewer than one-quarter of the therapists in that sample are psychiatrists.
Rigby-Weinberg (1986) has described quasi-consensual posttermination client-therapist sexual involvements that are accepted as
commonplace in some lesbian communities. Special issues that inhibit
reporting of sexual abuses in therapy by male clients as well as by clients in same-sex relationships are discussed by Gonsiorek (1989b).

Although surveys with small numbers of respondents, low response
rates, and reliance on self-reports are not conclusive, they do give us
an approximate statistical picture of the small minority of clinicians who
engage sexually with patients. Underreporting by therapist-abusers in
self-report studies remains a problem of unknown dimensions. Indeed,

honest disclosure in self-reports is likely to become more difficult to obtain as more attention is focused on the issue and more severe sanctions applied. Increasingly, therapists will be in the position of admitting to behavior judged unethical, damaging, actionable, and even criminal (Borys & Pope, 1989; Pope, 1988).

Documentation of Harmful Effects

It is more difficult to verify statistically the presumed negative effects of such practices. An initial attempt to do so was made by Taylor and Wagner (1976), who reviewed published cases of sexual relations between therapists and patients and tabulated the outcomes as reported by the therapists. They found negative effects on either the patient or therapist in 47 percent of the cases, positive effects in 21 percent, and mixed effects in 32 percent. Butler (1975) interviewed 20 psychiatrists and psychologists who had been sexually involved with patients. Of these all but one reported both positive and negative effects. However, given the definitional and methodological problems in assessing therapeutic outcomes and the divergent biases and inconsistent criteria employed by the therapists involved, these results should be considered suggestive only.

More systematic efforts to identify and document the damage done by patient-therapist sex began with Bouhoutsos et al.'s (1983) survey of California psychologists. Respondents indicated that 90 percent of their patients who had had sex with a previous therapist had suffered ill effects. In one-third of the cases these included one or more of the following:

> . . . increased depression, loss of motivation, impaired social adjustment, significant emotional disturbance, suicidal feelings or behavior, and increased drug or alcohol use. Eleven percent of the 559 cases were hospitalized and 1 percent committed suicide. (Bouhoutsos et al., 1983, p. 190)

Sexual, marital, or intimate relationships worsened for one-quarter of the patients. Understandably, nearly half were suspicious and mistrustful of therapists and had difficulty resuming therapy. Although the causal link between the sexual relationship and these sequelae is supplied by the judgment of subsequent therapists, we still see a decided pattern of negative outcomes following this brand of psychotherapy. Similar effects were found in a study that compared women who had sexual contact with their therapists with a control group of female patients (Feldman-Summers & Jones, 1984). Finally, in a subsequent review of Bouhoutsos et al.'s (1983) data, Holroyd and Bouhoutsos (1985) found that in a number of the 10 percent of cases for which "no harm" was reported by subsequent therapists, the reports were suspect because these therapists were themselves sexually involved with clients.

Pope (1988) has codified the commonly observed harmful effects of sexual involvement with a therapist into a "Therapist-Patient Sex Syndrome," along the lines of Post-Traumatic Stress Disorder and analogous constructions such as Battered-Woman Syndrome. We believe that such medicalized terminology sets up an overly rigid, all-or-none model for understanding personal and emotional experience. We concur, therefore, with Schoener (1989e, p. 45), who comments, "I do not believe that a clear pattern or syndrome can be found across the board in victims and thus I must reject the notion of a 'client-therapist sex syndrome.' . . . Many of the characteristics . . . noted are also characteristics of other syndromes or victims in general, and we see great variability among victims." Gonsiorek (1989a, p. 567) adds, "We believe strongly that client-victims require services that are carefully individualized to their experiences and needs."

In that spirit, Gutheil (1989b) concisely describes some damaging consequences that patient-therapist sex can have:

> Patients' responses to sexual misconduct may range from anger at being exploited to full-fledged post-traumatic stress disorder. Feelings of rage, betrayal, and humiliation may be aroused, and old traumas may be revived—especially since patients in these situations often have a history of similar boundary violations or sexual abuse by persons in positions of authority or trust. Time that might have been spent on valid therapy is lost, and the patient's attitude toward therapy itself is often poisoned. . . .
>
> Patients are often reluctant to abandon these relationships or report them. Like rape and incest victims, they may blame themselves, especially when they have been similarly abused in the past and the pattern is repeated. Furthermore, a shallow but pow-

erful feeling of specialness may make the relationship highly grat-
ifying in the short term. . . . A patient who feels this way may
become extraordinarily angry if the therapist loses interest and
tries to terminate, or if it becomes clear that other patients are
being treated in the same "special" way. (p. 4)

Jordan (1990) has listed several sources of guilt the victim may
experience—guilt for getting involved sexually with the therapist, for
continuing the involvement, for believing that she meant something
special to the therapist, and for not telling anyone sooner. These feelings may be exacerbated if a subsequent therapist attributes the
involvement to the victim's seductiveness or bad judgment. Self-blame
and the judgmental attitudes of others drive the victim further into
silence, which in turn isolates her from the empathy she badly needs.

The patient is also conflicted because to admit to herself and others
what is going on is to relinquish any positive memory of the therapy
and its value. Strasburger (1990) notes as well the loss of the "inner
therapist"—the benevolent internalized figure of the former therapist
with whom the patient may conduct an unspoken dialogue years after
therapy ends. Once a breach of trust such as sexual exploitation occurs,
this invaluable consultation is no longer available.

Increasingly it is being recognized that the patient who gets involved
sexually with a therapist is not necessarily the only victim of this abuse.
Spouses, partners, children, and other family members and friends may
be affected as well (Milgrom, 1989). The potentially destabilizing effects
on a primary love relationship are apparent. A therapist's other patients
also may suffer from the disruption of the therapist's practice resulting
from either true or false accusations of sexual involvement with a
patient.

Intimacies With Former Clients

On the question of sex (or other nonprofessional contact) between
client and clinician *after* termination of the professional relationship,
there is not so clear an ethical consensus as there is concerning sexual
or personal intimacy during therapy. Here a greater number of well-
intentioned practitioners wonder, "Why not?" The lack of clarity surrounding this question is reflected in a paper by Dahlberg (1970) which

is credited with being the first contemporary treatment of the issue of sexual acting out in therapy. Dahlberg (who takes a firm ethical stand against sex between client and therapist) describes a case in which a lovestruck therapist, "realizing that the situation was out of hand, . . . transferred the patient to another therapist and sought brief treatment for himself while maintaining a social and sexual relationship with her." According to Dahlberg, "This case illustrates the ideal way such a situation should be handled." He does not mean, of course, that it was ideal for the therapist to have permitted himself to act on a mandate from his feelings, but rather that, once this happened, both parties had a legitimate therapeutic channel for exploring its implications. Still, terminating therapy and giving the client another therapist does not resolve all the issues raised by the first therapist's sexual availability. Dahlberg presents another case in which the therapist, "as the case was drawing to a close, said that no sexual contact could occur during the course of treatment, implying that it might afterwards," as indeed it did. Dahlberg draws the appropriate conclusion: ". . . since the planned weekend seems to have been covertly in the therapist's mind for some time during treatment, it must have affected his judgment during at least part of the therapy" (1970, pp. 111–112).

With such considerations in view, Marmor (1972) comments on the rare case where a therapist genuinely falls in love with a patient and is therefore compelled to transfer the patient to another therapist:

> I must still affirm my clinical conviction that the therapist to whom this happens has failed in his primary responsibility to the woman who came to him as a patient. I make this statement in full knowledge of the fact that a number of prominent psychiatrists and psychoanalysts have married former patients. How many others who did not reach this honorable end-point, have nevertheless rationalized their loss of self-control on the basis of "falling in love" with their patients I do not know. My point, however, is that such a rationalization should not obscure the fact that whenever this happens, the psychotherapist has not been able to master his countertransference feelings. (p. 7)

The question is a controversial one. Silverstein (1977, p. 61), writing from considerable experience as a counselor, therapist, and human services administrator, categorically states, "I won't even date someone who used to be a client, for when can you say that the counseling relationship has stopped?" Herman, Gartrell, Olarte, Feldstein, and Localio (1987), who conducted a major nationwide study of psychiatrist-patient sexual relationships, strongly reaffirm this position:

> Neither transference nor the real inequality in the power relationship ends with the termination of therapy. In our opinion, the notion that exceptions to the rule of abstinence can be allowed in the name of love or marriage reveals either a naive romanticism or an insufficient understanding of the nature of the therapeutic relationship or both. Similarly, pragmatic efforts to define a post-termination waiting period, after which sexual relations might be permissible, disregard both the continued inequality of the roles of the therapist and former patient and the timelessness of unconscious processes, including transference. (p. 168)

Not everyone adheres to this position, in part because institutional sanctions against sexual relations with ex-clients have been inconsistently applied. Such sanctions would be difficult to maintain in most agencies because this behavior tends to be less visible than sexual contact with clients presently on the caseload. When it is visible, the informal sanction of peer disapproval may be as effective a restraint as any official policy. More often, though, it takes self-discipline to pass up these fringe benefits of the clinical vocations, and many otherwise honorable individuals see no good reason to do so.

In an effort to show that there are good reasons at least to stop and take a second look (and in almost all cases not to go any further), we will present some of the arguments pro and con. An examination of all sides of the issue, we believe, ultimately validates Marmor's, Silverstein's, and Herman et al.'s concerns.

Rationalizations and realities. The individuals interviewed for this book give a number of justifications for treating sexual contact with former clients differently from sexual contact with clients currently in treatment. Some of these justifications take the form of stipulations of conditions under which what would otherwise be antitherapeutic is thought to become normal social behavior. The explanations and exculpations reviewed here are the ones most commonly offered. To show that they do not answer several major objections to the practices in question is not to deny that, at a certain level of seriousness and integrity, they may cease to be rationalizations and become good reasons. But to cite any or all of them as if they could routinely countenance turning therapeutic relationships into sexual relationships is to accept uncritically the promptings of self-interest.

1. *"It's okay after 'X' amount of time has elapsed."* What makes this claim unconvincing is that X is so variable. Estimates of how long (after termination) a clinician and client must wait before commencing a sexual relationship run from three months to six months to one, two, or five years. (At the lower end of the scale they approach the facetious: "Let's see, we're terminating at one o'clock; see you for dinner at seven.") With so little agreement about the length of time required, it seems clear that there is no magic "cooling-off period" after which the personal relationship will no longer be affected by the memory of the therapeutic relationship. Nor does it matter whether (as some respondents specify with misguided scruple) the parties wait out the three months or three years before having sex or before beginning to date. All these distinctions evade the issue that, once the therapeutic intimacy has been supplanted by personal intimacy, the clinician is no longer available to provide the safe therapeutic space that the client-turned-lover may once again need. An ex-client who does need help again may, like a client who has been seduced during therapy, feel betrayed and hesitate to risk another therapeutic encounter.

2. *"It's okay once the ex-client is in therapy with someone else."* Referral to another therapist because of one's own inability to maintain a professional involvement with the client should be seen as a last resort, not as a routine escape hatch allowing one to further one's personal agenda. To engage in a therapeutic relationship with a person is to endeavor to provide whatever professional support the person needs. One must ask oneself whether one is really fulfilling that commitment by passing the buck to another therapist—and then becoming one of the issues the new therapist will have to deal with!

3. *"It's okay if it's with a former client of the same sex, since the relationship will have to be platonic."* A love affair is not the only kind of relationship that can compromise one's ability to provide therapeutic support for an ex-client. If one accepts the mandate of continuing availability (and wishes to avoid unnecessarily complicating one's own life), one will refrain from relating to former clients at a level of full equality

and mutuality, as by lending money or making personally revealing statements.

4. *"To disqualify a person forever from having a normal personal relationship with you is a form of labeling, like putting somebody in a slot."* When one meets a former client out on the street or at a party or a football game, it is appropriate to respond (up to a point) as one would to anyone else—to say, "Hi, how are you?" and shake hands, perhaps exchange a ritual hug (if hugs were part of the therapy in question), and then go about one's business. The assertion that declining to do more than that is labeling is as foolish as the contrary claim that doing even that much is a violation of confidentiality! Everyone has been a client of helping professionals (such as medical doctors), and many people (including perhaps the clinician in question) have been clients in some sort of therapy. A clinician may have love affairs or friendships with people who have been clients of other clinicians, and a former client of that clinician may have personal relationships with people who work as therapists, counselors, or whatever. What rules out fraternization between a clinician and a former client is not the latter's lifelong status as a client, but the special character of his or her relationship with that particular clinician. This relationship remains a fact in the lives of those two individuals even if the client becomes a clinical psychologist or a U.S. Senator.

5. *"What if the meeting is completely accidental? What if it happens five or ten years afterward?"* Then worry about it five or ten years from now when it happens. Unplanned meetings do occur. But the more the idea of "bumping into" someone a few years after termination is held out as a loophole permitting some form of personal relations with ex-clients, the more it can be used to rationalize meetings that are not altogether accidental. And who is to say that leaving open the hope of an accidental meeting years hence (even as distinct from planning to meet soon) may not influence the course of therapy? Even when the therapy and its termination are handled completely cleanly, other objections to personal intimacy with a former client still hold—namely, that the personal relationship is likely to be undermined by the prior therapeutic relationship, and that any future therapeutic relationship is ruled out by the personal relationship.

6. *"Mature individuals can decide for themselves."* Who decides who is mature enough to decide? When does a client in therapy become mature enough to decide to become involved with someone who has

seen and dealt with the least mature aspects of his or her makeup? As for the therapist, how many therapists disqualify themselves on the grounds of immaturity or incompetence? Does that mean that they are all mature and competent? Although mature individuals do occasionally decide to act counter to the norm, this justification is ready-made for abuse.

7. *"I've seen one case where it worked out well for both parties."* One case in how many years? Out of how many?

8. *"Therapy is really a form of love, and a love relationship contains a lot of counseling."* As is made clear earlier in this chapter, therapy involves a special kind of caring that depends for its efficacy on a commitment not to act out or become preoccupied with other aspects of caring that are normally expressed in a love relationship.

9. *"Any two people can fall in love."* It cannot be denied that people choose lovers unwisely and suffer the consequences of their folly in contexts far removed from clinical helping relationships. But why look for trouble in a place where it is almost sure to be found? Moreover, a professional helping relationship is not just another arena of "life." It includes a mandate on the clinician's part not to fall in love except in the form of countertransference, which is dealt with according to established clinical procedures. When the therapist loses control and crosses the boundary that separates countertransference from falling in love, there has been at the very least a therapeutic failure.

The rationalizations listed are articulations—for public consumption—of a wish, a fantasy, an unwillingness to let go. A young male social worker, when asked what he would do if he met an attractive female client at a singles bar after termination of therapy, muses, "Well, I don't think it would be a good idea to take it any further, but you know, it's a matter of the chemistry between two individuals. . . . Once she was out of treatment, perhaps the same problems wouldn't present themselves." His is the voice of the thousands of decent people who go about their clinical work wishing (almost in the manner of an alcoholic or drug addict who still resists "hitting bottom"), "If only there were some way, if only I could do this without violating my ethical contract to serve my clients. I just can't bear to give up the idea completely."

Ethical and policy considerations. From this discussion there have emerged several major grounds for concluding that, as a matter of ethics and policy, helping professionals should not form relationships involving sexual or personal intimacy with former clients. These can be summarized as follows:

1. *Compromising of the therapeutic process.* The expectation of a possible love affair after termination is bound to lead to self-aggrandizing behavior (including subtle bribes and the avoidance of difficult issues) not only during termination, but throughout the course of therapy. Such limit-testing is expected of the client in any case, but it is potentially tragic when the therapist's purposes are confused by personal longings and impulses. A professional who thinks it permissible to use a clinical practice as a source for the recruitment of sexual partners will tend to suffer lapses of judgment as to what clients to accept, how to present oneself to them, how much to risk alienating a client in the service of therapeutic goals, and when and how to terminate. One is less likely to be able to discipline one's countertransference feelings from the outset when one allows oneself the "out" of thinking, "Oh, if this goes too far I can just terminate therapy, and then it will be okay."

Usually this is not a question of sinister exploitation. Rather, it is a trap in which decent people ensnare themselves. A case in point is that of an alcoholism counselor in his forties, a sensitive man who has never sexually exploited a client in treatment, who reports,

> I've gone out with a couple of former clients when they had been sober for over a year and had been away from my agency for an equivalent period of time. I had introduced them to A.A., and by that point I thought of them as A.A. friends rather than clients. They were well into their recovery; it was almost as if they had become different people.

Although it is quite possible that no harm was done in these cases, an unintentionally self-serving pattern of thinking and behavior is evident here. The therapist takes on clients, takes them to A.A., terminates them as clients, meets them at A.A. meetings, and pronounces them friends rather than clients. Granted that this man does not terminate his clients prematurely, he nonetheless does take up social opportunities stemming from his professional exposure to vulnerable people. It is easy to see how a less scrupulous clinician could systematically rationalize the initiation and termination of therapeutic relationships for the purpose of sexual self-aggrandizement.

2. *Denial of future therapeutic support.* Both client and clinician invest a great deal in the development of a therapeutic relationship. All the work they have done to establish the trust that therapy requires is lost if they exchange the therapeutic relationship for a romantic one. Also lost is the security the client gains from knowing (even at times when the relationship is not actively maintained) that the therapist is there to be called upon if needed. Sacrificing that point of safety for the sake of a personal involvement not only makes the therapist unavailable for renewed therapeutic involvement, but also may lead the ex-client to distrust therapists in general.

3. *Corruption of the personal relationship by the privileged knowledge and inequality of the therapeutic relationship.* An alcoholism counselor married a man whom she had treated. During their divorce proceedings she confessed to "an almost irresistible tendency to hit him with below-the-belt shots in a fight." It is indeed only human, at moments of stress between spouses or lovers, to fall back on whatever "edge" one has, such as (if one's spouse or lover is a former client) a reminder of past inequalities: "What do you know? Who are you to talk? Remember what you used to be?"

Lovers normally get to know each other by sharing intimate information on an equal basis. A clinician gets to know a client by being given privileged, unreciprocated access to the most vulnerable parts of the client's being, including fears and insecurities about intimate relationships. The clinician reads the client's file; the client does not read the clinician's file. The power that resides in this inequality of knowledge remains ripe for abuse when the client and clinician attempt to make the difficult transition to a relationship of mutuality.

Those who wish to attempt this transition should consider carefully the obstacles interposed by the prior history of client-clinician transactions. To build one type of relationship on the foundation of another is to substitute (in large and small ways) one set of expectations for a very different set—for example, to demand reliable behavior of one's partner in life when one had previously accorded one's client infinite patience. Is it worthwhile to try to form an intimate relationship against such unfavorable odds? Although the caution recommended here might seem to represent a kind of discrimination against the ex-client, our interviews suggest that the former clients (e.g., in prisons or substance abuse programs) who have been most successful in getting their lives together are least likely to want or need any intimate involvements with those who have helped them professionally. A man who came out of prison to become a prominent human services educator put it this way:

> I certainly don't feel "branded" these days. I socialize as an equal with people like those who once counseled me. Some of them know that I was once a "recipient of services" in a correctional institution; some of them don't. But I have no wish now to go back and take up with any of the professionals who knew me as an inmate or a parolee. And if one of them wanted to take up with me, I'd be uneasy about how she viewed her motives and mine. It would smack of voyeurism.

An interesting reservation on the question of the ex-client's vulnerability is voiced by a female psychiatrist who cites the training analysis that psychoanalysts must undergo as an instance where privileged knowledge of a personal nature must be worked through as the relationship between the two parties evolves. Student-analysands and their analysts do make accommodations for what has passed between them as they exchange the analytic relationship for that of colleagues in the professional community. In this case, however, the dual relationship is unavoidable. Analysts must be trained, and the benefits of the training procedure exceed the costs of the shift in roles. The question remains why one would incur those costs unnecessarily when they are likely to exceed the benefits.

These considerations have been presented not as the last word on an admittedly controversial subject, but as questions on which responsible individuals should want to satisfy themselves before proceeding further. They at least would appear to set a very high threshold for undertaking personal involvements with former clients. Instead of focusing on the former client's supposed disabilities as obstacles to such a relationship, it makes sense to look at one's own motivations. One might ask oneself, "What is going on in my life that I need to take advantage of my privileged exposure to people's troubles? If I am coming from a position of strength in helping others, why am I looking for dates from among the pool of people who come to me for help? Is it in keeping with the values that brought me into the helping professions to do something that for several reasons is potentially destructive?" What, in other words, would constitute a good reason for overriding the ethical objections that have been raised here? Finally, will a jury or one's professional organization endorse this "good reason"? Increasingly, as we shall see in Chapters 6 and 10, professional regulations and the law are taking the matter out of the realm of individual discretion.

Are there any exceptions? Some serious, well-intentioned individuals hold to the belief that, very rarely, a clinical relationship can be transformed into a genuine courtship leading to a relationship of mutual love. Is this a realistic hope? Can organizational and public policy allow for this possibility?

First, in this respect it is difficult to generalize from the rigors of psychotherapy to the range of helping professions. In the teaching profession, for example, it is generally assumed that love affairs with former students are a private matter. Up to the present, accepted ethical standards for university teachers not only have differed from those in the clinical professions, but have varied greatly from one campus to another. Although even a wholesome teacher-student courtship can have a disruptive effect on other students (Kaslow, 1980), such liaisons have been tolerated at some colleges. Only recently has a consensus begun to develop that the patent inequality of power between teacher and student makes an intimate relationship between the two a breach of ethics on the teacher's part. And this prohibition generally is not taken to extend beyond the time when the student remains in the teacher's class or under the teacher's authority or influence.

One factor differentiating the two professional situations is that classroom teaching does not necessarily entail intimate revelation and emotional investment on the part of the student. A teacher is not ipso facto a repository of personal trust, as is a therapist. It is the student's choice whether or not to take the relationship beyond the structured classroom exchange. Moreover, the inequality between teacher and student is seen as merely chronological or else highly specialized. A client in therapy is a client by virtue of some acknowledged difficulty in coping; a student is a student by virtue of being less knowledgeable in the area under consideration. It is assumed that the student can outgrow or compensate for this inequality in experience vis-à-vis the teacher.

One type of teacher-student contact that is receiving considerable scrutiny is that which occurs in training programs and supervisory relationships in the helping professions (Brodsky, 1980; Conroe, Schank,

Brown, De Marinis, Loeffler, & Sanderson, 1989; Sanderson, 1989c). Studies of graduate students and clinical trainees in psychology (Glaser & Thorpe, 1986; Pope et al., 1979, 1980) have shown that those who had sexual contact with educators or supervisors tend to view such relationships more negatively in retrospect than when they occurred. They come to feel that it is unethical for teachers to use their position for sexual gain and regret that their training did not prepare them better to deal with such situations. Moreover, the researchers found evidence of a "modeling effect"—that is, those who were sexually involved with their teachers were more likely to be sexually involved with clients later on. Residents in psychiatry have been found to have similar experiences, although there were insufficient data to test the "modeling effect" there (Gartrell, Herman, Olarte, Localio, & Feldstein, 1988).

In recognition of these problems, the American Psychological Association in 1981 added to its ethical standards the principle that "psychologists do not exploit their professional relationships with clients, supervisees, students, employees, or research participants sexually or otherwise" (APA, 1981, p. 636). Gartrell et al. (1988, p. 694) recommend that the American Psychiatric Association adopt the position that "sexual contact between a psychiatric educator and resident is unethical as long as the educator has authority over the resident." Finally, Conroe and Schank (1989) conclude that any sexual intimacy between supervisor and supervisee in the clinical professions is inappropriate and destructive.

The legal profession, too, is only beginning to clarify the nature of the relationship between client and professional. Its code of ethics prohibits conduct detrimental to the welfare of a client. However, the implications of this injunction for sexual contact between lawyers and clients, or ex-clients, are a matter of dispute. Some observers emphasize that the range of concerns for which people seek legal advice includes many straightforward financial transactions involving no confidential personal revelations and no inequality of status between client and counsel. In such cases the hiring of the lawyer's special expertise is said to be just like other business dealings between equals (such as the collegial relationships among helping professionals discussed in Chapter 9) in which both parties are assumed to be capable of informed consent regarding sexual and emotional intimacy. Others maintain that the privileged information and one-sided financial and sometimes personal vulnerability that characterize the lawyer-client relationship put the attorney in a position of special trust comparable to that of a therapist (Coleman, 1988).

Lawyers do hear a great deal of confidential information about their clients' personal lives, particularly in divorce cases, where both the client's situation and the nature of the revelations made to the lawyer (here indeed a "counselor") leave the client vulnerable to exploitation. At the extreme, a person who seeks legal counsel after having been sexually abused by a family member or therapist is as vulnerable as one would be when relating the same painful experiences to a member of the clinical professions. It is not clear, however, that attorneys will ever be constrained from having intimate relationships with ex-clients or from terminating a professional relationship for the sake of initiating a personal one.

Medicine, too, presents a range of moral scenarios, although here the Hippocratic Oath sets a precedent for declaring sexual contact with current patients and their families off limits. The complex considerations an ethical physician faces are captured by Alex C., a family physician whose practice extends from pediatrics to geriatrics, from routine laboratory tests and employment physicals to marital counseling:

> The job of a clinician is to be with people, to witness their condition, to reflect them to themselves, to let them be safe in being expressive, in trying out different roles and behaviors, in having a relationship that isn't jeopardized by being examined. The clinician's purpose—if it really is one's purpose to be there for people in this way—is not easily reconciled with the practice of changing therapeutic relationships into friendships. When you have experienced what you can do by extending yourself fully for people in the role I have described, you have to have powerful reasons to want to take yourself out of that role. I have more than once seen the transition from a professional to a personal relationship negotiated successfully for all concerned. But I start with the strong presumption that this is not going to happen. When it does, it should always be a difficult decision.

As checks against glib self-justification and willful denial, Alex recommends that the physician seek peer review and confide in family and friends. He also suggests "a waiting period—one that's much longer than what would seem comfortable—to establish your compatibility outside the clinical situation and without sex."

It would be foolish to deny that the ethical obstacles are not as great for a nurse on a medical ward as for a family physician, not as great for a physician who sees a patient once to fix a broken arm as for a psychiatrist engaged in a course of therapy with a depressed patient. A broken arm, though, as physicians, nurses, and other medical personnel should be aware, represents one end of a continuum of complex dependency relationships between patients and healers. The pain, fear, and risk of danger that accompany patients on the most routine medical visits create more vulnerability than meets the eye (Bursztajn et al., 1990). It is for this reason that the ethics of the medical profession forbid touching—in the erotic sense—those whom one would heal.

The vulnerability we have been speaking of is nowhere greater than in psychotherapy. It is only with the greatest caution, then, that a responsible therapist can challenge the notion of ongoing therapeutic availability. Eric F., a psychologist in private practice whose moral and intellectual seriousness are not at issue, poses a provocative question:

> If we really believe our own claim that we can help people become capable of healthy functioning, then don't we have to accept, at least as an ideal, that an intimate nontherapeutic relationship could work out with a former client as it would with anyone else? Of course, some severe conditions would have to be met. But the purpose of therapy is for the client to be empowered, not to give power away permanently. I'm concerned that the notion of availability may be used as a cover for perpetuating the therapeutic dependency beyond termination as, in effect, a personal dependency. I wonder whether "I will be here for you" may not sometimes mean, "You will continue to need me."

In reality, however, the goal of restoring people to healthy, autonomous functioning is not always achieved. Moreover, the journey toward that goal is a process of approximation that typically does not have a decisive resolution, but rather continues indefinitely on an irregular path. Sometimes even a healthy person can use a little maintenance from a trusted therapist.

In any case, Eric's hypothesized "ideal" of an honorable transition from a psychotherapeutic to an intimate personal relationship is, in the present climate, likely to remain no more than an ideal. For example, in 1988 the Florida Board of Psychological Examiners ruled that, for the purpose of determining sexual misconduct, "the psychologist-client relationship is deemed to continue in perpetuity" (Schoener et al., 1989, p. 730). The following year the American Psychiatric Association added to its ethics code the statement that sexual involvement with former patients "almost always is unethical" (American Psychiatric Association, 1989, p.4).

Proposed guidelines. Even so, the clinical professions have not taken a united stand against liaisons with former clients. The Ethics Committee of the American Psychological Association has debated the issue seriously for several years without reaching a definitive decision. Part of the difficulty lies in the concern that a comprehensive ban against such relationships might be held by the courts to be an unconstitutional infringement of freedom of association (Schoener, 1989i). Acknowledging this and other constraints on policy, Gonsiorek and Brown (1989) propose detailed provisional guidelines for regulating posttermination relationships so as to honor both professional ethics and the civil and legal rights of clients and therapists. In their framework, sexual contact with former clients is "always and forever prohibited" in the following circumstances:

- after long-term therapy involving transference and a clear imbalance of power between therapist and client
- with severely disturbed ex-clients
- with ex-clients with a history of childhood physical and sexual abuse
- when posttermination romantic contact is initiated by the therapist
- within two years of termination
- when there has been more than incidental social contact during the two years following termination
- when the therapist has not obtained an independent consultation as to whether the above criteria have been met
- when there is any possibility of risk or harm to the former client

These recommendations, offered with cautionary language about the actual or potential harm attendant upon most posttermination sexual relationships and with no implied endorsement of those not explicitly ruled out, leave only the smallest opening for "innocent" relationships. The burden of proof is on the therapist to show that his or her conduct is nonexploitative.

Attitude surveys. An alternate approach is to take the empirical route—that is, to find out what practitioners actually believe about the ethics of various practices. A firmer empirical grounding would enable the professions (a) to identify areas in which better training and reme- dial education are most needed, and (b) to make policy with a view toward the complexities of actual practice. Several studies show a lack of consensus among practitioners with regard to the propriety of sexual relationships with former clients. In a survey of 456 psychologists, over 95 percent of whom regarded sexual contact with a current client as unethical, only 50.2 percent regarded sexual involvement with a former client as unquestionably unethical, while 34.4 percent believed that it was ethical under rare circumstances (Pope, Tabachnick, & Keith- Spiegel, 1987). Among 1,423 psychiatrists, 98 percent of whom affirmed that sexual contact between client and therapist is always inappropriate and always or usually harmful, 29.6 percent nonetheless said that such contact might sometimes be acceptable after termination, and 17.4 per- cent believed this conduct to be compatible with the American Psychi- atric Association's ethics code (Herman et al., 1987). Of the 84 psychiatrists in this study who admitted to having had sexual contact with clients (most beginning shortly after termination), 74.1 percent opined that sexual relations with clients could be appropriate after termination.

Conte, Plutchik, Picard, & Karasu (1989), surveying 101 psychother- apists (psychiatrists, psychologists, and social workers) on a medical school faculty, found that while 80.2 percent held that sexual contact with a patient in treatment is grounds for malpractice (the other 19.8 percent also thought it unethical), only 37 percent thought that termi- nating treatment for the purpose of having a sexual relationship is grounds for malpractice (another 52 percent thought this to be uneth- ical). And a mere 14 percent believed that having sexual contact with a patient after proper termination of treatment is grounds for malprac- tice (another 50 percent found this practice unethical). When marriage resulted from the liaison, the percentage finding malpractice dropped into single digits. Amplifying and commenting on Conte et al.'s findings, Schoener (1989i) noted several anomalies:

> One of the most interesting findings of this study is that the respondents differentiated little between situations involving clients who were seen for consultation or brief therapy versus long-term therapy. This runs counter to my expectations and to the model proposed by Gonsiorek and Brown (1989). Secondly, contact with a former client for the purpose of marriage is seen as far more acceptable than contact for sex alone. It is also surprising to find that having sex with a patient's spouse after completion of the patient's therapy is seen as *less* acceptable than having sexual contact with the patient [after completion of therapy]. (p. 268)

The tendency of a large minority of therapists to excuse sexual relationships with former clients runs counter to the increasing evidence that, in administrative proceedings and civil litigation involving therapists who have had sex with clients, prior termination of therapy is not a successful defense (Conte et al., 1989; Sell, Gottlieb, & Schoenfeld, 1986).

Empirical studies such as those cited here can be an invaluable resource as the various professions, courts, legislatures, and regulatory agencies confront the task of discriminating among a range of sexual and social behaviors in different professions, different types of client-family-helper relationships, and different stages of those relationships (Coleman, 1988). Do the same ethical mandates hold for physicians in an emergency room or acute-care service, physicians who provide personal or family counseling, and psychotherapists? Are nurses or medical assistants to be held to the same standards as physicians? Would a divorce lawyer be compromised by behavior that would be acceptable for a tax lawyer? Is it wrong for a stockbroker or business consultant to date a client? Should teachers in graduate and professional schools be subject to the same constraints as teachers of undergraduates? What relations are proper between a psychology researcher and a student who volunteers as an experimental subject? Does a writer who obtains privileged personal information in an interview have ethical responsibilities similar to those of a therapist?

In each of these cases, when (if at all) does the privileged relationship end and normal socializing become possible? What about family members of clients? Should a single mother go out with her child's pediatrician? If not, is it permissible for the doctor (as it would not be for a therapist) to find another pediatrician for the child so that he and the mother can immediately begin dating?

The Program in Psychiatry and the Law at Massachusetts Mental Health Center plans to study how different lay and professional groups would answer these sorts of questions. Such attitude surveys will not, of course, give us definitive ethical guidelines; the fact that something is common practice, or that people think it is the right thing to do, does not make it right. Nonetheless, as society begins to sort out these sensitive issues, a better understanding of actual practices and attitudes will provide a benchmark for ethical decision making. By examining the rationales for popular viewpoints and customary behavior, ethicists and policymakers will be on firmer ground as they assume their prescriptive roles.

Cases. Along with the institutional sanctions that a clinician who gets personally involved with a former client may face, there may be other disagreeable consequences, including the informal sanction of peer disapproval and the fact that relationships initiated in this manner tend not to work out very satisfactorily. The range of outcomes that can occur is suggested by two cases involving prison personnel.

The first case is an unusual one. A mutual attraction developed between a male prison guard and a woman who was serving 20 years for killing one of her children. Both were in their late forties. Although they may have been seeing each other on the woman's monthly furloughs, they handled their relationship so discreetly that no one at the institution saw any sign of it. After the woman's discharge they were married with the tacit approval of the prison administration, which arranged for the guard to be transferred to another state facility. To the people who knew them at the prison, this man and woman are "a nice, well-matched couple" who to all appearances have remained happily married.

The acceptance (formal and informal) with which this relationship between a state employee and a former client was received can be traced to three extenuating factors: (1) The inmate and guard were middle-aged. (2) They got married. (3) They behaved in such a way as not to arouse rumors while the woman was still incarcerated. Taken together, these facts created for this couple an image of "maturity," so that what transpired was not interpreted as disruptive of the purposes of the institution. The special circumstances surrounding this case make it an extreme exception, a marginal or "limiting case" against a background of less happy resolutions.

A far more typical case is that of a female staff member in her early twenties who took up with a recently paroled male inmate of about the same age. In this particular facility the administration regards relationships between employees and former inmates as a private matter once the ex-inmate is off parole, but not before. This attitude to some extent filters down to the personal reactions of fellow staff members, although the latter cannot be reliably predicted. Occasionally a female corrections officer or counselor forms a liaison with a parolee, and, in the words of our informant concerning this case, "is put through hell professionally." She speaks from having seen a friend of hers, Mary T., respond to the overtures of a "charismatic" inmate in the unit next to the one where she worked. This man was never on Mary's caseload, but she visited his unit and became friendly (though not intimate) with him while he was in prison. At this time Mary was having some personal problems and was concerned about being unattractive to men. Vulnerability, opportunity, and self-interest came together. After the inmate was released to a halfway house, Mary would pick him up for weekends, explaining to her co-workers that she was "just helping the guy." Before long she was living with him.

This is what Mary's life, as seen by her friend, is like now:

> I wouldn't want to be in her shoes when she walks in to work every day. She hates her job. The staff and inmates torment her, calling her "—'s old lady," and most of all she torments herself. She doesn't seem happy at home, either. She supports this man financially much of the time, and he even brings other women home. "Think about whether you're being used," I've told her. Mainly I'd just like to see her choose what would make her happier. Either she should give up the man and try to mend her situation at work, or go with the relationship and try to get a job transfer.

The ugly reactions Mary has gotten from some of her co-workers stem in part from racial prejudice. (Mary is white, her boyfriend black.) This, however, along with other sore points that have contributed to making her job situation practically untenable, could have been anticipated as part of the "givens" in the milieu where she works. She knew all along that she was not working among the Twelve Apostles. But her better judgment was overruled by the pressure to find an immediate, convenient answer for needs not being met off the job.

Attractions and, sometimes, liaisons between staff members and former residents of prisons, halfway houses, therapeutic communities, reformatories, and other live-in facilities (as well as between probation officers and their clients) are increasingly a matter of common observation. In a well-publicized case, a young relative of President Carter married a social worker he met while in prison, only to be divorced soon afterward. At one residential school for court-referred adolescents this phenomenon is referred to by the staff as "the 'Summer of '42' syndrome." Female staff members look at the male residents in their teens and make remarks like, "That one's going to be something else in 10 years. If there's ever going to be a 'Summer of '42,' I'll take him." Male staff members, meanwhile, deny any attraction to teenage girls and then "have their eyeballs fall out" when one walks by. It is natural to have such feelings and probably helpful to discharge them among one's peers. In the next chapter we will consider ways of dealing with them so as to make it less likely that looking will lead to touching.

Even in private practice, where the clinician is protected against some kinds of sanctions directed against agency personnel, relationships with former clients as often as not collapse of their own weight. A male psychologist in his mid-thirties tells this rueful tale:

A female social worker came to me as a client for therapy. After three sessions I realized I was so attracted to her that there was no point in even trying to work it through. I told her so when she came for the fourth session. She told me that she had been thinking along the same lines herself. I felt I couldn't be a good therapist for her, and she felt she couldn't be a good patient for me. So we terminated. A few months later we did have sex, and it was a terrible experience, though one that we both were able to talk and laugh about. Later we went into practice together and made a success of it for several years. I don't know whether I was right or wrong to terminate therapy with her, but I knew I couldn't be objective about her problems with men when inwardly I was panting after her.

Here the sexual relationship was no more successful than the therapeutic. Although this case by itself does not prove the unsuitability of therapists and ex-clients as sexual partners, it is representative of the experiences reported to us.

If anyone could be expected to be able to seduce ex-clients with impunity, it is the psychoanalyst, who sits at the pinnacle of the helping professions. That was not what happened when two leading New York analysts (one of them a former president of the American Psychoanalytic Association) married former patients some years ago. As Malcolm (1980b, p. 89) learned from an informant within the profession, an analyst of no particular renown who married a patient "would merely be frozen out of the referral network and allowed to sink into even greater obscurity. . . ." These two pillars of psychoanalysis, on the other hand,

> . . . were removed from the roster of training analysts, they were divested of their various functions in the ruling structure, they were dismissed from their teaching posts. Their careers in the higher reaches of establishment psychoanalysis were over. (Malcolm, 1980b, p. 89)

What motivated these men to take such a self-destructive course? According to the same analyst,

> These two men—as far as I can understand the rumors and the myths—were men whose marriages were breaking up in middle age. They were men in desperate straits. . . . It isn't the attractiveness and seductiveness of the patient; rather, it's that the analyst is in horrible shape in his own life and turns to the patient for help. (Malcolm, 1980b, p. 110)

Even so, what made them act so recklessly? The analyst speculates that although they may have acted with tragic indifference to consequences that they knew would come, it was more likely that they had become so famous and powerful that they thought they could get away with it. "And they figure, as they say in Yiddish, *'Der Reb meg'*—'The Rabbi is allowed' " (Malcolm, 1980b, p. 115).

From prison worker to psychoanalyst, the story is the same. Vulnerability, opportunity, self-interest.

6
Morality

Bob, Alice's upright fiance, seems to many people the least likeable of the characters who survived our shipwreck. Like all the others he is a caricature of one point of view, but there is something particularly disagreeable about a caricature of morality. When Alice compromised herself to get the raft that enabled her to join him, Bob responded with moralistic disapproval rather than with empathy. This kind of response seems particularly inappropriate in the helping professions, which (we like to believe) are built on a foundation of empathy. Yet it is a response from which no one, including the sainted helping professional, is exempt. Moral considerations are very much in point for people who earn their living by trying to do good. But what is really moral? Bob's inflexible standards of conduct? Alice's loyalty? Charlie's keeping an unsavory agreement? People have different conceptions of what is good and what is right, and we must allow for those differences while, as helping professionals, we seek to distinguish between unhelpful dogmatism and humane ethics.

Moralistic Reactions

A pregnant 19-year-old woman sought advice from a minister about whether she should get married. The minister asked her, among other things, whether she was pregnant by the man she intended to marry. The woman felt as if she had been intruded upon, attacked in terms of her sexuality. Of course, since regulating sexual conduct is a function of the church, the woman might have served her own purposes better by going to a secular counselor. Even in his counseling role the minister may have had good reasons for exploring the question of paternity, which might affect the prospects for the marriage and the bond between father and child. However, in the absence of a pastoral relationship strong enough to allow the woman to hear his questions as constructive, the minister's probing was not helpful (Glasser, 1965). As she experienced him, he was substituting his agenda for hers.

The same can be said of a female therapist in her forties who, upon learning that a young man who came to her for treatment for alcoholism was homosexual, virtually ignored his alcoholism in her zeal to treat his homosexuality (for which he did not desire treatment). This therapist was willing to set aside the presenting problem and impose her own priorities on the client and on the agency employing her. Although she saw herself as concerned with the welfare of the client (he described her as "feeling sorry for me" and "wanting to mother me"), she was attending to what she, not he, found uncomfortable. It was an assertion of control in the guise of sympathy.

The same bias—and its detrimental effects on those being "helped"—can be observed on a larger scale in the attitudes of prison staff toward homosexuality among inmates. A female social worker who worked for several years in a women's prison describes the conditions she observed there:

> The relationships women formed in prison usually were not sexual in the full sense. Sometimes two women would just lie on a bed together with their arms around each other as they watched TV. Women met their emotional needs in jail by forming little "families"—father, mother, and child, all of them actually grown women.
>
> Officially even the most innocent physical expressions of affection were forbidden, but the strictness of enforcement varied from shift to shift. Some staff members, myself included, tolerated the sexuality as long as it was not coerced. Although some subtle psychological coercion might have been operating, on balance it seemed that if that was how the women made it a little less unpleasant for themselves to be in jail, and if they didn't fight about it, it probably was more beneficial than otherwise. There was, however, a distinct minority of staff members who considered this behavior unnatural. What seemed to bother them most was

that they might walk into one of the rooms and see something embarrassing. One woman who had good relationships with the inmates took it personally that they didn't have enough consideration for her to post a lookout so that she wouldn't walk in on two women making love.

The issue was discussed incessantly at all levels of administration—cottage staff meetings, meetings of counselors from throughout the prison, and high-level conferences. They were especially concerned about behavior at outside activities such as picnics and softball games. In a bizarre example of the selective enforcement that occurred, they once stationed cars at the crossroads to keep women from holding hands while walking to and from their cottages.

Those who work in a prison can expect to see things that will make them uncomfortable. Instead of accepting the responsibility of adjusting to what there was to adjust to in that milieu, some administrators and staff members at this prison rationalized their discomfort into an issue of morality. The inconsistent enforcement that resulted, while indeed one of the "givens" that the inmates for their part had to adjust to, could not be characterized as beneficial to them.

Sometimes this moralistic rationalization on the part of staff members has positively harmful consequences for clients, as in this account by a female "rap group" leader at a reformatory for male adolescents:

Earl was a very short 12-year-old "street kid" who, in part to protect himself, did sexual favors for other kids in the cottage. What he was doing was first discovered by a male staff member who failed to report it to the coordinator as was called for. This man was also black and a "street person," and there was a bond between him and Earl. Then Earl expanded his activities beyond his own cottage, and eventually the whole thing came to light when some kids who didn't want his favors assaulted him. Once the news got out, all the kids in his cottage were ashamed and intimidated; they became known as the "homo group."

The male staff member who kept quiet about what he had discovered exemplifies one typical response to adolescent homosexuality in a residential institution—that is, protective overidentification. Predictably,

Earl and his peers suffered from this well-meaning concealment. Other typical staff responses are dramatized as the group leader's account continues:

> To me this behavior seemed not so uncommon; it's what you can expect wherever adolescents or young adults of the same sex are thrown together. I was angry at the man who suppressed it, which allowed the situation to deteriorate, but I was also concerned about the overreactions of other staff members. As in other such cases, they ignored it as long as they could, to the point of not picking up on obvious clues that something was happening. Then, when they couldn't avoid it any longer, they became hysterical in their condemnation: "Oh, this is horrible, disgusting—anyone involved is sick, they're crazy, send them away, have them tarred and feathered . . ." The men on the staff raved and ranted more than the women did. They seemed threatened by something they hadn't dealt with in themselves. They even tacitly approved of (and possibly precipitated) the way the kids ostracized and brutalized Earl, so that he had to be removed from the cottage temporarily for his own safety. I heard staff members say things like, "I don't blame them. He deserved the beatings."
>
> I actually had an easier time dealing with the kids over this issue than I did with the line staff. At first the rap group in the cottage was demoralized with guilt because so many of them had been involved. They picked up words like "sick" and "not normal"—as applied both to Earl and to themselves—from what staff members were saying. But after a few days of working it through, they were able to look at one another and say, "I did this, you did this. We're not sick just because we enjoyed it." Most of the male adults at the facility never did reconcile themselves to what had happened.

Here a staff member who was both better trained and, in this instance, more objective (by virtue of being a woman) could understand and report the dynamics of the male staff members' reactions. These men, predisposed by their own backgrounds to overidentify with the young residents, responded to a threatening situation by avoiding it. When forced to confront it, they resorted to sympathetic overprotectiveness or (more frequently) moralistic rejection. It is a common pattern and not a helpful one.

One inevitably makes moral judgments about clients, just as one does about anybody one comes across. It is only natural sometimes to look at a client as one human being would look at another and to think, "How revolting! How could anyone do such a thing?" It should, however, hardly need to be stressed that to communicate such judgments to someone with whom one is working in a professional capacity is unethical and antitherapeutic. How one can deal with negative reactions to clients (whether these are based on morality, taste, or temperament) will be considered in Chapter 7. When it is specifically moral disapproval that gets in the way, though, one may be able to gain some detachment simply from the realization that most moral judgments, far from being universal, are greatly influenced by the time, place, and point of view of the person making them.

For one thing, moral values change. In recent years there has been a liberalization of attitudes concerning homosexuality and marijuana use as other moral concerns—such as wife battering—have come to the fore. A female attorney comments, "Prosecutors used to stay away from family abuse, but once there is enough notoriety they get interested." She elaborates on some unspoken considerations that influence the moral principles on which judges act:

> Male judges tend to feel about incest the way they felt about homosexuality five years ago. At one time men couldn't deal at all with homosexuality because they weren't used to examining their feelings toward other men. Now there's been some breakthrough on that. What still isn't talked about is men's feelings of attraction to their developing daughters. Without this awareness, the human beings who constitute the legal system cannot cope with the subtleties of incest—such as that it is sometimes done as a gentle, loving act, and that it is almost never the violent, assaultive act that rape is.

Moral passions vary in intensity depending on how close one is to the victim. Consider the abuses we have documented in public treatment facilities, where teenage female residents are sexually coerced by male counselors. As a taxpayer one might be moderately concerned ("We aren't getting all that we're paying for; our limited appropriations aren't being wisely administered"). As a human being one might be appalled, and as a parent imagining one's own children victimized one might well be outraged.

Finally, moral principles may conflict, even as they guide the actions of one person in a given situation. Lawyers, who (according to the attorney quoted above) "are expected to be bastions of ethics and at the same time to go beyond the bounds of all propriety to win for their clients," experience the conflict of values especially keenly. To the lay person a "good" lawyer is one who is "sharp," "shrewd," "knows the angles," and can be dishonest when it is to advantage. This split image reflects the contradictions inherent in a system of law that seeks to achieve just outcomes through the partisan exploitation of technicalities. As a result, concludes our informant, "lawyers either are very concerned with integrity or not concerned at all."

In another example of conflicting moral imperatives, many (perhaps most) child molesters are never prosecuted because to do so would require subjecting the abused child to the trauma of testifying to the abuse again and again—first to a caseworker, then to agency staff, then to police, and finally on the witness stand. Meanwhile, the abuser is released pending trial to return home and intimidate the child. It would be more humane to tape the child's statement and play the tape whenever the testimony had to be repeated (with the caseworker present to certify and interpret it), but this may not satisfy the requirements of the law. Here two moral perspectives are painfully in conflict—the helping professional's wish to spare the child further suffering and the legal system's concern to safeguard the rights of the accused. How does one choose which morality to follow?

Against this background of moral complexity, let us compare two vignettes concerning homosexuality in the U.S. Navy, leaving it to the reader to decide which approach exemplifies a morality that can usefully guide those who work with people. On the one hand, a major scandal occurred when 21 Naval women of various grades were accused of being homosexual by several men on their ship. All but one contested the charge. Most of the women had the charges dropped, and the remaining few were cleared by courtmartial. Only when national publicity led to comparisons with the Salem witch trials was an investigation begun into the credibility of one of the men who brought the charges, who, it turned out, had previously made "improper advances" to these women.

A male substance abuse counselor at a Naval base takes a more understanding view of homosexuality:

> I've worked with four or five homosexuals with the presenting problem of drug or alcohol abuse. Actually, who knows, maybe I've worked with 40 or 50, but these are the few that I know about. I report homosexual incidents or the fact that someone is having a problem with homosexuality (if that's the problem for which he comes for help). But I don't feel compelled to put in someone's record the mere fact that he is homosexual—which, if anyone pulled the record, would get the guy kicked out of the Navy. Instead, I advise him that it's against regulations and leave it at that. Some of the old-time career men say, "Homos ought to be taken out and shot." But as I see it, if the guy can do his job, who am I to say he has a problem? I don't want to bring down any extra burden on him. Anyway, one of the guidelines they give counselors is, "If you can't remember it, you can't write it down."

Probably the best response to dogmatic moralism in clinical situations is the traditional injunction to medical students: *primum non nocere* (first, do no harm). The following can serve as a working definition of morality in the clinician-client relationship: It is ethical always to do what is in the interest of the client, consistent with the integrity, well-being, self-respect, and privacy of the clinician as well as with the clinician's responsibilities to society and to concerned agencies. This definition does not resolve all the complications that occur in practice (such as the clinician's conflicting obligations to the client and to others whom the client may be likely to harm), but it does rule out the imposition of the clinician's personal agendas, whether "immoral" or "moral."

Ethical Responses to Feelings of Attraction and Seductive Behavior

What does one do when one finds oneself distracted from the clinical work at hand by feelings of attraction to a client? By provocative behavior on the client's part? By some unfathomable combination of the two? How does one respond to gestures, overtures, "leading questions"? How can one maintain a therapeutic commitment to the client when (to quote from the case that begins Chapter 2) "everything is going to hell in a handbasket"?

The guidelines offered here are based on the assumption (controversial though it may be) that the helping professional is capable of choice. When the client (as is often the case) has not learned to make appropriate choices, it is the clinician's responsibility to teach that vital skill by modeling as well as by other therapeutic methods. On the clinician's side, although one may at times be under stress from what is melodramatically called "temptation," one learns from experience (if one is to remain in the field to good purpose) that one invariably can choose to act responsibly. The inner resources that one calls upon in order to do so go by many names: maturity, professionalism, clinical ethics, detachment, rational thinking (Ellis & Harper, 1975), acceptance of reality (Glasser, 1965). When these are insufficient, the trained clinician knows when, where, and how to seek the support of fellow human beings (often fellow clinicians who have dealt with the same issues).

The following "dos and don'ts" are a distillation of what experienced clinicians have found to be helpful and not so helpful ways of negotiating the sexual dynamics of the client-clinician relationship.

DO acknowledge your own feelings. When helping professionals (including the most astute, well-trained therapists) are asked how they react to seductive clients, they tend to focus on the therapeutic techniques they employ rather than on their own emotional reactions. It is, of course, the theme of this discussion that helping professionals must act toward clients therapeutically rather than out of feelings of attraction. But the poise required to do so is not always easily achieved. As psychotherapists (of all people) ought to recognize, it cannot be achieved by the shortcut of evasion, as exemplified by the all-too-common retreat to the safe ground of medical jargon. Sometimes this denial stems from personal discomfort, sometimes from improper training in which the injunction not to act out feelings of attraction to clients is misrepresented (whether by the trainer or trainee) as meaning that one must not admit to having such feelings. In either case, timely supervisory intervention can be helpful.

What frees the clinician to act with clear ethical purpose is an acceptance of and comfort with the normal human feelings that are incidental to the clinical interaction. Surely it is not abnormal for a physician, social worker, or counselor to desire a client sexually when a psycho-analyst matter-of-factly states,

> There have been many times when I've entertained fantasies not only of dating and marrying patients but of having sexual inter-course with them. These are common countertransference reac-tions. Yes, I have had these fantasies. Every other analyst has had them, too, and they're not the issue. (Malcolm, 1980b, p. 110)

The analyst deals with his fantasies by analyzing them in the same man-ner as with a patient's material. Other helping professionals do not, however, need to learn analytic techniques to keep their fantasies from becoming disruptive, destructive realities. What amounts to a clarifi-cation of purpose will suffice.

DO separate your personal feelings from dealings with the client.
Winnicott (1960, pp. 18–19) distinguishes between "professional work" and "ordinary life" by noting that clinicians, when engaged with clients, must be more than just the "unreliable men and women we happen to be in private life." The duality the psychotherapist must observe is to "remain vulnerable, and yet retain his professional role in his actual working hours." "In other words," concludes Dahlberg (1970, p. 121), "the therapist must remain human but try to *behave* ideally."

The realization that one can be, when appropriate, both human and professional is understood by each individual in his or her own terms. A male social worker says, "When I'm attracted to a client I register the attraction, but since I know it's impossible I don't get invested in it. Instead of dwelling on it, I move on to something else." A male psy-chologist in private practice articulates the therapist's dilemma in this way:

> The compassionate empathy that I as a therapist feel for all my clients does not depend on their physical beauty, or even on whether they are male or female (especially as time goes on), but it does nonetheless have a potential sexual component. The issue is to recognize the line beyond which compassion can turn to pas-sion. There's no easy way out of this, since I doubt that good ther-apy can be done unless the risk is taken and the therapist's vulnerability exposed. On those infrequent occasions when the

risk becomes imminent, I check out the sources of my vulnerability—namely, the feelings of deprivation and frustration (romantic, financial, whatever) that I bring into the hour. Then I hold the line by experiencing dignity, wholeness, and pleasure in my occupation and in the fact of my being a professional.

The tone of this statement captures an ennobling, empowering quality in the awareness that one has the capacity to choose which parts of one-self to express in the service of clients. In the following account a female psychologist relates a moment of revelation early in her career. The revelation was of her own strength and commitment to purpose.

I had a client whose attractive qualities were immediately appar-ent in the initial sessions. He was an exuberant, caring, sensitive person who could appreciate what was valuable about people regardless of the ups and downs of his relationships with them. Even as a client he was a stimulating person to be with. I kept thinking about him and looking forward to our next session with an excitement that I felt as sexual. The turning point (and it was a turning point in my career as well) came when I had him do a gestalt exercise in which he spoke to an empty chair representing a woman he loved. He said, "I'd do it better if you sat in the chair." Here I was, placed in a dramatic situation that symbolized my desires as much as his. I wondered if my fantasies would interfere with my role-playing. As I sat there, though, I became the char-acter I sat in for. I did what needed to be done therapeutically and left my feelings behind. I learned that my commitment to therapy was greater than the sexual excitement I felt for this man. And in subsequent sessions the sexual excitement died down as the work of therapy became more satisfying.

What happens when one fails to achieve this clarity about one's dual identity as human being and clinician is illustrated in the following case, presented by the director of a halfway house for adolescents:

A 17-year-old male resident made approaches to a 21-year-old female counselor. He was good-looking with an air of maturity and a "hippie" look, which she, too, cultivated. She kept putting him off by telling him she had a job to do, but she didn't feel comfortable enough to give him a yes-or-no answer. It was clearly a trauma for her, and she showed it in a way that gave him a double message. She even brought it up at a staff meeting, saying, "I just don't know what to do with this." The resident, after he was discharged, kept writing her letters as he went about the business of finding work and going to school. At first she did not respond, but after four or five months she began writing him notes. Within a year after they had met they were living together.

The counselor in this case (who was young and lacked formal training) apparently believed that as long as she made her personal conflicts an open issue at staff meetings, she was entitled to act them out. Actually, she should have given the resident a clear "no" answer and *then* come to the staff for help in dealing with her own conflicts. Clinicians, like ordinary mortals, sometimes need counseling and emotional support. But the resolution of personal issues cannot be made a precondition for maintaining appropriate professional behavior. The client with or against whom the clinician "sins" is not helped by the clinician's "confession."

DON'T make the client's problems your own. Overidentification occurs when the clinician's judgment is affected by emotional involvement in the outcome of therapy or treatment (Edelwich with Brodsky, 1980). Although countertransference reactions are normal, to act them out by overidentifying with a client is not normal. It is a clinical error.

Students of therapeutic skills are taught this useful reminder: "The client has the problem; you have the job—which is to do your best to help the client deal with the problem." Failure to take this responsibly detached stance can lead to a deepening spiral of overidentification, with damaging consequences for both clinician and client. First, the clinician becomes upset when the client relapses or shows a lack of progress (e.g., by drinking, taking drugs, violating probation, breaking agreements, etc.). Seen through the distorting lens of overidentification, the client's failure to self-actualize becomes a reflection on the clinician's competence and credibility. The client, sensing the clinician's vulnerability to self-blame, plays upon it by offering the implicit bribe of good behavior in return for acquiescence in the client's fantasies. The clinician, anxious to avoid further discomfort, plays along to a greater or lesser degree. Whether what results is a sexual liaison or a more subtle form of complicity in the client's evasions, the clinician's role is compromised. By encouraging false hopes in place of realistic coping, the clinician takes on the client's dependency needs at an extratherapeutic level. It is no favor to the client. In the very act of taking on the client's problems, one burdens the client with a problem of one's own—that is, the inability to provide therapeutic support by representing reality clearly to the client.

DON'T give your problems to the client. Words or gestures addressed to a client should be governed by a therapeutic purpose. Even a clinician who feels only compassion (as opposed to passion) for a client must be careful not to express that feeling in self-indulgent, antitherapeutic ways. A social worker in her mid-twenties took the following dilemma to her supervisor:

> I find it hard to keep the intimate content of therapy from leading to intimate behavior on my part. When a client spends an hour talking about his loneliness and sadness over his personal losses, he can really get down to some raw emotion. Along with all my analytical observations I find myself feeling moved. My impulse at the end is to stand up and hug him. But I hold back because I don't know how it will be taken.

Her supervisor told her:

> Comforting gestures can be fine, but they can invite misinterpretation unless you really know what you're doing. In this case you correctly see that in hugging the client you would be responding to your own need to take care of him and to discharge the tension built up over the hour. It would be understandable for the client to interpret your reaching out to him as something more than it was. He might carry away the memory that "She hugged me!" and forget everything else that happened in the session.

The supervisor then described a somewhat different situation which, he felt, did permit some demonstrativeness on his part.

> I had gone through an intense, intimate session of family therapy with a mother, father, and two children. At the end everyone was

crying. I asked them what they needed to do to close themselves up and walk out of there, but they couldn't focus on the question. So I said, "Well, I can tell you what I need so I won't walk out of this session raw, too. I need to know where all of you are at and how you feel about me for having done this with you." One person responded by coming over to me and squeezing my hand. That helped heal the intimacy for me. Therapists tend not to ask for energy from clients. No textbook ever taught me how to say, in effect, "Now that I've given to you for an hour, how about giving to me for five minutes?" But I think it's important to learn when and how to take those risks.

This instance differs from the previous one both in the "when" (it was a family rather than one-to-one therapy session) and the "how" (the therapist explicitly defined his needs *as a therapist*). Clearly, one cannot make a set of definite rules governing emotional revelation by therapists. But the examples given here do indicate a need for considerable caution and care.

When the clinician is feeling not only compassion, but passion as well, the guidelines are clear-cut. It is wholly inappropriate to tell a client about one's sexual interest in or fantasies about that client. To do so is to take one's own problem and give it to the client, which is obviously countertherapeutic. Psychologists, for example, report that therapy tends to be harmed if the client is aware of the therapist's attraction (Pope et al., 1986). There are other places where one can discharge and clarify one's own feelings.

Some therapists object that "if I have to hold something back, then I can't be completely natural with the client," or "I don't have to say anything about being attracted because the client will pick up my vibes anyway." The clinician's job isn't to be natural, just responsible. One can be natural with one's supervisor, peers, or therapist. And while the subtleties of verbal and nonverbal communication and the sensitivity of many clients to unconscious cues are not to be denied, one need not simply resign oneself to being an open book. One can and should maintain therapeutic propriety in one's overt behavior while seeking help elsewhere to master the feelings that may be unintentionally communicated. If the client brings up the perceived "vibes," then the client's perceptions and reactions should be discussed as a therapeutic issue.

There are times when the clinician may need to confront a client about disruptive sexual undercurrents that appear to have an element of mutuality. In such cases one must first work through one's own emotions with colleagues or other sources of personal support so as to be able to deal with the client from a position of integrity.

DO confide in your supervisor, peers, or professional consultant. There are at least three constructive channels for the overflow of personal energy that a clinician may experience in the course of therapeutic encounters, as well as for the clinical uncertainties presented by the seductive client. Usually it makes sense to draw upon these sources of support in the following order:

1. *Supervision.* Supervision is set up specifically for the purpose of helping the clinician deal with questions of therapeutic technique, including the relationship between a therapist's clinical behavior and personal motivations. It offers an ongoing opportunity to share with a more experienced colleague the problems stemming from seductive client behavior or feelings of attraction to clients. At the supervisor's discretion, the supervisory consultation may lead to a conjoint session to work out the issue with the client. (How a supervisor deals with these issues is discussed in the final section of this chapter.)

2. *Peers.* When supervision is not available or is not helpful, one may consult with one's colleagues, as in the case of physicians in a group practice or fellow staff members at a hospital or other institution. Again, someone who has had similar feelings and experiences can offer an informed objectivity to help one past an emotional stalemate. Simply making the issue explicit and bringing it to someone else's attention can raise it to a conscious level, thereby either neutralizing it immediately or making it accessible to further examination. This can be done with a matter-of-fact, even joking remark, such as "Boy, she looks nice!" One's colleague may then say, "Yes, I think she looks nice, too," or "Do you think this is a problem for you?" or "If you need some support with this, maybe you should have a chaperone." Through such an exchange the depth of the problem can be measured and necessary steps taken. When one seeks deeper scrutiny of one's handling of a case, this may be obtained from a peer as well as from a supervisor. Professional support groups as well as informal contacts can be used for this purpose.

3. *Professional consultation.* If support from supervisors or peers proves elusive, some form of therapy or counseling is always available. Helping professionals, whose job is to provide such services or make

referrals to those who do, ought not to feel compromised if they sometimes need to avail themselves of the same services. If the clinician's
feelings are at issue, then the clinician may appropriately assume the
client's role in a therapeutic exploration.

These remedies, like any others, carry no guarantee of efficacy. Just
as an insensitive therapist or counselor sometimes makes a client's problem worse, supervisors and colleagues do not always provide the support sought by the clinician. For supervisory or peer consultation to
work, the clinician must be given permission to raise delicate issues
(Bursztajn, 1990). In an expression of the guardedness that exists
between the genders at many agencies, female clinicians sometimes
sense a lack of such permission from male staff members. Some women
say flatly that they never discuss sexual questions with a male supervisor, no matter how sensitive that individual may appear to be (cf.
Woolley, 1988). A female counselor at a halfway house for male
ex-prison inmates under 21 years of age reports what unfortunately is
not a unique experience:

> I worked closely with a smart kid who I thought had considerable
> promise. I felt that he really needed affection, but I thought it
> absolutely inappropriate for me to be physical with him because
> it could easily be misinterpreted. (I've seen too much of what hap-
> pens when mothers are seductive with their teenage sons.) When
> I brought this up at a staff meeting, the male staff members were
> quite critical of me. They said that my concerns were ridiculous
> and that I should be more physical with the kid. "You guys are
> nuts!" I said. I did not go along with what they recommended.

In seeking a staff consultation this woman acted according to our recommendations, but it didn't do her any good. Her fellow staff members
were part of the problem rather than the solution.

When the channels of consultation break down, it is of no avail to
be judgmental about the supervisor or others who are insufficiently
supportive. Blaming the problem on a bad supervisor doesn't solve the
problem. If one recourse doesn't bring satisfaction, try something else.
If nothing works, accept the problem as a "given" and live with it or
leave the job.

The protocol for taking job-related personal issues first to supervision, then to peers, and finally to therapy is applicable to many prob-

lems besides sexual attraction to clients. It will be cited again in relation to other "sexual dilemmas" discussed in this book.

DO set limits while giving the client a safe space for self-expression. Clients who act seductively are testing limits. They will do what they can get away with. The clinician must set clear limits to acting out without denying the client the space needed to engage in the many forms of self-expression and self-discovery that constitute therapy. In practice these two aims are not contradictory, but quite compatible. It is by being only a therapist, rather than a lover or potential lover, that one can be fully a therapist. It is when a boundary is clearly drawn that the client can most thoroughly explore the space within the boundary. The following examples illustrate sensitive limit-setting behavior in different clinical contexts.

A young psychotherapist in private practice gives his clients the "behavioral mandate" that "anything goes except acting out." The "anything" involves delicately defined boundaries and free space:

> One of my clients, a self-described bisexual man in his forties, compulsively gives out "body language" that he isn't aware of. At this early stage of therapy it has become clear that physical contact is what grounds him in reality. In our sessions (as, undoubtedly, in other contexts in his life) he regularly flexes his body and even gets up from the chair and walks around in an exhibitionistic manner. For him the line between anxiety and sexual expression is very thin. It makes me uncomfortable when he walks around, but I have not set limits on that. I remain seated and calm, facing the empty chair. If he wants to come back into my focus, he has to come back into the chair. And that has worked.

A male social worker in his thirties who directs a therapeutic community for youthful drug abusers finds himself an object of attraction for some of the female residents. He is able to deal with this in a personally and therapeutically self-confident way:

> I suppose that in the eyes of the residents there is always that challenge: "Can I break his wall?" But there is also another feeling that I do my best to nurture. It comes up, for example, with a 16-year-old who is actively seductive with me (once to the point of sitting

on my lap) and who gets jealous when she sees me talking to a female staff member. She's a sexy kid, and part of me likes the seductive treatment. What takes precedence, though, is the security she gets from knowing that I'm the one man in her life who won't sleep with her. She can be playful with me because there is no question in her mind (except at an extreme level of fantasy) that I won't ever touch her.

Limit-testing situations requiring tact and flexibility occur every day in medicine. People who are placed in the dependent role of a bedridden patient commonly overcompensate by being sexually provocative in order to regain the feeling of control that is lost through illness. Those who suffer from disabling or disfiguring conditions are the most likely to do so. Nurses, who bear the brunt of such behavior, need to cultivate a less rigid set of responses than psychotherapists. In a typical example, a young male patient laid hands on a young female nurse. "What a charmer!" she said with a smile while deftly lifting his hands from her body. The nurse's response was a wise one. She defined physical contact as being off limits, yet took care not to assault the patient's self-esteem. In recommending this approach as most considerate of the patient, however, it is only fair to acknowledge the job stress that nurses experience from constantly having to fend off physical advances.

DON'T be rejecting. Understandably, helping professionals often respond with disgust to sexual advances on the part of clients. Consider the following scenario: An elderly man living in a nursing home pinches a female staff member. She recoils, thinking, "How could you!" Her supervisor might answer, "Because he's an old man placed in a humiliating situation where he experiences unaccustomed feelings of helplessness." Or, as a 45-year-old nurse with a wide range of professional experience has learned:

> I've had many male patients get cozy and start hugging me, especially after something as demoralizing as a heart attack. I used to find this repulsive. After I went back to school and learned about the dynamics of ego-insecurity, I realized that the "dirty old men" I had condemned were just acting out.

The clinician's dilemma is that to respect the client's self-esteem one must not invest oneself personally in responding to behavior normally thought of as assaultive to one's own self-esteem. A cold, rejecting manner on the part of the clinician may communicate to the client that his or her sexuality is not acceptable, rather than that it is simply being directed at the wrong person. This ego-deflation runs counter to the purpose of the clinician as clinician. But the clinician as human being still has feelings about the matter. To get past these feelings, it helps to keep in mind that sexual overtures and attempted seductions are among the "givens" of working with people. They "come with the territory." The awareness that one will inevitably be the object of such behavior can reduce the stress associated with it and thereby make it easier to set firm limits in a gracious rather than a defensive manner. Sometimes the latter can be done wordlessly, through gesture and implication. When a spoken reply is called for, words like the following usually suffice: "I appreciate your interest in me—it's flattering—but if you've found our conversations helpful to you, I think I can continue to be helpful by staying away from any other role. I've found from experience that it's most useful to stick to a professional interaction." Or simply, "That's not what therapy is."

DO express nonsexual caring. As often as not, the client who approaches a clinician sexually is seeking nurturance, which is what the clinician is there to give. It is a mistake to react to the sexual overture by withdrawing from the nurturing role. On the contrary, the clinician should strongly reaffirm that role in a nonsexual context. It is important to empathize with the sense of loss that lies behind the client's compensatory assertion of sexuality. Wherever possible, one should reaffirm in human terms the attractiveness the client seeks to confirm in sexual terms. (It may require some delicate clinical judgment to decide when and how this kind of communication can be made comfortably as well as unambiguously.) In the words of a female psychologist quoted in Chapter 3, "I respond to the need underneath the bravado by giving the client the feedback he's looking for (i.e., letting him know he is attractive) while conveying that he doesn't need to act out sexually to obtain warmth and caring from me."

DON'T be drawn into answering personal questions or giving the client other "double messages." An error frequently made by the inexperienced or insufficiently trained clinician is to make excuses for turning down a personal relationship with a client. Thrown into confusion and discomfort by the client's sexual gambit, the clinician interposes a real or invented obstacle instead of explaining straightforwardly the nature of a therapist's ethical commitment. The client is left with the impression that, were it not for that one obstacle (perhaps a temporary one), an intimate relationship with this or another clinician might be possible.

Even the proper-sounding response that a social or sexual involvement with a client would be "against the rules" can (depending on how it is said in context) be an evasion of the issue. Indeed it is against the rules, and it is reasonable (though not necessary) to indicate that the clinician's scruples are backed by a strong ethical tradition within the profession. The clinician should, however, speak from having internalized this tradition, rather than appear to be chafing against an external restraint. To say "I can't do it" instead of "I won't do it" is to pass the buck. Again, just say, "That's not what a therapist does."

It is even worse to "put off" a client as one would an eligible dating partner. A female clinician who tells a male client that she is "too busy" to go out to dinner with him can expect to be asked out again, since there could be a time when she wouldn't be too busy. A sure way to get in trouble is to answer questions about one's personal life, as Marty P. (a substance abuse counselor in Chapter 2) did when he was drawn into this sequence: "Are you married?" (Yes.) "Are you happily married?" (Yes.) "How happy?" Another respondent reported having engaged in the following dialogue:

Client: "Do you have a lover?"
Clinician: "No, not at this time."
Client: "Do you miss it?"

This sort of probing is like quicksand. Each reluctant answer legitimizes the next intrusive question. The deeper the discussion gets into the clinician's life, the farther afield it wanders from the client's.

It is immaterial whether the excuse given by the clinician is a real or a fabricated one (although dissembling in itself is patently inimical to therapy). In either case there is a lack of candor on the clinician's part about the actual reason for avoiding a personal involvement. A male social worker, for example, tells seductive male homosexual clients that "I'm very heterosexual." Since he also does not go out with female clients, one might question the logic of his defensive strategy. He wouldn't say to a female client, "I'd like to, but I'm homosexual." A female colleague of his does, by her own testimony, stoop to falsehood in her anxiety to shield herself from unsettling overtures. "I make perfectly clear," she says, "that I have a steady relationship with a man—even if I don't." On reflection she admits that this is "a copout."

What must instead be made clear is that the clinician's personal life is not an appropriate subject for discussion in a therapy session. It is not something that the client needs to be concerned with. The failure to get this message across (when necessary) compromises the clinician's role, in that the clinician may appear to be colluding in the client's fantasy that such a relationship may someday be negotiable.

DO confront the issue straightforwardly. There is some disagreement about whether avoidance can be an appropriate technique for dealing with sexually provocative behavior on the part of the client. Some physicians prefer to deflect unwanted interest by cultivating a detached professional manner or by performing examinations in the presence of a chaperone (such as a nurse or medical student). Others believe that to ignore seductive mannerisms is to undermine patient-physician rapport and to leave unattended a manifest clinical problem. As obstetrician-gynecologist Marc Lowen stated at a roundtable discussion of the seductive patient:

> I'm a firm believer in confronting the patient shortly after one is aware that one is being seduced. I think in the long run the patient doesn't really want to seduce or be seduced. She really appreciates your attention and your awareness. Without destroying her, without rejecting her, you can explain why she is having such feelings and this will nip the seductiveness in the bud, yet allow a deeper understanding between the patient and the physician. (Shochet et al., 1976, p. 99)

Physicians not directly concerned with psychotherapeutic issues sometimes use avoidance to test whether a patient's seductiveness is a light diversion or a serious issue. For patients who are not deeply invested in the fantasy, it can be therapeutic simply to offer an opportunity for self-confrontation without embarrassment under conditions that discourage acting out. If, however, the behavior persists and even escalates, it must be confronted. It is best to do this, in the words of a family physician with a special interest in interpersonal dynamics, "without pejorative labeling, without imputation of motive, but simply as a perception of your own that you are willing to have corrected."

In psychotherapy nothing ultimately is avoided or ignored. Seductiveness is a therapeutic issue like any other, to be dealt with when and in the manner the therapist deems appropriate. The consensus among the therapists interviewed is that the issue should be confronted as soon as it becomes a problem. In the words of one psychologist, "When you start getting the dinner invitations and requests for your phone number, you have to make the distinction between kindness and romance. It may feel cruel and withholding, but the clarity can be quite helpful to a person." In keeping with Glasser's (1965) method of direct communication, it is best to state matter-of-factly what one perceives to be going on, emphasize that a personal relationship between a client and therapist cannot be negotiated, and reaffirm the purpose of the session while leaving room for the client to explore the issue further. If the client's behavior is distracting, it may (depending on the client's condition and the stage of therapy) be appropriate to ask that it be modified (e.g., by requesting that the client pull down a dress that has been raised to provocative heights).

The words used to negotiate this delicate issue reflect the personal style of the individual therapist as well as the tenor of the relationship with the client. A female psychologist (in Chapter 3) responds to aggressive physical advances by saying, in effect, "Okay, so you needed to do this; now let's get past it." A female counselor at a drug treatment center speaks as follows to a male client who seeks her out regularly even though she is not his primary therapist: "I'm concerned about you. I think you're coming to talk to me because you have feelings for me. Is there something going on with you in relation to me?" She expresses this concern, she explains, "for me as well as for him, so that I can let go of my anxiety about his being infatuated with me." An older man working in a similar agency tells seductive clients, "Yes, you are attractive, but that's not what we're here for. It's just not going to happen, so let's move on to something else." A male psychologist at a university clinic describes his handling of the difficult issues presented by a young female client:

In addition to the usual seductive moves of sitting close to me and striking poses, she would reach out and touch me when she made a point. Then, each time, she would apologize for doing it. Finally I said, "Look, do what you want. It doesn't bother me." After that she never touched me again. She also loosened up therapeutically and began to speak more revealingly about herself.

On the rare occasion when the clinician must acknowledge a mutual attraction, it is essential to alert one's colleagues first, both to remove the option of acting out and to avoid making the client act as therapist for the clinician. The discussion with the client can then focus on the implications *for the client* of the options of talking out the issue or altering or (in rare cases) terminating the relationship.

DO explore the client's behavior therapeutically. The very act of calling attention to the client's seductive behavior opens up therapeutic questions for discussion. Since the therapeutic interaction tends to reflect the client's habitual patterns of coping, the therapist should take the opportunity to explore underlying issues revealed by the client's acting out in therapy. Thus a psychiatric social worker asks clients who give exhibitionistic accounts of their sex lives, "What kind of reaction do you want to get from me?" A psychologist in a marital counseling session, perceiving the husband's attempts to win her over against his wife with seductive mannerisms, gains insight into the mechanisms of control by which the husband and wife deal with matters ranging from sex to household finances. A psychiatrist replies to personal questions from clients by saying, "Hey, my life doesn't have anything to do with your therapy. What's going on here? Let's talk about it. What do you expect to get out of knowing me personally?" In this way he allows clients to explore their unrealistic expectations and subsequent disappointments in relationships outside of therapy.

In two reported cases therapeutic benefits were achieved by following up the implications of the client's romantic interest in the therapist. In the first, a female school psychologist was working with a 16-year-old boy who was phobic about school. He came to school only on days when he knew she would be there; on other days she arranged to be in telephone contact with him. After this pattern had been established, she asked him, "What's the issue? What is your goal—to see me, to come to school, or to drop out?" By addressing the question she helped him face what he had been using flirtation to evade, that is, his inability to define and pursue a goal. Subsequently his school attendance improved.

The second case was that of a middle-aged man who was hospitalized for major surgery which necessitated significant changes in his lifestyle. Clinically depressed after his return home, he continued to have weekly outpatient sessions with the female social worker he had seen in the hospital. He confessed to her that he was obsessed with her image, as if he were in love with her. She supported his sense of reality by making statements such as, "Gee, when you think about it, you really don't know anything about me." He replied, "That's true; it's just that you've been so kind and so helpful to me." She then drew him out concerning his feeling that he had not previously known many people to be kind and helpful to him. As he regained ego-strength, the issue of his attraction to the social worker became less salient.

A practitioner who takes therapeutic exploration to its outer limits is Eric F., a male psychologist in his thirties who elicits highly charged sexual fantasies focused on himself. In his words,

> In confronting seductive manifestations one must distinguish between a conscious sabotaging of therapy and an unconscious bringing forth of sexual material that gets directed at the therapist. In the latter case, where the sexual issues are important ones in the person's therapy, I find it worthwhile to explore them as deeply as possible, using whatever openings I am given. Thus, although I draw the line at any acting out of a client's fantasies about me, I permit and even encourage anything short of that. If a client expresses a sexual interest in me, I may, for example, ask, "What is it that you would like to do with me?" and pursue it until it gets pretty specific. When I first considered doing this, I was surprised that my supervisor accepted it so readily. But in practice I find it to be as legitimate a therapeutic tool as any other.

What makes it legitimate, Eric explains, is the seriousness with which the questioning is conducted, in contrast to an "atmosphere of titillation" in which "the therapist gets off on the fantasies."

> Admittedly the client starts out with an investment in the fantasies that is other than therapeutic. But whereas sexual banter can con-

tribute to arousal in a context where it is reciprocated, talk in an atmosphere of clinical examination can demystify. Fantasies tend to lose their power when brought out into the light of day. Moreover, the safe sharing of sexual material in therapy, with a contract prohibiting acting out, can help the client become less defensive about his or her sexual intentions. It also can start a process of looking at one's behavior more objectively.

The technique is legitimate, but it takes considerable poise to carry it off. One must have confidence in one's skills as a therapist to take the risks it entails.

DON'T "refer out." When a clinician feels attracted to a client or has difficulty dealing with the client's seductive behavior, it would seem simplest for the clinician to refer the client to a colleague. This solution not only is widely practiced by individuals, but is countenanced by many agencies. A counselor at a state-run alcoholism treatment facility matter-of-factly reports, "Three times this year at staff meetings someone talked about being embroiled in some kind of sexual dynamic with a client, though not to the point of acting out sexually. Those individuals were all told to refer the client to another staff member, with no questions asked." This policy (parodied as "when in doubt, refer out") is typical in such institutions—and typically misguided.

Here as elsewhere, the simplest solution is not the best. If the referral is followed by the initiation of a love affair between the client and the clinician who made the referral, then it is subject to the ethical objections detailed in Chapter 5. Even without this self-serving denouement, though, it is questionable whether one can best discharge one's responsibilities to a client by what amounts to passing the buck. Although there may be another qualified clinician to pick up the slack, there is no guarantee that there will be one. In any case, the client suffers the consequences of discontinuity of care, including uncertainty, loss of time, and possible feelings of rejection. These issues can, to be sure, be dealt with in therapy by both the referring and receiving clinicians. But why add more issues to an already ample therapeutic agenda? Should the client suffer on account of the clinician's problem?

There is still another important reason to resist the impulse to refer out. When therapy is blocked, an experienced therapist looks for the meaning of the feelings that get in the way. A therapeutic impasse, when turned to advantage, can lead to a therapeutic breakthrough. If, instead, the therapist's response is driven by discomfort, fear, and expediency, both therapist and client miss the challenge of overcoming the obstacle and learning what is to be learned from it.

As a limiting case, consider this statement by a female psychologist: "When I meet a client for the first time, I assess the feelings between us as well as any unresolved issues of my own that might make me vulnerable. If I sense the danger of an attraction, I don't take on that person." Two considerations make the "referral out" acceptable here. First, it is done immediately, *before* the therapeutic relationship gets underway. Second, this therapist, being in private practice, can choose her clients.

In a public agency all clients who meet the criteria for eligibility have a right to receive services. One can better serve these clients by taking one's own personal and clinical difficulties to one's supervisor, peers, or therapist than by dismissing the client along with the problem. If necessary, the issue can be taken up with the client either in conjoint session or subsequent to the professional consultation. Only when none of these measures achieves satisfactory results should a referral be considered.

A male psychologist sensitively describes the difficult choice that a referral entails:

Although I have not had to face the need to make a referral on the grounds of attraction to a client, I would not rule out the possibility. Since therapy involves the risk of vulnerability, and since I am only human, I must admit that I could be "decoded." If I saw that happening I would first test the ground with my clinical supervisor, who probably would ask me, "Exactly how vulnerable do you think you are?" If the risk had gone beyond acceptable limits, I would make the referral along with some self-searching for my own growth.

In the rare instance when a referral is called for, one must do everything possible to remove any implication of rejection or abandonment of the client. While validating the feelings of self-incrimination normally experienced by the client in these circumstances, one must take upon oneself the blame for being unable to provide the support the client needs. The responsibility for the decision to terminate is one's own, not the client's. Whenever possible, time should be allowed to explore what the referral means to the client, especially when verbal or non-verbal cues indicate a troubled response.

The ethical implications of referral will be analyzed more fully in Chapter 7, in the context of aversive reactions to clients. In this, perhaps the most controversial application of Reality Therapy to clinical practice, the professional caregiver is deemed to be capable of choice, that is, of assuming the responsibility of serving clients regardless of any distractions and temptations presented along the way. Although the urgency of this responsibility is greater for clinicians employed by public agencies, it is also a relevant concern for the private practitioner, as the therapist quoted above acknowledged in his reference to "self-searching for my own growth."

The Limits of Involvement: Boundary Violations

A psychiatrist of highly reputable background and credentials leaves a university teaching hospital and sets up a private practice at the far end of town. Taking over an old house on a large estate, he turns it into a drop-in center where clients in therapy can read, mingle, hold group sessions, and become a "family." Individual therapy takes place in the psychiatrist's private office, from which a client may emerge to resume a volunteer job elsewhere in the "learning center." In time these tasks evolve into explicit bartering arrangements, and clients who do well in therapy are invited to sign on as paraprofessional "helpers." Clients feel free to drop by the psychiatrist's house and meet members of his family, who in turn visit and work at the center. Friends and employees become clients as clients become employees and friends. As part of the center's atmosphere of quasi-familial support, the psychiatrist begins to engage in "therapeutic touch" (mainly hugs) and encourages clients to do likewise with one another in their group activities.

Towering above his charges in self-assurance and prestige, his opinions and directives unchallenged, the psychiatrist assumes the role of a therapy guru. As his enthusiasm for this innovative approach to therapy grows, his professional contacts at the local university and psychiatric association fall away. At the same time, not all goes smoothly at the center. With clients swapping work roles, some begin to wonder who (besides the psychiatrist) has access to their files. A pecking order develops as clients, especially women, compete for the psychiatrist's attention. After a while one female client begins to wonder just what *is* going on when the psychiatrist spends what seems an unusually long time behind closed doors with another woman associated with the center.

If this psychiatrist is sued for malpractice or brought before a licensing board for alleged sexual involvement with a client, he faces an uphill battle for vindication *even if he is innocent.* Because he has traversed numerous other boundaries of accepted practice, the credibility of his claim that he has continued to respect the final boundary is severely damaged. He may lose his liability insurance, his license, and his livelihood well before he has his day in court.

Boundary violations in therapeutic relationships have a way of escalating to the appearance or actuality of sexual misconduct (cf. Nielsen, Peterson, Shapiro, & Thompson, 1989). Gutheil (1990) gives clinicians three axioms to keep in mind:

1. Most sexual misconduct in therapy begins with other boundary violations.
2. Boundary violations do not in themselves prove sexual misconduct.
3. Finders of fact give more credence to allegations of sexual misconduct in the presence of boundary violations.

When for example, the Massachusetts Board of Registration in Medicine revoked the license of a physician who admitted that he twice met socially with a patient (once at the physician's home) but denied the charge that he had had sex with the patient, the Board concluded, "There was an undisputed level of intimacy between the two which supports the inference of sexual relations" (quoted in Mohl, 1989, p. 7). Whether or not this physician was falsely accused (as colleagues who established a defense fund believed), the lesson for clinicians is to avoid even the semblance of boundary violations.

What kinds of contact, physical and social, are appropriate between client and clinician? How much of oneself should one reveal to a client? These questions have perplexed therapists ever since Freud sardonically took his colleague Sandor Ferenczi to task for kissing his patients. Freud himself gossiped with patients, lent them money, and accepted birthday gifts from them (Malcolm, 1980a, p. 95). Since then more rigorous standards have evolved. Although one cannot make judgments in individual cases by appealing to rules set in stone, the following guidelines show how clinicians can be responsible without being unnecessarily harsh or remote.

Physical contact. Traditionally, the "laying on of hands" has been regarded as a vital ingredient in the art of healing. Neither modern medical technology nor contemporary psychotherapeutic techniques have eliminated the value of handholding, nonerotic stroking, a pat on the shoulder, or a hug at a strategic moment. Supportive physical gestures can be essential in helping someone through a painful or difficult passage (as with a woman in labor) or in giving reassurance that a person's humanity and individual identity are intact in the face of illness or injury. Nonetheless, the potential for misinterpretation inherent in physical expression must not be underestimated. In one study, 69 percent of the psychiatrists and 40 percent of the internists responding believed that nonerotic physical contact would occasionally, frequently, or always be misunderstood by patients (Kardener et al., 1973). Therefore, in deciding whether or not to communicate with a client through touching, one must take into account the nature of the client's condition (medical, surgical, psychiatric), one's confidence in one's own motives and in one's ability to convey them unambiguously, and the level of trust between the client and oneself (Marmor, 1972). Caution is especially advisable in view of Kardener et al.'s (1976) finding that male physicians who engage in nonerotic physical contact with patients are more likely also to engage in erotic contact. As for the nature of the contact itself, this commonsense rule will serve the clinician well: *"Nothing should be done when alone with the client that could not be done in public."*

Social contact. However warm and friendly one's relations with clients may be, one must not lose sight of one's special role as a person hired (by the client or agency) to assist the client in specified ways. One must take care not to act in a way that might lead the client to confuse a paid clinician with a personal friend. With experience, each individual learns what to do and what to avoid with clients (and former clients) in general as well as with particular clients. For example, one might send a client a birthday or Christmas card, but let Valentine's Day pass without acknowledgment. Lending money is certainly not a good idea, while the advisability of accepting a gift depends on the spirit in which it is given. (People do sometimes give gifts to therapists as therapists rather than as romantic objects.) One should avoid doing things for clients that they can do for themselves—for example, making phone calls, checking bus schedules, managing finances.

Lunch and dinner invitations present a dilemma for many clinicians (other than in some formal psychotherapeutic situations where such meetings would be out of the question). The two are very different, in that the lunch hour is bounded as to time and place by the constraints of the business day, while the dinner hour is not. For this reason it is almost never appropriate to join a client for dinner or any other leisure-hours activity away from the office. Even if a sharp line is drawn between dinner and a love affair, the after-hours contact may confuse the client as well as other clients and staff members in the agency who may not be able to set such clear limits. When it comes to having lunch with a client, one likewise must consider how one's actions are likely to be interpreted by the client and by one's peers in terms of the mores of the agency. Obviously, sitting down opposite someone in the agency cafeteria is different from making a lunch date. One clinician may feel professionally compromised after meeting a client for lunch, in the sense of not being able to approach that client with clinical objectivity and firmness. Another may say, "I can learn more from a client at lunch than with a desk between us" (which may reflect shrewd clinical insight or the clinician's own insecurity and need for intimacy). A female clinician may find that she, unlike her male colleagues, cannot have lunch with male clients without being presumed upon. To recognize and heed such reactions on the part of clients is prudent. One must, on the other hand, be alert to one's own patterns of selection, especially those suggesting that the lunches are more than a matter of convenience. One's supervisor may well have some questions if one's lunch companions are always attractive clients of the opposite sex.

Extracurricular therapy. A related boundary violation is the therapy session that "must" take place outside of normal hours or off-site (for example, at the clinician's or client's home, or at a restaurant or bar) because there seems to be no other time or place to meet. (At whose behest and in whose interest is that decision being made?) A therapy session that looks like a date may well turn into one—in reality or in court. Beware of "mobile" therapy, too. You don't want to have a malpractice suit hinge on what was said or done when you drove the client home in a snowstorm and stayed parked for an hour in front of the client's home with the car windows steamed up.

Money and employment. In the context of the growing public and professional concern over sexual exploitation of clients in therapy, a range of potentially unethical "dual relationships" between therapists and clients is coming under increased scrutiny (Kitchener, 1988). Unusual financial transactions as well as deviations from normal financial arrangements (such as unpaid therapy, barter, and the accumulation of vast unpaid bills) are part of the maelstrom of irregularities out of which sexual misconduct may arise. These practices in themselves may also be construed as compromising or exploiting the professional relationship. Reflecting the views of a substantial proportion of psychologists, psychiatrists, and social workers (Borys & Pope, 1989; Pope et al., 1987), the ethics codes of these and other professions (such as marriage and family therapists) proscribe or warn against such boundary-blurring transactions (Schoener, 1989d).

Indeed, "money dilemmas" may come to rival "sexual dilemmas" as a professional concern for clinicians. For example, therapists who benefit financially from privileged information divulged by a client during a therapy session (regarding, for example, the prices of stocks) may be subject not only to "insider trading" regulations, but also to malpractice liability. Although here the client is not harmed directly as the sexually exploited client is harmed, there may be a similarly corrupting effect on therapy. For example, the client may lose trust in the therapist as a result of the therapist's self-interested exploitation of their relationship. Moreover, the therapist's objectivity and concern for the client may be undermined when the therapist takes financial risks on the basis of information obtained from the client.

Follow-up with former clients. While the guidelines given here apply equally well to present and former clients, there are also some special concerns in relation to the latter. A client should be able to come back and see a former therapist or counselor without being in trouble or having a specific therapeutic agenda. As one therapist puts it, "You don't have to be messed up to see me." Nonetheless, the contact between clinician and ex-client should continue in the spirit of the clinical relationship, with the same boundaries observed. To socialize or "hang out" with a former client is not appropriate.

It is essential, then, to distinguish between continuing professional involvement as a reality and as a rationalization or "cover" for personal involvement. The clinician who follows a former client's progress in another institution or out on the street and offers support when called for is doing something not only proper, but admirable. A young woman who counsels prison inmates describes her readiness to lend a "helping hand" to one who has been discharged:

> Sometimes a man I've counseled in prison will call and say, "I'm going through a difficult time at the halfway house." If I think he's about to run away or violate parole, I'll ask, "Do you need a visitor?" He may say, "Would you really come down and see me?" I'll reply, "Yes, and at the same time I'll see another gentleman down there whose case I'm following."

This counselor informs her supervisor of all such contacts with ex-inmates and shows him the letters they send her. Not to do so, she feels, would be "to set myself up." For guidance as well as for self-protection, it is wise to carry out follow-up missions only with the knowledge of one's supervisor.

Self-disclosure. As numerous cases in this book have shown, clinicians may be drawn into compromising positions with clients when they answer personal questions about themselves. As in setting limits on physical and social contact, one learns to make judgments about when self-disclosure ceases to be therapeutic and becomes an invasion of one's own privacy. Here is where one experienced clinician draws the line between what he reveals to clients and what he keeps to himself:

> If establishing a relationship with a client means telling him what teams I root for, what movies I like, what food I enjoy, I'll tell him. My sex life, how much money I make—these are no one's business. . . .
>
> When I work for an agency, my qualifications are a matter to be settled between me and my employer. They are not subject to discussion with clients. I am not obligated to justify myself to clients by telling them what degrees I have, how long I have

worked in the field, or whether or not I have been an addict. Self-disclosure is a tool of the trade that I employ at my own discretion. . . . (Edelwich with Brodsky, 1980, pp. 68–69)

A question that frequently comes up is that of the clinician's vacation plans. When a therapist spends several weeks preparing a client for a two-week interruption of therapy in August, it is only natural for the client to be curious about where the therapist is going. Inexperienced therapists sometimes react to this question in an overly prim and proper way. They reply, "What is your need to know?" which makes the question seem irrelevant, or "We're here to talk about you, not me," which makes the question seem impertinent. It is unnecessary to create distance over so small an issue. As even some psychoanalysts have come to accept (Malcolm, 1980a, p. 103), it makes sense just to tell the client where one is going (though not with whom) and proceed with the business at hand.

The Supervisor's Role

Good supervision is an essential component of clinical work in all of the human services. Its importance in fostering effective and responsible interaction with clients cannot be overestimated (Shapiro, 1982). Specifically, clinical supervision plays an essential role in preventing and/or responding appropriately to sexual abuse of clients, for the benefit of the client, the clinician, and the agency (for detailed guidance see Schoener, 1989g; Schoener & Conroe, 1989). Case management, which involves larger groups of staff members in administrative deliberations, is wholly inadequate to address issues of such intensity and sensitivity, which require one-to-one and small-group supervisory relationships for adequate monitoring.

Clinical supervisors must know and adhere to state laws and agency policies governing client-clinician relationships and the reporting of infractions (see Chapter 10). They must be aware of transference and countertransference and trained in recognizing the dynamics discussed in this book, such as double entendres, passive and active seduction, and "fragile" and "intimidating" sex roles. Supervisors in many settings think of sexual exploitation of clients as an exotic phenomenon with little relevance to their day-to-day responsibilities. On the contrary, client-therapist sex reduces to issues that are of the essence of therapy. Observing when the sexual energy between any two people rises above a certain threshold is a dimension of all clinical supervision. It involves familiarity with the varieties of seduction by client and clinician (Chapter 2) in the contexts of power, opportunity, self-interest, and morality (Chapters 3 to 6).

Supervision comes into play not only when a suspicion of wrongdoing arises, but, more important, in the normal, ongoing vigilance that keeps both individuals and the organization out of trouble. Clearly, supervisory intervention becomes more focused when (on the basis of a complaint, rumor, staff member's observation, or tip from another agency) there is reason to believe that a clinician has some personal stake in his or her relationship with a client. Nonetheless, the same skills of observation and inference are to be deployed in routine weekly supervision.

With respect to the sexual dynamics between client and clinician and the clinical and ethical issues they raise, several features of the supervisor's and administrator's roles are salient.

Methods of supervision. Typically, supervision is conducted in one of four ways: blind supervision, one-way mirror, audiotape, and videotape. Each has advantages and disadvantages.

Blind supervision. The clinician reports on the case to the supervisor both orally and with a written case record or notes. This is the least elaborate, most convenient medium for supervision, but it does not meet the challenge presented by sexual misconduct. Blind supervision tends to be self-serving; the clinician tells the supervisor what the supervisor wants to hear. Such selective presentation is obviously problematic when there is suspicion of wrongdoing. The supervisor must either take the clinician's word for it or probe with leading or direct questions. The latter path has problems of its own. Requiring the supervisor to ferret out the evidence of an ethical compromise places the supervisor in an investigatory role. Investigation is not, however, part of the supervisory process; in fact, it is incompatible with the supervisor's role, in that its adversarial nature undermines the supervisory alliance. Rather than take on the responsibility of investigation, it is best for the immediate supervisor to report the concern, along with the documentation or other evidence on which it is based, to appropriately designated superiors.

One-way mirror. Direct visual monitoring of a therapy session permits observation of body language, innuendo, and all the subtle nonverbal and verbal communication that is lost to blind supervision. On the other hand, it leaves no permanent record for subsequent legal or administrative proceedings. In addition, it is possible only when the client is presently seeing the clinician, as opposed to when the therapeutic relationship has been ruptured by the client's filing of a complaint. The one-way mirror is used, therefore, in normal, preventive supervision or when irregularities are suspected in an ongoing relationship.

Audiotape. Audiotape provides a permanent record of a session at the cost of losing the participants' body language. Although videotape is preferable, low cost and ease of setup make audiotape a more practical medium for regular use. Audiotape should be employed at least periodically to supplement other means of supervision; how frequently it is used will vary with the needs and resources of the agency.

To illustrate the value of an audiotaped record, we can imagine a situation in which a clinician's actions are called into question. A male therapist is meeting with a female client after hours on the grounds that that is the only time they both are available. Because the office is closed at that hour, they meet away from the agency. At this private site, after weeks of resistance on the client's part, a therapeutic breakthrough is achieved. The clinician, meanwhile, is inexperienced and insecure in his abilities. Just when he is thinking of changing careers, he experiences his first breakthrough as a therapist. Moved by the client's newfound awareness and his role in it, he spontaneously hugs her. The client, for whom the hug takes on sinister overtones in the isolated setting, lodges a complaint, saying that the therapist made sexual advances and propositioned her.

Circumstantial evidence weighs heavily against a therapist who should not have been allowed to exceed boundaries in the first place. The investigators confront him: "You admit that you met at 8 P.M. at the student lounge in the dormitory. You admit that you gave the client an unsolicited, affectionate hug, which you never did before. Are we to believe that you didn't do more than that?" Without a taped record of the session, he doesn't have much chance of exoneration. Admittedly, he is less likely to have made a tape away from the agency than at the agency. If, however, he does have a tape, he can defend himself by presenting evidence of the clinical context in which the impulsive hug occurred. He would have an even better defense, of course, with a taped record of a session conducted in his office during regular hours.

Videotape. Videotape provides the most complete record of a session for supervisory and evidentiary purposes. In normal supervision, as a rule, it is not cost-effective to review an entire session on videotape. Rather, the clinician identifies both successful and problematic portions of the session and presents these to the supervisor for review. In normal supervision by videotape (as in blind supervision), the supervisor accepts the clinician's good-faith selection of material. When, on the other hand, there is suspicion of misconduct, it may be useful to have a videotaped record of a full session.

Counseling clinicians individually as well as conjointly with clients. Clinicians who cannot communicate comfortably among themselves about sexual issues are unlikely to be of much help to clients in this area. A major function of supervision is to provide both a forum for the airing of the clinician's doubts and a model for effective communication with clients. When a therapist or trainee tells the supervisor, "I'm falling in love with a client; I want to terminate the relationship," the supervisor (rather than simply recommending a "referral out") should look into what is interfering with the therapist's professional performance. Balanced against the costs of burdening the client with the therapist's problem are the insights a conjoint session can yield into the depth of the difficulty in this particular relationship, as well as into the therapist's overall suitability for clinical work. Although one such instance of vulnerability should be seen as an opportunity for learning rather than as grounds for disqualification, a trainee who shows a persistent inability to differentiate personal feelings from professional responsibilities may need to be counseled out of the field. The supervisor should make clear to the trainee that to fail to achieve the helping professional's stance of caring detachment is not a fundamental human deficiency. It is no disgrace not to have the special gifts required to make good use of privileged access to people's inner lives.

Avoiding the role of personal therapist. The support provided by a supervisor is professional, not personal. The supervisor deals with personal feelings to the extent that they relate to job performance. One cannot, however, expect those whom one supervises to observe this boundary as a matter of course. For some clinicians the supervisor may seem an all-knowing, larger-than-life figure, just as the clinician does to clients. With or without this quasi-therapeutic image, the supervisor's office is an irresistibly convenient place to bring personal problems for which there is no other outlet, problems such as the following:

- "Working here is creating trouble for me at home because it changes the way I define myself."
- "I can talk about sex more openly with my clients than with my spouse."
- "I feel more intimate with my colleagues than with my family."

Issues like these blur the distinction between supervision and therapy. It is better to clarify one's role as a supervisor by listening to the complaint and, if it is not germane to the job situation, recommending that the person go into therapy. One must make clear that the roles of supervisor and therapist are incompatible; a therapist cannot give grades or job evaluations. A failure to maintain this distinction not only compromises the supervisor's legitimate functions, but also leaves the supervisor vulnerable to burnout from the added emotional strain of trying to be a therapist. In the words of an agency director who supervises 20 people, "My office is the deposit box for all the emotions in the agency."

The highly charged supervisory relationship, with its overtones of power, dependency, vulnerability, and trust, is also incompatible with a sexual relationship between supervisor and supervisee. However, as with other teaching (as opposed to therapeutic) relationships, this restriction generally does not persist once the formal relationship is concluded.

Serving both the individual and the agency. Just as a clinician sometimes feels conflicting loyalties to the client, the agency, and victims (actual and potential) of the client's behavior, a supervisor or agency administrator may wonder whose moral standards to act upon (one's own or the agency's) in cases of possible ethical violations. It may be difficult to reconcile the different interests—moral, legal, practical—at stake in the clash between formal and informal definitions of morality. Although there is no single rule for sorting out one's priorities in such complex situations, one should aim to meet one's responsibilities to the agency without imposing one's personal morality on subordinates or making oneself liable for their mistakes.

The chairman of an academic department explains how he would attempt to reconcile these various considerations were a member of his department suspected of being sexually involved with a student:

> How I would act on information of this sort would depend on what kind of information it was. If I received a complaint of exploitation (say, from the student concerned or from another student), I would have to initiate a formal hearing. If I learned about it informally, and if I thought I alone knew about it, I would tell the faculty member (without being menacing) that I knew, but that in the absence of a formal complaint I would not take action. I would also warn him or her that if I knew, others might know, and that if anyone found out who couldn't avoid taking action, he or she would likely be out of a job. If it were more public, that is, if others knew and if they were in a position to inform an official of the university who would be legally bound to fire the professor, I would make clear to everyone involved (the professor, the student, and the others who knew) what the consequences of the official's finding out would be. Finally, if I received credible evidence that a faculty member was being profligate to the detriment of his or her job performance or that of others, I would follow the "one warning" rule. I'd say, "I know what you're doing; here's how I know it; it's causing grief. Stop it or don't get caught again, because the next time it's called to my attention I'll institute formal proceedings."
>
> In all of this my concern is with the public matter of malfeasance of duty. There I have no choice. If I don't deal with something right under my nose, it will become my problem, and I'm not about to pay the price for someone else's sex life. The personal relationship between two people, on the other hand, is not my business. I'm not about to trust my unaided judgment about when someone is being damaged by a love affair. My own view of the moral issue is that it's essential to differentiate between the systematic exploitation of one's role and the possibility of error. I don't believe in hanging some poor fool for one mistake.

This is a well-considered administrative stance. It should be noted, however, that an administrator or supervisor would have less discretion on this matter in the clinical professions, where a sexual liaison is ipso facto a serious violation of ethics. There such an affair would be assumed to be damaging to the client.

Supervisors and administrators are responsible not only for meeting the agency's responsibilities to clients, but also for documenting abuses for the protection of clients elsewhere. However sympathetic one might be to the "poor fool" who has made one mistake, one would be remiss not to report that mistake to a personnel manager who asks for a prior employment record. That the man is, say, a bisexual communist who has orgies away from the work place with personal friends is not relevant. The fact that he has had an affair with a client or student, on the other hand, is information bearing upon his job performance. This does not mean that he should be automatically denied any future jobs in the field. But those who have the responsibility of hiring him should be given a chance to make an informed choice. As Chapter 10 will show, such reporting is becoming not only an ethical, but a legal obligation as well.

Chapter 4 concluded with a case in which the administration of a state mental hospital failed to document a year-long pattern of sexual abuse for fear of exposing the hospital's lack of vigilance. This is an example of a widespread tendency to protect individuals, institutions, and entire professions by concealing what should be publicly aired. This failure to clean house has in recent years become more clearly counterproductive for the professions concerned, since the abuses that flourish in an atmosphere of complicity are sensationalized all the more when they do come to light.

7
The Question of Personal Regard

In the movie *Death Wish* Charles Bronson plays a man whose wife and daughter are brutally raped, the wife murdered and the daughter driven insane. In reaction, he roams the streets of New York as a lone vigilante, attracting the attention of muggers and then executing them on the spot. A social worker with 30 years' experience who saw the film found herself in sympathy with this personification of vengeance. The force of her reaction surprised her and made her uncomfortable. "In my head," she recalled, "I knew all the 'right' answers—that the perpetrators of these crimes are victims themselves, that everyone deserves a fair trial, and so forth. But in my heart I said 'Right on!' to the revenge killings."

A young counselor in a drug treatment program had difficulty dealing with some recurring personal styles among the clients he faced, such as seductive women, militant blacks, those who hardly spoke, and those with "machine-gun raps." On top of his discomfort he felt guilty, since he had heard during his brief training that he was supposed to love all his clients. "Positive personal regard," they had called it. That wasn't what he felt, but he feared that if he admitted it to his supervisor he would get bad evaluations and even lose his job. So he took the path of least resistance. He lacked the confidence to confront those intimidating clients by telling them, "Hold it; that's not the way to get what you want in this office." Instead, he gave them whatever would get them out of his office quickly and without fuss. "You want methadone? Okay." "You want a letter to the court? Here it is." What did it matter? Sooner or later they'd be back in jail anyway. With that attitude the counselor reinforced the very behavior that had put his clients behind bars in the first place.

These two vignettes illustrate the gap between what helping professionals think they should feel toward the people they serve and what they actually feel. Feelings of aversion can as readily disrupt the equilibrium of clinical detachment/involvement as feelings of attraction. The clinician learns to resolve the conflict intellectually, but the resolution tends to break down in the face of some particularly abhorrent form of behavior. A seasoned clinician sums up the issue in words reminiscent of our discussion of sexual attraction to clients: "There are those who have trouble dealing with child abusers and pedophiliacs, and there are those who lie about it."

Aversion in clinical personnel is aroused by a wide range of human frailties. Clinicians experience dislike for clients with alien or unsettling personal styles, clients who seem too dependent, clients who are difficult to work with, clients who fail to show progress, clients who present an unappealing image of themselves and their relationships with others, and clients who engage in deviant or even taboo practices. Now there is a new variation on the distasteful client—the clinician who is referred for therapy after sexually exploiting clients (Stefanson, 1989)! "I just can't work with that person," the clinician says ruefully. Whether it is a matter of "can't" or "won't" is the theme of this chapter.

It is in the sensitive places where sex and violence (as well as family dynamics) intersect that the clinician's attitudes and beliefs are most likely to interfere with professional relationships with clients. Prejudices concerning deviant or destructive forms of sexual behavior tend to be more difficult to admit than racial or ethnic prejudice. The costs of these prejudices, though often hidden, are substantial for all concerned. Clients suffer the consequences of punitive treatment, cynical indifference, or "benign neglect." Clinicians, pleading "personality clash," routinely engage in buck-passing referrals which in some agencies have an absurd resemblance to an active trading market in baseball cards: "I'll swap you a child molester for two second-round draft choices—and I'll buy you lunch." The clinician who resorts to evasive maneuvers (whether that of transferring a client or misplacing a file) to avoid facing difficult situations suffers as much as the client does, both in anxiety and in lost opportunities for professional growth. For example, the drug counselor who gave his clients what they wanted in the hope that they wouldn't make trouble for him spent his working hours in a state of constant insecurity. He expended considerable energy just to stay even. Clinical supervisors, trying to protect both client and clinician, compound the problem by permitting "no questions asked" referrals instead of confronting the issue with both parties. As a result, the work of the human services agency is hampered.

Supervisors would do better to help clinicians face and work through their negative feelings toward clients so that these feelings would not interfere with the provision of services to all eligible clients. In place of the common strategies of avoidance detailed in this chapter, clinicians can and should learn that, although human feelings cannot be denied or suppressed, professional behavior can be controlled in the interest of the client, the clinician, and the agency.

Common Evasions

Clinicians who have negative feelings toward clients may engage in a number of understandable, but unproductive, evasions of the therapeutic mandate. These include reaction formation (by which one bends over backwards to indulge and protect the client), denying to oneself or concealing from others what the client has done, dismissing the client with a pejorative label, overidentifying with the victim instead of treating the perpetrator, or withdrawing into cynical indifference.

It is especially futile for the helping professional to fall into the vigilante reaction of "the man on the street"—a self-righteous condemnation that requires no skill, knowledge, or empathic imagination. The desire to exact retribution is no less a normal human feeling than attraction or distaste. But the place for the imposition of punishment is in the courts. To advocate that cases now referred to human services agencies should instead remain under the authority of the criminal justice system is to take a legitimate political position. As a citizen one may favor severe punishment of criminals, but as a helping professional one must be able to honor the offender's humanity so as to provide unconditional therapeutic support. Teachers and supervisors in the helping fields have the responsibility of seeing that this mandate is carried out.

"Referrals Out": Rationalizations and Realities

One strategy of evasion is so widespread in its incidence and so pervasive in its effects as to warrant special emphasis. This is the practice of "referring out" disagreeable or troublesome clients to another clinician. Understandably, most of our interviewees (and perhaps many of our readers) see referral as a viable and convenient solution—indeed, a first rather than a last resort in uncomfortable situations. Many supervisors and agency administrators readily accept it. In contrast to much other teaching in the human services, we believe that routine referrals constitute a hollow panacea, and that referral without compelling justification is damaging for both the client and the clinician. Any prior personal relationship with the client or with a victim of the client's behavior (e.g., if it is one's own child who has been molested) constitutes adequate cause for referral. If one considers oneself to be physically endangered by the client, then the client plainly requires a different sort of attention. Other alleged indications for referral should be rigorously scrutinized.

Clinicians cite reasons such as the following to justify referring elsewhere those clients whose behavior lies outside the clinician's value system:

- "I'm too emotional about these things."
- "It's too close to my personal issues."
- "I couldn't be objective about such cases."
- "I wouldn't be fair to that kind of client."
- "I'm not an expert in that area."
- "They should be seen by a professional."
- "It's for the client's own good."
- "Some people just aren't well matched."
- "It is dehumanizing for therapists to have to disregard their feelings."

Are these good reasons or rationalizations? For anyone who is prepared to accept them, either from oneself or from one's trainees or subordinates, the following considerations are offered as food for thought.

Everyone has "human feelings." The argument that clinicians should make referrals to avoid the "dehumanizing" experience of assuming professional responsibilities in the face of strongly aversive feelings toward clients is based on two contradictory assumptions: (1) that the clinician making the referral, having human feelings, must act upon them to avoid being dehumanized; (2) that the clinician getting the referral does not have human feelings or does not need to act upon them to avoid dehumanization. It is as if the referring clinician were saying, "I'm rough on child abuse, so I'll find someone who is soft on child abuse." Who wouldn't be appalled by child abuse? Helping professionals are, after all, human beings who care about other human beings. But they are also professionals, and the profession they represent does not exist merely to serve unobjectionable people. A professional is not a person without feeling, but one who can work effectively irrespective of feelings.

"Unconditional positive regard" is a therapeutic stance, not a personal feeling. It comes as a relief to many clinicians to learn that they don't have to love their clients to care for them professionally. In the words of the drug counselor whose dilemmas were portrayed at the beginning of this chapter,

> I used to think something was wrong with *me* if I didn't start out feeling positive regard for a client. Then I learned that the animosity, like the attraction, is normal. The question is, "What do I *do* about it?" If I transfer out any client I don't like, my professional development will be stunted.

A psychiatrist whose experience has included university teaching and directing community service agencies as well as private practice comments, "It is a mark of maturity in a therapist to say, 'I'm not comfortable with this patient,' or even 'I don't like the bastard.'" One can then work through these feelings, with the help (as needed) of a supervisor, colleague, or therapist, and learn to set them aside.

One cannot be taught to have good feelings; one can be taught to take a positive therapeutic stance (Wolf, 1974–75). One can learn to manifest a professional attitude; whether or not one does learn is a choice. A seasoned psychotherapist candidly cuts through reams of rationalizations when he remarks, "I could work with anyone if I wanted to." It is when one doesn't want to that the machinery of justification is brought into play.

A public agency is open to all comers. An attorney who refused to defend a particular client said, "I conduct my own practice, so I make my own choices." Does one have the right to make one's own choices while conducting the state's practice? A public agency exists to serve all who meet its eligibility criteria. Individuals are entitled to services by virtue of their place of residence, financial need, or the judgment of a court of law. By refusing services to an eligible client, one engages in prejudicial, discriminatory behavior and fails to meet one's responsibilities to the agency and to the taxpayers.

Unnecessary referrals are an abdication of responsibility. Even private practitioners, who do have a right to refuse clients, recognize ethical constraints on the exercise of this right. A female attorney who will not defend men who admit to sexual violence or exploitation nonetheless defended a rapist who had been denied due process. Whatever her feelings about what he had done, she supported his right to equal treatment under the law. Other helping professionals face similar ethical choices.

At the very least, one should critically assess one's reasons for rejecting, referring, or terminating clients. Before accepting the explanation that "I'm doing it for the client's own good, since I'd be too emotional, unfair, not objective, etc.," one might ask oneself, "Who would be less emotional, more fair, more objective? Where are these paragons to be found?" When the voice of textbook training directs, "Refer them out!" the voice of experience replies, "Refer them *where?*" If everyone is entitled to send the client on down the line, there can be no assurance that someone better able to help the client will take the case. An exasperated agency director, his desk covered with referral requests, exclaimed, "Where does the buck stop? Do we refer them out to Jesus?"

Since it is hardly beneficial to the client to be passed from one clinician to another, it would seem that the referrals made "for the client's own good" are actually being made for somebody else's perceived benefit. It can be convenient to be too emotional, unfair, or subjective. When a white man who burned a cross in front of a black family's home was assigned to a black probation officer, the client bitterly resisted being placed under the authority of a black man. The probation officer sought a referral, saying, "I don't want to see him, and he doesn't want to see me." One might question whether honoring the client's prejudice was good for him. Why let him have his way? It would have been better to give him a dose of reality that he couldn't manipulate or intimidate. But it was not for his sake that the referral was made.

A clinician may have deep currents of personal experience running counter to the therapeutic mandate. Something about a client may touch off the memory of having been in a concentration camp, of having been raped or molested, or of having been the object of the particular brand of prejudice displayed by the client. One will not want to burden the client, who has enough problems already, with these problems of one's own. It is this very consideration that may seem to justify a referral, as in the case of the black probation officer. Nonetheless, in light of the risks clients suffer in being given over to an uncertain fate, "referring out" can be seen to be just another way of burdening a client with one's problems. The way to avoid "dumping" one's own traumas on the client is to learn the professional skills that make it unnecessary to "dump" the client onto someone else's caseload.

There are no "professional experts." Faith in the power of professional credentials to resolve difficult situations is maintained most fervently by those who do not have the credentials. It is a convenient faith, for a lack of professional standing or "expertise" can be as easy an "out" as "strong personal feelings." At all levels of the clinical hierarchy, clients are referred "upstairs" to "the psych people" or other mythical experts who, sitting back confidently in their swivel chairs, can dispose of the most vexing issues with objectivity and insight. As a check on the reality of this image, we might heed the old Packard car slogan: "Ask the man who owns one." A psychiatrist who has been in practice for 12 years (and who ought to know as well as anyone) notes, "There are no experts in child abuse and molestation. You learn through experience—by working with these cases." Nor are credentialed personnel insulated by their degrees from the uncomfortable feelings aroused by the behavior in question. We therefore suggest a different definition of "professional" from the one that depends on having three letters after one's name: "A professional is someone who gets paid for services and is accountable for performance." To find the nearest professional expert, look in the mirror.

This definition confers a higher standard of responsibility on those who, lacking advanced degrees, are referred to as paraprofessionals. These are the people who, despite their lack of formal training and often under far from ideal conditions, provide more therapeutic and counseling services overall than do M.D.s, Ph.D.s, and M.S.W.s. Consider this juxtaposition of images: (1) a psychiatrist in a downtown office pronouncing that inadequately trained and supervised people should not be seeing clients; (2) Gloria G. (in Chapter 3) out on the front lines, encircled by threatening adolescents while cut off from telephone contact with her colleagues. Society has given paraprofessionals the same privileged and not-so-privileged access to people in need of help that professionals have. Yes, many of them are inadequately trained and supervised. They should be exposed to the best possible training and supervision under existing conditions of limited resources—an effort to which this book is dedicated. This includes training in the professional skills needed to work with difficult clients. For although paraprofessionals (like professionals) may well make damaging mistakes in working with clients they dislike, to encourage referrals on these grounds is to denigrate the paraprofessional's capacity to learn professional skills, to deny the paraprofessional the opportunity to practice such skills, and to ignore the often unsatisfactory outcomes of referrals for clients in the chaotic world of front-line counseling. A psychiatrist or psychologist may at least be able to make an appropriate referral to a qualified colleague. But if a paraprofessional counselor in a public agency doesn't take responsibility for a client's case, who will?

In cautioning against passing the buck to professionals or "experts," we do not mean to question the value of either intake screening or specialized consultation, to the extent that these are available. Of course, clients coming into an agency should be assigned to suitable clinicians. But once a client and clinician have begun to work together, this primary therapeutic involvement should be maintained, just as a primary-care physician continues to see patients during and after referrals to specialists. For example, a woman who had abused Valium for 15 years came to a drug abuse clinic and announced her intention to go "cold turkey." The counselor, thinking this unwise, consulted a psychiatrist, who agreed that it would be safer for the woman to taper off. The counselor, while continuing to see the client, sent her to the psychiatrist for prescription of decreasing doses of Valium. This was a medical consultation in which the psychiatrist's expertise was appropriately deployed. A counselor might properly refer a client for psychiatric consultation for many reasons besides drug prescription—but not to get rid of an irksome client or to hide behind the psychiatrist's imagined ease in dealing with sexual deviance and misbehavior.

One cannot anticipate all the issues that may arise in treatment. The disclaimer of "expertise" runs up against the necessity of having to deal with interrelated problem areas. What happens when a family therapist sees substance abuse issues emerging during a course of therapy, or when a substance abuse counselor runs up against family issues? The therapist may be tempted to refer the client(s) out to an "expert" in the newly discovered problem. But the referral is an unrealistic solution because the family issues cannot be understood without reference to the substance abuse issues, and vice versa. It would be more supportive to bring to bear the second therapist's perspective by using a team approach. Certainly one should take advantage of the knowledge and skill of colleagues and the services of community agencies, but not at the cost of abandoning one's involvement with the client. The team approach also exposes the clinician to new issues and methods and thus fosters the professional growth to which helping professionals are presumably committed. One becomes an "expert" by facing unfamiliar problems, discussing them with colleagues, reading about them, and monitoring the results in the field.

Sometimes what comes out in the course of therapy is the kind of damning information which, because it presents a personal problem for the clinician, would have precipitated an immediate referral if it had appeared on the client's initial workup or Pre-Sentence Investigation. For example, suppose a client whose presenting problem is alcoholism drops this bombshell during the third or fourth session: "One thing I'm struggling with is the sexual relationship I'm having with my 10-year-old daughter." Suppose a therapist who can accept a presenting problem of incest with a child finds out along the way that the client has previously escaped prosecution in the violent death of another child. Now it is too late to refer the client out without conveying a message of rejection.

A psychiatric social worker, when asked how she would cope with such a delayed revelation, replied, "I suppose I would look at the context of the act in the person's life and see what had been going on for him at the time." In other words, she would try to find grounds to excuse or justify the behavior. This approach is wrongheaded. One will not always find the behavior easily justifiable; sexual violence is not supposed to be justified. Finally, if this were an effective way to assimilate unsettling information about a client, it would be just as effective for a clinician who got the information initially rather than later on, so that it would obviate the whole question of referral. In fact, the need for referrals is obviated when one learns that one can work with people who do unjustifiable things.

Working with the client may help prevent a recurrence of the behavior. If separating one's personal feelings toward the client from one's professional dealings with the client's behavior is a form of expertise, it is one well worth learning. Turning away from the harsh facts doesn't make them disappear. Those who detest rape, incest, wife beating, or child abuse should welcome the opportunity to do something about these destructive acts by working with the individuals who commit them.

Recommended Approaches

To separate one's feelings from the job at hand is a choice that anyone can make. Even so, it is easier said than done. One's resolve can melt quickly when one gets out into the field, a client's history in hand, and one's thoughts turn to one's own five-year-old daughter. Professional poise, or caring detachment, does not work like a perpetual-motion machine; it requires maintenance. The following guidelines are useful for alleviating the conflicts that inevitably occur. Some of these suggestions closely parallel those developed in the previous chapter for dealing with seductive dynamics between client and clinician.

Support from supervisor, peers, or therapy. Problems in relating to clients should not be held in and turned against oneself. They should be brought out into the open and shared—not with the client, but with those in a position to lend support—one's supervisor, peers, or therapist (in that order).

Treating the client, not the victim. It is important always to keep in mind whose case one is handling. Sometimes an inherent ambiguity attaches to this question, as when one is hired to serve clients under the aegis of a court of law. Probation officers, for example, report conflicting loyalties to the individual client and to the state. But when one is counseling individuals about their relations with other individuals (as in family therapy or in dealing with perpetrators of violent crimes), clarity of definition is essential. For example, a therapist on a military base is likely to see women who have affairs while their husbands are overseas. If the therapist is male and if he dwells on thoughts such as "I wonder if my wife would do this to me if I were overseas" or "If I were in his shoes, I'd rather come back and have a chance to work it out with her in family therapy than come back and find a note on the door," he is allowing his personal identification with the husband to compromise his therapeutic commitment to the wife.

Therapists who have learned to separate their professional commitments from their emotional reactions find it helpful to remember that the choice is not between accepting the behavior or rejecting the person. One's loyalty is to the person, not to what the person has done. As one therapist puts it, "I advocate for the best part of a person, the part that shows the capacity for change."

Contracts with clients. Although it is antitherapeutic to discriminate against a client on the basis of attitudes or past behavior, a therapist is entitled to make a contract with the client specifying the conditions under which therapy can proceed. The contract sets limits on acting out in therapy—limits which are therapeutic for the client and which permit reasonable working conditions for the therapist. The contract may focus on dress, deportment, physical restraint, and so forth. A male social worker recalls,

> I once had a client who weighed three hundred pounds, smelled like dead fish, and had a personality to match. By addressing the question of why I didn't like him I was able to make some rules for the therapeutic hour that enabled me to work with him.

A colleague of his, who is Jewish, was called upon to handle the case of a young man who wore a Nazi symbol on a chain around his neck. The social worker took the case, but insisted that the client not wear the chain in his office. Note that the stipulation concerned behavior, not attitude. "Sometimes," says the social worker in retrospect, "I had to remind myself how much I hated that guy."

The supervisor's role. A supervisor can support the clinician in identifying and working through any resistance to dealing with a particular client or type of client. Sometimes this is done in conjoint session with the client, where the supervisor can observe the pattern of therapeutic interaction and perhaps demonstrate a more fruitful approach. A supervisor can employ such exercises as listening to tapes of sessions and pointing out variations in the therapist's voice, manner, or method with clients with whom the therapist is or is not comfortable.

The core of what a supervisor must make clear to clinicians and trainees is conveyed in these passages from Maltsberger and Buie (1974, pp. 628, 630, 632):

- We conceive ourselves to be compassionate, caring, and non-judgmental, and often predicate our professional self-respect on not being rejecting, punitive, sadistic, murderous, and disgusted with patients. An able therapist cannot permit himself to behave according to such feelings, but neither can he afford the illusion that he differs from other human beings and has no id.
- The therapist . . . has chosen to bear what the relationship requires in electing to treat such a [hostile] patient. The therapist is simply the object of the necessary and inevitable hate of his patient, but out of choice, and in that sense he is not in fact a victim.
- The best protection from antitherapeutic acting out is the ability to keep such impulses in consciousness. Full protection, however, requires that the therapist also gain comfort with his counter-transference hate through the process of acknowledging it, bearing it, and putting it into perspective. Guilt then has no place in his feelings, and the therapist is free to exert a conscious loving self-restraint, in which he places a higher value on the emotional growth of his patient than he does on his own tension discharge.

Our interviews are replete with testimonials to the value of supervisory intervention in helping the novice come to grips with personal reactions to clients, as in the following case examples:

- A *psychiatrist:* "A middle-aged man presented as a child molester. The therapist, a mature and to my mind quite capable one, said that she was uncomfortable with the case because she lacked experience in that area. We had some discussions, and after her third session with the patient she said, 'This is not what I expected. I'm learning something, and the patient is learning something.' The year-long course of therapy worked out well for the patient, and the therapist emerged confident to handle future cases. She no longer pleads inexperience."

- A *psychiatrist:* "In group therapy we had one person who was terrified to acknowledge that he had been a child molester. My cotherapist, who was squeamish about being involved with child molesters, was most compassionate toward this man once he revealed himself. Direct exposure made what she had feared seem much more manageable."

- A *psychologist:* "When I was studying for my doctorate I used to tell seductive female clients, 'What you need is a woman therapist.' The client took the path of least resistance by being seductive, and I took the path of least resistance by referring her out. Fortunately, my supervisor did not allow me to go on doing that; instead, he helped me work it out. Not only did I learn from that, but it was better for the client not to be able to say that she 'got another one' under her belt."

- A *psychologist:* "My supervisor allowed me to realize that I wasn't a bad man and a bad clinician for feeling hate toward poor helpless people."

- A *social worker:* "During my internship at a university student health service, I saw a 21-year-old man who was molesting his 11-year-old sister. There must have been a reaction on my face when he told me about it, because after that the relationship broke down. The easiest course for me was to transfer him to group therapy—in effect, to terminate him. The next semester I saw him in a colleague's waiting room. At that time I was too insecure about my professional development to ask how the client was doing and to reassert my involvement with him. In retrospect I can see that this kind of avoidance was neither satisfying nor productive. I can see it now because I subsequently had a supervisor who pulled my feet to the fire and showed me that I could face the kinds of cases I had been abandoning."

Referrals. Only after every other avenue (including conjoint sessions among the client, clinician, and supervisor) has been exhausted should a referral even be considered. The burden is on the clinician, not the client, to show that referral is necessary. Referral must be on the basis of the likelihood of harm to the client, not the clinician's convenience. In the rare instance when a referral is decided upon, it must be appropriately explained to the client and, if necessary, treated as a therapeutic issue.

Clinicians who continue to request referrals for clients they find disagreeable may need to be counseled out of the field—not for the inability to feel unconditional positive regard for all clients, but for the unwillingness to adopt and practice unconditional positive regard as a working tool.

8
Like Client, Like Clinician

With the growth of racial, ethnic, and gender consciousness, there has been an increasing tendency for helping professionals to identify selectively not only with victims, but with clients as well. In some agencies it is considered preferable—or even mandatory—that clients be treated by those with whom, on the basis of having a similar background or lifestyle, they can share a special experiential bond. This bias provides yet another supposed justification for "referrals out." In the current climate it seems advisable to reaffirm the professional therapeutic role—its responsibilities, its prerogatives, its scope. A paid clinician is not a peer-consciousness-group leader—a distinction which has implications for determining both what clients the clinician can usefully serve and what stance the clinician should take in advising clients on sexual questions. It is also relevant to assess the various grounds on which clients in treatment or correctional facilities are or are not segregated from one another, as some of these practices have a more valid basis than others.

Matching Clinician to Client: Who Should Be Seen by Whom?

The issue of client-clinician matching is generally couched in terms of race, sex, sexual preference, and (in the case of substance abusers) clinical history. It rarely arises for practitioners with M.D., Ph.D., or M.S.W. degrees; rather, it is directed toward those lower in the hierarchy, those without professional credentials. It is most passionately argued on behalf of groups that have suffered a history of discrimination: blacks, women, homosexuals. More of a question is raised about white staff members working with black clients, and about male staff members working with female clients, than vice versa. (Although the role of female staff members in institutions serving male adolescents is sometimes questioned by male staff members, in many such instances the issue is complicated by the fact that the women are white while the adolescent residents and the male staff members are black. As a rule, the male staff members are more likely than their female counterparts to share with clients a "street background" of addiction and/or crime.) With homosexuals the bias cuts both ways, since they are both a recently aroused minority and the object of continued open prejudice.

It is not surprising that clients express and act out preferences for clinicians with whom they can identify. For example, a gay male psychologist meets resistance from "straight" clients who ask, "What do you know about heterosexual love life?" (Echoes of "What can he know—he, a Jew?") A female therapist working in a men's prison reports that inmates tell her about their prowess with women, but that they "regard it as taboo to violate their masculinity, their machismo, by talking to a woman about whatever homosexual relations they may have among themselves." A female counselor in a residential treatment community for drug abusers describes a similar reticence on the part of her male clients: "They'll reveal problems like impotence and homosexuality in a group led by a man, but to me they always come on macho." A female psychologist describes a male client's reaction to her:

> This man resisted everything I tried to do. "How can you know what a man feels?" he would say. "Besides, I wouldn't tell you anything about my sex life anyhow." I replied that, true, I was a woman, but I could also bring in another viewpoint. I asked him whether the real issue was that I couldn't understand or that he was feeling uncomfortable about it. If he was uncomfortable, I suggested that we talk about it and see what was happening to make him uncomfortable. His solution was that therapy cost too much for him to continue. I don't know whether I made a mistake in confronting him or whether he had decided to get rid of me one way or the other.

It is more troubling when staff members take the same line. A white social worker can expect clients to say, "How do you know? You're not black," but it is surely distressing (as has been reported in our interviews) to hear this from a co-worker. (Imagine a helping professional saying, "How do you know? You're not white.") A male probation officer who brought a client to a school for court-referred adolescents insisted that the youth be assigned to a male staff member because, as he told the female director of the agency, "He's been worked over enough by women, including his mother." (The director disregarded this request.) Staff members at human services agencies expend considerable energy at meetings in heated debates about whether male or female clinicians (in the abstract) can deal more effectively with male or female clients. Helping professionals are pressured to cultivate an identification with clients in dress and appearance, as in this account by a female social worker in a therapeutic community for female drug abusers:

> The women I treated, who ranged in age from 16 to 30, had trouble accepting me because I wore suits. In this they saw a contrast with their own disadvantaged status. The director asked me to come to work in jeans. I replied that if the residents wanted to make something of their lives, they could look at me as a role model. The director said, "Yeah, but they can't relate to you that way." I think it was he who couldn't relate to me.

She goes on to describe how staff members at this treatment center projected their own insecurities onto the clients, who responded predictably:

> I came to the therapeutic community with a B.A. in social work and a two-year associate's degree in drug and alcohol counseling. The residents were quick to pick up that I was not a former addict, and this made a big difference in their behavior toward me. If I noticed from someone's affect and body movements that he was high, he'd deny it. If an ex-addict counselor confronted him on the same thing, he'd admit it. The ex-addict counselors (who were male) credited themselves with special knowledge, but I don't agree. Many people have similar manipulative skills; they just use them for different purposes. Among the ex-addict counselors it was those with no other training who most insisted on their unique insight. They would even say to clients, "I know. I've been

there. Maybe that college woman doesn't know." This effectively isolated me from the clients, especially the men, but it did get them to open up to the ex-addict counselors. They would talk to those counselors about their craving for drugs, while they sought me out for nurturance, telling me about their illnesses and their problems with their wives and girlfriends (but not sexual problems).

The male staff members who were least confident that they had anything else to offer used their "street background" to underscore the polarity between themselves and the more highly trained female therapist. In so doing they reinforced—indeed, aggravated—whatever tendency the addict clients had to do likewise. Treatment suffered as a result. "Like client, like clinician" can be a self-fulfilling prophecy as well as a convenient refuge for inadequately trained clinicians and diplomatic administrators. When a homosexual therapist is hired by an agency as "the therapist for gays," for whose benefit is this done?

There are numerous grounds for discouraging the practice of trying to match clinicians to clients in terms of personal characteristics. Among these are the following:

The professional therapeutic role is different from peer support. Women, racial minorities, homosexuals, substance abusers and their families, food and gambling addicts, and those suffering from certain illnesses have consciousness-raising groups for mutual support in dealing with the special issues they face. Helping professionals should by all means inform clients of the existence of such groups and encourage participation. A human service agency should not, however, be staffed on the basis of sharing clients' personal concerns. To say that an alcoholic can benefit from attending meetings of Alcoholics Anonymous while seeing a therapist is not to say that the therapist, even one specializing in alcoholism, must also be an alcoholic. Professional counseling is concerned with the universal human dilemma of learning to satisfy one's needs without being destructive toward oneself or toward others. Any person can, with empathy, training, and (where necessary) collegial support, relate to any other person over this issue.

Empathy transcends differences. To maintain that "only an addict can help another addict" or "it takes a gay person to understand another gay person" is to deny both the universal aspects of human suffering and people's capacity to communicate in a common language. A white female social worker, confronted with the claim that she could not understand a black woman's special trauma, replied, "I don't have to have cancer to know that it's painful." It is a professional's responsibility, with the help of supervision, to adjust to the differences that may obscure this commonality of human experience. One who cannot adjust to certain clients—for example, a therapist from an elite background who cannot deal with "street people"—should not continue in the employ of an agency that serves those clients.

It is impossible to take into account all of the potentially relevant variables that set people apart. Once race, sex, and sexual preference are admitted into consideration as qualifications for a professional therapeutic relationship, where does the qualification process stop? What about age, socioeconomic status, educational level, and ethnic background? Can an Italian do good therapy with an Irishman? Age in particular has been mentioned in several interviews as a barrier to communication, in that older clients may be reluctant to divulge intimate material to someone who calls to mind a son or daughter. Whether in staffing an agency or in screening clients, one cannot anticipate all the traits in a clinician to which a client may respond positively or negatively. The answer, therefore, lies elsewhere than in seeking perfectly homogeneous matches between clients and staff. It lies in training clinicians to work through (or around) whatever transference issues do arise. The energy that in some agencies goes into a version of computer dating is better devoted to training and supervision. Intake screening can identify, for example, those clients who need psychotropic drug prescription or hospitalization as well as those who do not speak English. But one should not have to be lefthanded or a Yankee fan to work with a client who is similarly inclined.

A team approach can be used when special insight or familiarity is desired. The assumption that a clinician is competent to work with any client does not preclude consultation with other staff members who can serve as resource personnel for particular clients. For example, if a client wishes to speak with a female therapist about women's issues, or if the primary therapist thinks it beneficial for the client to do so, this can be arranged in the context of a team effort where the primary therapeutic involvement is maintained.

Clients benefit from positive models of both sexes. A client in a professional helping relationship is likely to have had problems in past relationships with both sexes. After treatment the client will be going out into a world that is not exclusively male or female. For these rather obvious reasons it is good for the client to work with clinicians who can be positive models of the opposite sex as well as of his or her own sex. Let the male client see that not all women are like his mother or wife. Let the female client see that not all men are like the ones she drank or took drugs with. In the case of the youth whose probation officer described him as having been "worked over" by women, that would be all the more reason to give him a chance to develop a positive relationship with a woman. The probation officer might more reasonably have said that the youth had problems with sexual identity that he needed to work out with a man. In that event, if the primary therapist was a woman, a team approach could be employed as discussed above.

Transference and countertransference feelings do arise when the client and clinician are of opposite sexes (as they do when the client and clinician are of the same sex). When necessary, the clinician must be prepared to deal with these straightforwardly, indicating that "We're not here for you to become dependent on me. You can work these things out with me as a person who happens to be male." If issues still come up for the client, it can be a positive experience to confront and work through them as preparation for coping with other complex realities. If, on the other hand, it is the clinician's discomfort that is in question, then it is the clinician's responsibility to work through it in the ways recommended in the previous two chapters, so as not to add to the client's problems or deny the client effective treatment. A client is expected to manifest difficulties in relating; that is what therapy is about. A professional is held to a higher standard of accountability.

That this standard is not always met has been the burden of this book. We have documented the sexual exploitation of clients in settings ranging from therapeutic communities to psychiatric hospitals to private practice. Most of the victims are women, although among incompetent institutionalized patients men are also sexually exploited. While liaisons between male clients and female psychiatrists or psychologists are not treated in the psychiatric literature as a problem of any consequence, our interviews in public institutions such as prisons, halfway houses, and drug abuse treatment centers have revealed a recurrent pattern of attractions between young white female staff members and (often younger) black male clients (as in the case of Mary T. in Chapter 5). Responsibility for dealing with these antitherapeutic dynamics is shared by the individual clinician and the employing agency. Given the risk of abuse, male staff members working in facilities for female clients and female clinicians working in male units should be carefully selected and trained. The selection, though, should be made neither on the basis of academic degrees nor on the "matching" principle. To insist that clients be treated only by personnel of the same sex is to do an injustice to the great majority of helping professionals, as well as to reduce drastically the available pool of clinicians. Selection should instead be on the basis of the clinician's ability to assume a professional role—that is, to be nonseductive, to have his or her reactions well in hand, and to be able to confront the client's issues forthrightly.

Matching has not been shown to result in better therapeutic outcomes. The experiences of our interviewees admit of no generalization about the effectiveness of matching female clients and female clinicians, black clients and black clinicians, and so forth. Some clients respond better to the transference that develops with a clinician of the same sex (or race, or whatever); others respond better to the transference that develops with a person of contrasting personal characteristics. Some clinicians show greater empathy, insight, and involvement with clients with whom they have some outward reason to identify; others are overprotective and fail to confront, or else overreact punitively. For still others it makes no difference at all. A male therapist may seem better able to handle a potentially violent male client, yet the presence of a woman may actually have a calming effect on such a client. Whereas one female clinician believes herself incapable of sympathy for the perpetrators of rape and incest, another finds that working with the victims of rape and incest brings her uncomfortably close to her own vulnerability. The same female psychologist who reported a male client's "parting shot" of "How can you know what a man feels?" was accused of being unsympathetic and "jealous" by a female client in group therapy when she confronted the client on her seductive behavior. On the other hand, a white female therapist in a halfway house for male ex-offenders aged 16 to 21 describes her qualified success in working with these young men, most of them black:

> I was more effective than the male staff members in getting the clients to do what I wanted, more effective in having them fulfill their program plans, more effective in terms of control—at the cost of reinforcing their stereotypes of white women. If one of my goals was to have them question those stereotypes, I did not have the luxury of achieving it. I was tough; I wouldn't brook disrespect; in effect, I exploited their fear. When one of the kids screamed profanities at me because I wouldn't give him a ride, I got out of the car, marched him into the house, and told him that a real man wouldn't act that way. The black male staff members reinforced my position by treating me with a respectful aloofness which the kids probably took as a model.

Note that here, unlike the drug therapy situation described earlier in this chapter, the male staff supported rather than undermined the female therapist's position with the younger male clients. Put simply, the transference can cut both ways. It is best, therefore, to accept as a "given" that there will be some form of transference and to work with whatever comes up rather than to attempt to predetermine the client's reactions.

Some ancillary issues that arise in connection with client-clinician matching are referrals, therapist shopping (or client-initiated matching), and exclusionary or prejudicial (as opposed to preferential) hiring.

Referrals. Referrals are no more justified on grounds of a "mismatch" than on grounds of attraction or aversion. In a case in point, a black male psychiatrist at a health maintenance organization had a white female client who insisted that she be referred to another therapist because she believed that black people had too many problems of their own to help anyone else with theirs. Her attitude was so persistently abrasive that the psychiatrist finally acceded to her wishes. He made clear, however, that it was her attitude that made it impossible for him to help her, and that in making the referral he was not accepting her prejudiced view that he was incompetent. The psychiatrist was right to disassociate himself from the client's belief that she needed a therapist of her own race, but his judgment in permitting the referral can be questioned. Whatever he said, what he and the agency did may well have reinforced the woman's feeling of being "right" in her negativism.

Clinically, the psychiatrist would have been on firmer ground had he refused the referral. If the woman had then complained to his supervisor, the latter might have told her, "In a public agency, race is not an acceptable reason for referral. Our therapists are all well trained, competent, and ethical. We make sure of that by investigating all complaints of improprieties. Dr. Black's race does not bear upon his competence to treat you. If he makes a pass at you, whether he's black or white, male or female, I want to know about it. Otherwise, if you have an issue about his being your therapist, let's all talk about it. If you want to be seen here, you'll have to be willing to work it out with him." This did not happen not only because of clinical error, but because the health maintenance organization would rather grant referrals than see its clients take their business elsewhere. Such economic constraints, however real they may be, do not alter the wisdom (or lack of it) of the clinical decision.

Therapist shopping. The woman who did not want to see the black psychiatrist at the HMO had the option of not coming to that agency for psychotherapy. If that particular psychiatrist had been in private practice, she presumably would not have gone to him, or else would have excused herself once she saw that he was not what she wanted. Either of those situations differs fundamentally from the one where the HMO honored the woman's insistence on making a prejudiced choice of therapists within the organization. In private practice, where both the therapist and client enjoy freedom of choice, therapist shopping is part of the natural flow of therapy. When confrontation becomes painful, resistance may take the form of shopping around, with some shoppers eventually returning. Our concern in this chapter is not with such exercise of free choice, but with the tendency of clinicians and institutions to evade responsibility while permitting clients to do likewise.

Exclusionary hiring: The homosexual clinician. Our emphasis thus far has been on the inadvisability of preferential hiring of staff members whose personal characteristics match those of the clients they are to serve. Exclusionary hiring, by which an individual with particular personal characteristics is deemed thereby unfit to work with people in a clinical capacity, is even less justifiable. Currently it is the homosexual who is the primary object of such discrimination and the focus of public debate about it. The illogic of refusing to hire homosexuals as teachers or therapists because a few homosexuals (like a few heterosexuals) seduce children and adolescents is illustrated by this imaginary vignette:

Employer: "Are you homosexual or heterosexual?"
Applicant: "Heterosexual."
Employer: "I'm sorry, then, we can't hire you. You see, we've had a few incidents where heterosexuals have seduced our students."

Although homosexuals are less likely than in the past to lose their jobs because of their sexual preference, they may suffer other consequences if they announce that preference on the job. This state of affairs is not ideal. But clients are clients precisely because of their capacity for irrationality. Staff members, too, have been known to be less than paragons of fairness. As a rule, if staff members dress in gay attire on their own time away from the job site, it is regarded as their own business. If, however, they flaunt their private behavior during working hours, then it is no longer private, just as when a heterosexual clinician makes an issue of being heterosexual with self-revealing statements such as "I've never had a homosexual experience." Any autobiographical revelation on the part of a helping professional invites clients to take liberties. This is not to say that "coming out" is right or wrong, but simply that it is a choice which (especially on the job) has consequences.

Advising Clients on Sexual Questions

As a helping professional (meaning, again, one who is paid and is accountable), one is responsible for making one's services available to clients without prejudice and keeping one's own attitudes and beliefs about sexual behavior as far removed from the clinical interaction as possible. This professionalism is expressed not only in setting aside one's personal feelings about a client, but also in engaging in a therapeutic dialogue aimed at clarifying the issues of concern to the client. There is, of course, no way to anticipate the many ramifications of this complex subject as they occur in practice, but there are a few basic guidelines that can give order and direction to one's efforts as one gains experience.

Limit intervention to areas of clinical concern. One of the moralistic reactions to which clinicians are susceptible, as described at the beginning of Chapter 6, is the insistence on dealing with something that the clinician, not the client, regards as a problem (e.g., homosexuality). Instead of imposing one's own agenda in this way, one should limit one's concern to those areas defined as problematic by the client or by a court of law or other referring agency. As new aspects of the client's life are revealed for discussion, the therapist should address them in the spirit of "What is the issue for *you*?" It is of the essence of therapy that new issues will make themselves felt, but these should emerge as discoveries by the client (albeit with guidance from the therapist's interpretations) rather than as impositions by the therapist.

A common pitfall is the desire to impose the helping professional's own agenda of self-knowledge, sensitivity, or sophistication on clients to whom these concerns are irrelevant and whose immediate concern is with bread-and-butter survival issues. Clinicians who have no difficulty accepting homosexuality in clients may be put off by the stereotyped sex role behavior of clients who have a more conventional outlook. "I hate to see women present themselves as less than they are," said a female social worker. At a personal and political level she is entitled to this reaction. But the issue should be addressed in therapy only to the extent that it bears upon the defined clinical agenda. For example, a woman's "learned helplessness" may contribute to her reluctance to leave a man who abuses her. In itself, though, learned helplessness is a trait shared by many "normal" women and men who do not seek therapy. The same social worker, irritated at men who open doors and pull out chairs for her, remarked, "That's how they treat women in Europe!" But the resistance to the Equal Rights Amendment shows that many Americans outside the sphere of influence of the helping professions are holding on to their "European" ways.

Helping professionals also object to the "street language" of some adolescent males and the down-to-earth view of relations between the sexes that it expresses. "They have no concept of intimacy; they think of sex as if it were the same as basketball," said a female staff member in a reformatory. It is appropriate for this woman to model a different style of language, manners, or dress that her clients will need to learn if they are to adapt to a larger world than the one they have inhabited. But this choice is theirs to make. Their matter-of-fact conception of sex and their indifference to intimacy are shared by many other young men from the same cultural backgrounds who show a normal social adjustment in those contexts (and, for that matter, by people who are not thought of as disadvantaged). Should they all be reformed? Those who are in prison are given counseling so that they can get a job, stay out of trouble with the law, and learn to make their way in the world. It does them no favor to obscure these priorities.

In the Navy, women who remain on bases in the U.S. while their husbands are on Pacific duty are referred to as "West-Pac widows." Every so often one of these women comes to a therapist on base for guidance about whether to have an affair or, having found a boyfriend, whether to leave her husband. To the male therapist she presents a temptation to advocate his own morality, favoring loyalty to the husband, rather than to help her clarify what she believes to be right, what she is comfortable doing, and what consequences she is willing to accept. In such a situation the therapist should not pressure the client to make value judgments that she is not prepared to make. In the interplay of conflicting moralities, it is the client's morality that the therapist is committed to discovering.

Give the client support in questioning choices rather than easy validation. If a moralistic response is the Scylla on a therapeutic voyage with a "West-Pac widow," Charybdis is the impulse to grant absolution: "It's okay. Do whatever you want." Although the client may be hoping that the therapist will give her an "okay" to do what she is contemplating, she wouldn't be coming to the therapist if she didn't have doubts. Automatic validation leaves the doubts unresolved and therefore is not therapeutic. Just as it is the client who must decide that it would be wrong to be unfaithful or to leave her husband, so it is the client who must decide that such a move would be right for her.

When it comes to sexual conduct, people spend their lives searching the bookshelves for a guidebook that has never been written. Clients come to therapy in an uncertain, vulnerable state, seeking answers to questions such as "Am I acting out enough?" "Am I acting out too much?" "What is preventing me from acting out more (or less)?" "How am I being received in terms of my sexuality?" Clients believe that therapists have answers to these questions. A therapist who encourages this blind trust or who rubber-stamps the client's own superficially held "answers" is doing the client a disservice. Whether the issue is homosexuality, adultery, or multiple relationships, it is in the best interest of the client to question without judging. It is, however, relevant to consider how others will judge the client's choices and how the client is likely to react to such judgment. If the client feels bad as a natural consequence of acting out, the bad feeling should be examined, not dismissed. Ultimately, the only meaningful validation is one that the client has worked for.

With the homosexual client, an issue of great moment is whether or not to "come out" (i.e., to acknowledge one's homosexuality to others who are not homosexual). The therapist's role here is not to jump on an ideological bandwagon. The client can get immediate validation and ready-made support for "coming out" from a homophile consciousness group. Knowing this, the client has come to a professional adviser for more objective advice. Facing two risky choices—to "come out" and risk rejection from family, friends, and employers, or to continue to feel the emotional weight of concealment as well as isolation from other homosexuals—the client needs to decide which choice he or she can more easily live with. As therapist for such a client, one can easily gain the applause of homophile groups and satisfy one's own liberal instincts by saying, "Sure, come out!" But it is the client who must walk the lonesome road afterward. A better clinical intervention is to explore the client's relationships with the people who are important in his or her life and to assess the likely consequences in each case. If some of these people are likely to accept the client as a homosexual while others (e.g., parents) are not, one might recommend "coming out" selectively (telling some people but not others), at least as a first step. In any case, there can be no assurance that the world will be fair.

Frame alternatives in terms of concrete choices rather than global self-identification. The concerns people have about their sexual identity often reflect a tendency to attach global meaning to individual acts. The question "Am I a homosexual?" can be an agonizing one. A therapist can help unload this loaded question first by validating the client's confusion ("No, you're not crazy"), and then by shifting the focus from vague labels to concrete alternatives. Instead of "Am I a homosexual?" the client can be encouraged to ask, "Do I want to act on my attraction to this particular person? What will be the consequences? Do I want to take the risk?" A male social worker tells clients, "I know what it means to do something or not to do it, but I don't know what a homosexual is, and I'm not going to do brain surgery to find out." A female psychologist relates how she helped a young woman make the question of her sexual identity a less oppressive one:

> The client, a 16-year-old girl, told me that she was a lesbian, although she didn't want to be one. She had acted on a physical attraction to another woman. Others had caught her at it and labeled her, and she had labeled herself. I told her that it was perfectly normal for a woman to love other women and even to have sexual feelings for women, and that her having acted on those feelings once did not automatically define her as a lesbian. I think it was a great relief for her to hear that.

Like Client, Like Client

In residential treatment and correctional facilities, particularly for adolescents and young adults, there is disagreement about whether male and female clients should be separated from one another and whether homosexuals or those likely to be ostracized because of the nature of their crimes should be segregated for their own and others' protection. On what grounds is the segregation of clients good policy? When should a prison, reformatory, halfway house, or therapeutic community be set up to resemble the outside world, and when is it prudent for the institution to take a more protective stance? The suggestions that follow are intended to guide the thinking of administrators and staff members on these delicate matters.

Coed treatment. There are, of course, numerous contexts, such as couple and family counseling, in which men and women participate in therapy together. Voluntary, adult clients in group therapy can share their feelings with and about the opposite sex, and learn more appropriate ways of behaving. But with vulnerable young people who are where they are because they have not yet learned a successful adjustment to life, coed treatment is inadvisable. Advocates of coed treatment say, "That's life," or "It reflects the real world." But residents of institutions have not been able to function in the real world, and they are less likely to learn to do so when peers of the opposite sex present a constant distraction as well as a challenge to their egos. They need to deal with survival issues before they can take risks involving sexuality and intimate relationships.

Some pros and cons of coed treatment are presented in this favorable account by a woman who directs counseling programs in a woman's prison:

> When we had an experimental co-correctional program, we did have a couple of pregnancies and people sneaking off into the bushes, and the women sometimes got into fights over men. But there were fewer escapes, and the women looked better and took better care of themselves. They seemed more interested in their lives than after the men left.

The female inmates already knew how to make themselves look good for men and would attend to that as a matter of course upon their release. We are not told whether their enhanced aliveness translated into the learning of useful skills and behavior. All that we know for sure is that the presence of men made the inmates more manageable and life more pleasant for the staff.

It may seem inconsistent to advocate separate treatment units for males and females while opposing gender-based distinctions in the assignment of clinical staff to clients. The critical difference is that fellow residents do not act like trained professionals. A therapist or counselor of either sex is expected to serve as a model of constructive behavior and positive relationships. The staff member's role is supportive, not stress-inducing.

Physical protection and peer pressure. A correctional institution is a microcosmic society polarized along racial lines, with a barter economy, a code of unwritten regulations and reprisals, and a pecking order based on (among other things) skill in gambling and obtaining drugs as well as on the nature of the crimes one has committed. The workings of this society are strikingly dramatized in the film *Short Eyes*, where a child molester is ostracized and finally murdered by fellow inmates in a men's prison. The reality behind this fictional portrayal comes through in the following account by the director of a residential treatment center for female alcoholics:

> In addition to its primary function, our agency occasionally provides emergency shelter for women. Recently the city police

called and asked if we would shelter a woman who, with her boy-friend, had locked her two children (aged one and three) in a room for a month and abused them to the point where they had to be put in an intensive care unit. The police put the man in jail and were going to take the woman to the state farm, but then changed their minds and called me. I told them, "The women who live here would do such a number on her that she'd be better off else-where!" The police tried to get me to take her on the grounds that she had an alcohol problem. I think they were afraid of the same thing happening at the state farm that I was afraid of here.

It appears that the police and the agency director, voicing their own discomfort in the name of the residents of their respective institutions, were passing the buck back and forth to each other. To the extent that they were actually concerned with the residents' reactions, they were assuming a more protective role than in fact was called for. The administration of either the state farm or the alcoholism center would have two primary responsibilities toward this woman: (1) to protect her from *physical* abuse by fellow residents; (2) to make sure that *staff members* did not "do a number" on her. But verbal abuse by her peers would simply be a natural consequence of her unacceptable behavior. If anything, it would be therapeutic for her to experience people's reactions to what she had done, provided that the reactions did not come from clinical personnel.

Segregation of homosexuals. It is the institution's responsibility to protect residents from coerced homosexuality, as from other forms of physical abuse. (It hardly needs to be acknowledged that this responsibility often is not met and that rehabilitation efforts suffer as a result.) Does this mean that avowed homosexuals should be kept apart from their peers in residential institutions? We believe not, for the following reasons:

First, it is unjust to withhold services to which a person is legally entitled unless the person manifests disruptive behavior. Second, homosexuality is not always a visible trait, and many homosexuals may blend in smoothly without the agency's being aware that they are gay. Third, self-labeled homosexuals are more often the victims than the perpetrators of coerced homosexuality in institutions. Fourth, exclusion from treatment on grounds of homosexuality is stigmatizing, whereas the separation of male and female residents is not. Fifth, if a homosexual does try to seduce residents, those residents have some responsibility for the way they respond—a manageable challenge compared with that of constantly attending to the demands of the opposite sex.

These distinctions have, for the most part, empirical rather than logical force. Other observers may disagree, and there may be special circumstances where these recommendations do not apply. Surely, institutions are responsible for protecting all inmates and clients from physical harm. Beyond that, our experience with various institutional policies and their consequences indicates that sexual preference should not be treated as equivalent to gender in determining the placement of residents. Coed treatment, on the other hand, creates a visible polarity that colors every aspect of the residents' daily lives and can easily lead to systematic exploitation of women. As with questions of client–clinician "matching," the clinical priority is not to "please the customer" by indulging clients' preferences, but to create a therapeutic environment that allows for adaptation and growth.

9
Relationships Among Staff Members

That a helping professional's relationships with clients may have sexual overtones is not earthshaking news. Clinicians more or less expect some sexual acting out from clients. But they usually do not expect to have more trouble over sexual issues with fellow staff members than with clients. One does not, of course, have to be a helping professional to experience this. In any job one may face the pros and cons of "mixing business with pleasure" by becoming intimately involved with a co-worker, the interweaving of gender and sexuality with the polarities and power struggles of the work environment, and outright sexual harassment. If these dilemmas present themselves with special intensity to the helping professional (and the "if" here is not merely rhetorical), the reasons may lie in an emotional runoff from the human vulnerability to which helping professionals are exposed, as well as in the situational stresses and opportunities of working together at close quarters, often for long hours and in isolation from other social contacts. In any case, the sexual dynamics of relationships with co-workers can be as subtle or unsubtle, as challenging and perilous, as those that arise with clients. And one's professional training and formal orientations are likely to be of no greater help in coping with them.

Liaisons Between Staff Members

Sexual involvements between staff members at an agency, when they occur without coercion, lie in a narrow border zone between being the private business of consenting adults and a potentially disturbing force in the interpersonal dynamics of a human service organization. They tend to occur most frequently and most visibly, and therefore with the greatest impact on client services, in treatment settings where long hours, live-in arrangements for the staff, and/or geographical isolation create an incestuous atmosphere (cf. White, 1986). A female psychiatric social worker describes such an atmosphere at a community mental health center located in a small rural hospital:

> The inpatient service was a mess. The staff were almost all people in their twenties who were dating each other. One was fired for having sex with a patient. When everybody is living and breathing the same atmosphere, you forget that the outside world exists. Your options become limited, and you lose your objectivity and your sense of boundaries.

Although rural isolation predisposes to this sort of social milieu, it is not a necessary condition. In *Burnout* we described an inpatient ward at an urban psychiatric hospital where socializing among the staff took on a similarly ingrown character. There, under the pressure of patient overload together with the frustrations of dealing with the annual turn-over of resident physicians, the psychiatric nurses and technicians (both groups including males and females) turned to each other for comfort. As one of them reflected,

> With the crazy hours we work and the intensity of our involve-ment with patients, who else could support us, who else could understand, who else could put up with us but another one of *us*? . . . That's why, at least during our first year or so here, just about all our social and sexual gratification comes from the others in the group. (Edelwich with Brodsky, 1980, p. 85)

A male psychologist reports, "At a psychiatric residential program where I worked during my training, all of the four or five married cou-ples who came in as live-in staff were divorced by the time they left. All of those who came in as singles coupled up with someone in the same position."

There is a great deal of popular mythology about the goings-on between physicians and nurses. Our interview reports are very incon-sistent on this point. Strong confirmation of the risqué image of the busy hospital comes from a male psychologist (who, though not directly involved in the nurse-physician encounters, is a credible source):

> I was just amazed by the amount of this stuff that actually did happen. Some of it I could observe for myself, but I also made friends with a licensed practical nurse who showed me how it was done through the hospital's paging system. A doctor and nurse would arrange to meet in the emergency room, where the nurse would get a room ready and then page the doctor. My friend said that she had had affairs with 25 doctors that way. When she heard the pages, she could tell which ones were for sex. I imagine it's thrilling to page someone or be paged for a tryst in the presence of a couple of thousand people.

Some nurses indignantly reject such stories. One explanation for the widely discrepant accounts (aside from variations in hospital and community mores) is that the frenetic coupling between doctors and nurses occurs disproportionately in surgical and emergency services. Those who do not work in those facilities may not appreciate the way stress plus opportunity can touch off a natural tendency to seek sexual outlets.

Sexual contacts between staff members, whether in the form of expedient liaisons in a pressured atmosphere or simply two people becoming romantically involved in a normal office setting, present issues both for the individuals concerned and for agency administrators. For the individual: Is it wise to act on this impulse? Is it worth suffering the consequences? Should it be done discreetly? For the administrator: Does this detract sufficiently from the work of the agency to justify declaring it "against the rules"? One of the most sensitive tasks of human services administration is to decide what practices should be proscribed as inherently or regularly detrimental to clients, and what practices are best left outside the province of agency regulation except in those cases where they do affect services (in which cases it is the effect on services that should be addressed). Thus we have distinguished between telling a client about one's favorite sports team and about one's sex life, between protecting clients from physical abuse and from verbal abuse by peers, between entrusting clients to therapists of the opposite sex and to peers of the opposite sex. Some agencies have policies forbidding cohabitation or dating among staff members; if two co-workers become intimately involved (or even marry), one must leave the agency. Despite the difficulties that intra-agency love affairs can cause, a restrictive policy on this matter seems unwise in view of the ethical implications of attempting to dictate the personal choices of competent adults, the damage to staff morale from such intervention, the difficulty of enforcement (in the words of one administrator, "I could call the spirits from the deep, but would they come?"), and the loss of skilled personnel through forced transfers. For an agency to involve itself in the sexual behavior of its employees (except where clients are involved) will be seen by those employees as a moralistic interference with their lives. Assuming that there is no issue of coercion, the agency should limit its concern to effects on job performance.

It would be naive to deny that such effects may occur. Although intimate socializing among staff members can be mutually supportive, the consequences can also be deleterious. For this reason, helping professionals often prefer to avoid romantic involvements with co-workers. A 30-year-old male psychologist articulates a wariness that many of his colleagues share:

> I can't work well with someone in a helping capacity when there is sexual tension between us. It's not good for clients, and I don't have a good time. When I was attracted to a social worker at a mental hospital where I worked, I waited a few months until she gave notice before I asked her out. No supervisor has ever told me to lay off like that. I made the decision myself, not primarily for the sake of client care, but for the quality of my own experience.

What perceived difficulties, what awkward memories, lie behind this statement? The following are some ways in which sexual tensions among staff members can compromise both job satisfaction and services to clients:

Loss of privacy. Mixing one's personal and professional involvements can cause trouble on both ends. Several interviewees have described the claustrophobic feeling that sets in when co-workers who are dating spend their evenings together talking about patients and second-guessing clinical decisions. Equally uncomfortable is the feeling of having too much of one's personal life exposed on the job. "It's hard to have a sexual encounter in a closed environment," says a female school psychologist, "without leaving tracks behind you, ranging from 'I wonder if . . .' to 'I saw them at. . . .' " The social worker who was courted by her psychologist colleague only after she left the hospital where he worked gives her own perspective on the situation:

> If he had asked me out sooner, I would have responded cautiously. I can't identify the reasons why, but I know I didn't want to divulge to anyone at the hospital that this attraction was developing. When he took me back there for a staff party some weeks after I left, I picked up a general feeling of embarrassment together with glee at the revelation of our involvement.
>
> Previously I had had an affair with a graduate student who was interning at the hospital. Even though I was not directly responsible for his training, it would have been awkward (I felt) if my supervisors had found out. They never made this explicit, but it would have been impolitic.

Our recommendations notwithstanding, some agencies do impose sanctions, formal or informal, against liaisons with co-workers. One should consider carefully what the "givens" of a particular situation are and what consequences may ensue.

Favoritism. Client care suffers when clinicians do not manifest professional objectivity toward one another. When professional relationships are complicated by personal ones, a clinician may become overly protective by failing to confront a colleague/lover on clinical issues. Clients may receive arbitrarily unequal apportionments of time and energy from a clinician distracted by the desire to please or impress a colleague. A psychiatric social worker candidly admits, "When a physician I'm attracted to refers a patient to me, I try to do an especially good job to gain his notice." A psychologist says, "In a relatively unstructured setting like a halfway house I've seen myself shortchange clients by spending too much time with a staff member I was attracted to." Individuals who are as honest as those two can note these patterns and check themselves before they go too far. There are times, though, when similar motives lead to gross abuses, for example, in referral patterns. In a serious lapse of clinical integrity, the director of a psychiatric inpatient service gave every halfway house referral at her disposal to a house manager with whom she was having an affair.

Personal awkwardness or prejudice. Sexual dynamics can introduce a negative as well as a positive bias into professional relationships. Two staff members may have difficulty working together after they have ended an intimate relationship or after one has suffered a perceived rejection at the hands of the other. Understandably, the emotional barriers between them may affect their clinical judgment. A female coordinator of a training school for the mentally retarded describes her tense relationship with a male co-worker whom she had declined to date:

> I tried to be as nice as I could about it, but since then he hasn't been able to face me. To this day he will argue with or dismiss anything I say. Recently, when my supervisor was on vacation, this man fell behind on his routines, which in turn threw off my schedule. I approached him (as my supervisor later confirmed I had every right and obligation to do) and reminded him what the procedures were. His reaction was: "Who the hell are you?" When I came here others had resented my having a "man's job," but only this one man kept up that attitude.

Group dynamics: polarization and projection. In addition to these tensions between individuals, entire agencies and departments can be polarized over policy issues by underlying sexual tensions. The agency can become a combat zone for disputation, with battle lines drawn around the unspoken agendas of demonstrating personal loyalties and outmaneuvering rivals. Another symptom of disruptive sexual undercurrents is the projection of attitudes onto clients. In facilities with ingrown staff interaction patterns, therapists may be seen at clinical case conferences devising life plans for families with whom they may have little acquaintance. The "family dynamics" that they role-play are actually their own.

Antitherapeutic effects on clients. Clients who have sexual fantasies about a clinician are quick to identify other clinicians as real or imagined rivals. Even the presence of a supervisor in (say) a group therapy session may be resented by clients who see the supervisor as a suitor of the attractive group leader. In the irrational realm of client fantasies, a spouse or lover who (even if known to exist) is not physically present at the agency interferes less with therapeutic transference than one who is right on the scene. As Kaslow has observed,

> Patients fantasize about the nature of the relationship between a cotherapy pair and are apt to intuitively sense if their suppositions are based on reality rather than fantasy. If the former is true, and the cotherapists are sexually involved with each other, this can implicitly give permission to patients to also act out sexually. (1980, p. 7)

A female social worker at a drug abuse treatment center found that some of her male clients were alienated when she began dating another social worker at the center:

> Some of the guys who had been doing "good" things to impress me stopped showing progress. Their infatuation turned to resentment. "What does she see in him when she could have me?" they would say. One of them even told the social worker I was going out with, "Since you came into the picture I don't have a chance"—as if they ever did.

Not all clinicians, however, view the disruption of clients' fantasies as a bad thing. A male therapist offers this counterargument:

> It doesn't really matter how discreet you are, because patients always know. But I don't see why they shouldn't know. In a psychiatric unit, fantasies are best undone, not indulged. Let them see what the reality is. Besides that universally therapeutic effect, the immediate effects in a particular case can be therapeutic as well as not. When female patients suspected that I was having an affair with a nurse (I was not), it seemed to make them feel safer with me. This can be especially true for women who previously have had to pay for kindness from men.

This argument has some force; it is one of the reasons why liaisons between staff members need not be considered in and of themselves antitherapeutic. However, the clinician who regards such liaisons as positively therapeutic for clients should pause to examine (in consultation with a supervisor) the self-serving implications of this viewpoint and its potential for abuse.

These, then, are some consequences of intra-agency liaisons which must be dealt with when they reach troublesome proportions. A common problem that is not specific to clinical situations is that of public displays of affection among staff members. One who is offended by this behavior can do nothing about it or take the risk of saying, "I'd appreciate it if you didn't do this in public." Depending on the mores of the agency, the informal sanctions may go against either the lovers or the person raising the objection.

Sex and the Pecking Order

Staff polarization along lines of sex, age, race, level of professional training, and hierarchical position is a fact of life in human service organizations (Edelwich with Brodsky, 1980). Although staff members may air legitimate differences about treatment decisions, client care issues too often are a smokescreen for other dynamics as clients suffer amidst an abrasive conflict of egos among the staff. Thus a female therapist at a drug rehabilitation center whose master's degree in psychology was used to impress outside funding agencies was told, "Don't bring your psychology shit in here," by male ex-addict counselors at the center. In a prison where 80 percent of the inmates were black, white staff members spread false rumors of improprieties on the part of the one black corrections officer employed there, who came from the same neighborhood as some of the inmates and knew their families. A white male unit supervisor in a halfway house for adolescents became suspicious whenever a white female staff member went into a room alone with a black male student. At the same facility, black male staff members would undermine treatment by telling students, "Don't listen to that white———; black is where it's at!" In a women's prison administered by women, male staff members complained about being used as a "Gestapo force" to keep order. A power struggle between a male family therapist and his female supervisor (who was older but less credentialed) became so apparent to a family in treatment that the family dropped out. The male director of a crisis center, whose female staff was known as his "harem," felt threatened by a new staff member, Susan Q., who got through to young female clients with a feminist appeal.

The two came into open conflict over a flirtatious female therapist, Susan charging that she was setting up male clients for disappointment, the director contending that she was "giving them ego-regard."

Susan, the feminist therapist, did something about the abuses she witnessed. Consistently outvoted at staff meetings, she brought the matter before the board of directors. When the board sidestepped the issue, Susan threatened to resign and report the whole affair to the agency that funded the crisis center. Eventually the center was closed. Susan was willing to make "waves"—and enemies—by acting responsibly. The actions she took were appropriate ones for a staff member caught in the middle of a power struggle that seriously affects the welfare of clients. Faced with the choice of letting the situation deteriorate or taking some risks, one who decides to act can most usefully do the following:

First, air the dispute in a conjoint meeting with a supervisor. Concreteness and specificity are vital here. Vague expressions like "bad vibes" and "there's something going on here" only obscure the substance of the conflict. The discussion should focus on issues (preferably, a list of specific issues), not personalities. The relevant agenda is: (1) What happened? (2) How did it sabotage treatment? The "bottom line" always is the effect on the client.

Second, if discussion fails to bring results, and if a breach of ethics is involved, document and report the abuse. Initiate a formal complaint—first with an immediate supervisor, and then up through channels if necessary. Concreteness and specificity are every bit as important at this stage.

Another woman who took action, in this case on an issue of job discrimination rather than improper treatment of clients, was Alison H., a correctional training officer in the state prison system. She explains:

> I share a civil service rank with a handful of men in the same field around the state. In a recent reorganization it was decided that, as an incentive to take on new duties, these men would all be promoted to the next higher rank, which would mean a jump in status plus a pay raise of a few thousand dollars. I, on the other hand, was to get the pay raise without the title, even though people with the higher rank have held my particular job. When I inquired about why I was being singled out, it turned out that they were afraid that, with my seniority, I might bump a male officer of equal

rank out of a male institution when my training job expired. I threatened to go to the State Commission on Human Rights if they went ahead with their plan. In the end, no one was promoted. Instead of being a "good girl" and going along, I sacrificed the pay increase to stand up for my rights.

Although Susan Q. and Alison H. provide useful models of taking action, their cases also illustrate the depth of the often dysfunctional conflicts of interest between men and women in the workplace. Even in the human services the proportion of women in management positions is far less than the proportion of women in the total work force. The ranks of female physicians and attorneys are noticeably growing, but a preponderance of female nurses must still work with a preponderance of male physicians, and female social workers can expect to present their cases primarily to male attorneys and judges.

In the polarities based on gender, age, race, training, and position, in the politics and manners, the opportunity and self-interest of the work environment, sexual attraction between men and women acts as an explosive catalyst. Sexual conquest gives people who are unsure of their status a tangible way of posing and answering questions such as "On what grounds am I the equal of that individual? On what grounds are we unequal?" It is used to clarify power relationships in agencies where credentialed staff members are subordinate to managers who have less formal training. This pattern occurs, for example, when a clinician (usually male) with a "street background" directs a rehabilitation program staffed by psychologists and social workers (often female) as well as paraprofessional counselors. Sex is the equalizer for the person whose organizational status has not been earned by professional training, as in this account by a female master's-level psychologist who trains counselors in a drug program:

My position is subordinate only to that of the director, which puts me above other men as well as women in the agency. After I had been there for several weeks I learned that one staff member had bet another that within two weeks the director would have me in bed. It turned out that this man, who is black, had seduced almost every woman (either that or almost every white woman along with an occasional black woman) who worked in the program. Once a woman went to bed with him, he had a lot of power over her. After about six months I started wondering why he hadn't even asked me out to lunch. I suppose it was that I came across as unapproachable. Still, even in our strictly professional contacts I noticed tests and provocations in his manner. He would, for instance, throw out some idea while knowing exactly how I would react. In my view he was sublimating the physical seduction. I believe that, for him, to win an argument with a subordinate who was female, white, and better educated had a sexual payoff.

As she perceived the situation, the racial dynamics reinforced the sexual. However, it would be a mistake to assume, on the basis of a case such as this in which the racial dimension was present, that the latter is an essential part of the phenomenon observed here. The interplay of sexual and organizational oneupsmanship occurs across the board, irrespective of racial differences.

Sexual Harassment

Sexuality as a weapon in the struggle for power and position leads into the question of sexual harassment, defined by the American Psychological Association as "deliberate or repeated comments, gestures or physical contacts of a sexual nature that are unwanted by the recipient" (Dietz, 1982). Chapter 3 ended with a case of harassment in which a nurse found herself the object of false and embarrassing innuendos after she rejected the advances of a resident physician. A female staff member in a men's prison was introduced to the grim reality of sexual harassment in a briefing by a deputy warden on her first day on the job. "The inmates won't give you much of a problem," he told her. "Oh, they'll have their wolf whistles and their flowers and so forth. But your real problems will be with the staff. Remember, you aren't one of the boys, so don't try to be one of them." More trouble with the staff than with the clients—a disturbing truth for many women.

As an aid in recognizing harassment and the sexually polarized atmosphere in which it develops, the following are some characteristic ways in which men relate to women in human service (and other) organizations (most of these, of course, do not in themselves constitute harassment):

Favoritism in hiring, promotion, and case assignment. For a woman
to be hired in preference to other candidates because she is attractive
can make her feel both fortunate and uneasy. A counseling supervisor
in an addiction treatment program reflects,

> I think there were others who were more qualified for the job—
> people with master's degrees as opposed to my bachelor's in social
> work—but I was hired after a man in the state office who was
> infatuated with me pushed my application through. He probably
> wanted a sexual payoff, but he didn't ask for it.

The favoritism accorded her has continued on the job:

> Some men do me favors to impress me with their power. "I'm
> going out of my way to release this client to you," they'll say. I
> recognize this when it happens and use it to advantage.

A schoolteacher speaks of "the principal's favored daughters—
physically attractive, high-sexual-energy women who get the most
attention regardless of their professional capacity." Usually this preferential treatment does not signal overt harassment, but it is still
a non-work-related agenda that leads male administrators to discriminate in favor of young, attractive women over other job applicants
or staff members (thereby treating clients, too, as pawns). The personal agenda may simply be a feeling of pleasure and stimulation in
the presence of an attractive woman. It may also involve a hope of
an actual liaison.

A more serious form of discrimination is that which gives preferment
after the fact as a reward for sexual favors. Everyone has heard rumors,
substantiated or not, about (for example) a woman who suddenly
became a head nurse after having an affair with an influential physician.
This is one step away from coercion, where the quid pro quo is spelled
out in advance.

Jealousy and protectiveness. Some male staff members imagine it to
be their mission to protect their female counterparts from the advances
of predatory male clients. In their view, women in the helping professions are naive "bleeding hearts," easy prey for clients' sinister designs
(which are a projection of the staff members' fantasies). This attitude

may be expressed as either old-fashioned gentility or tasteless suggestiveness. Either way, it is stifling and patronizing. As a female social
worker exclaimed, "I can't make a move with all the protectors I've got.
If I don't want the boys to touch me, *I'll* tell them."

Criticism of sexual expressiveness or its absence. If a man wears tight
jeans and a half-open shirt, he is said to be macho. If a woman does
the same, she is said to be sexually provocative. If a man wears a business suit or overalls, he is said to be properly dressed for the job. If
a woman does the same, she is said to be suppressing her sexuality. The
double standard signifies that women are perceived much more in
terms of their sexuality than men are. Sexuality is taken to be the center
of a woman's existence, and everything she does or does not do is understood in relation to it. If she flirts, she is "loose." If she does not flirt,
she must be a lesbian. She can't win.

A textbook case of harassment with sexual overtones is contributed
by a staff member at a psychiatric halfway house, a woman in her
mid-twenties:

> My immediate supervisor is a man with a strict Old World back-
> ground. He adheres to a tradition which holds that the woman
> should follow behind the man. Recently, after several days in
> which I had felt a lot of strain around him, he came in one morning
> and blew up at me, saying that I had been incompetent and uncon-
> trollable for two weeks. It was an unprovoked outburst. I've seen
> him work with men, and he would never yell at a man that way.
> The scene went on for a couple of hours. I wanted to bring it down
> to the issues, but he insisted on generalizing that I was wrong and
> he was right. I was in shock; I almost resigned right there. After-
> ward I went to the director, but so did he, with a completely dif-
> ferent story. He had cleverly done his act when there were no
> witnesses, so it was his word against mine. The three of us then
> had a meeting which I thought resolved things, but as soon as we
> walked out he started in on me again. The director has assured
> me, however, that she knows I'm highly competent and considers
> me an asset to the house. She also can't help but notice how much
> more open I've been to resolving the issues than this supervisor
> has. It's good that I have the director's support, since the super-
> visor has given me a bad evaluation.

As far as I can see, all this goes back to some stories I had told him earlier when I hadn't realized how unsympathetic he'd be. My personal life, my morals, are not what he approves of. Because I've dressed comfortably, sometimes without a bra, in an appropriately casual manner for the setting, he's accused me of trying to entice him. My response now is to hold everything back, to divulge nothing further about my personal life.

This woman was attacked for both her gender and her sexuality. The lesson she learned is one that many women in human service agencies feel they must heed—namely, to shut off personal communication and to speak and dress self-protectively.

Disrespect and lewdness. Attributions of "looseness" that men make about women in certain situations serve to permit (in the eyes of the men) disrespectful conduct. Prime targets of this treatment are nurses, whose "Hot Lips Hoolihan" image (from the sexy nurse in the television show "MASH") is bitterly resented by many in the profession. Nurses complain of being "grossed out" by men who feel entitled to take linguistic liberties with women who see and touch the bodies of sick people (Edelwich with Brodsky, 1980). A pathologically extreme instance of this behavior was revealed when three young Boston-area physicians were convicted of raping a nurse they met at a party in 1980. Although the motivation of a criminal act is not subject to simple explanation, it is likely that the image of female nurses as fair game for male physicians contributed to this abuse. That image can be so destructive in its consequences that nurses are organizing to combat it. The television series "Nightingales" was taken off the air after nurses protested against the libertine image it conveyed.

Another setting in which women are subjected to nasty innuendos is the men's prison. In the nearly exclusively male world of a correctional facility, not only the inmates, but also most of the staff are not likely to have access to young, attractive women. A woman who is young and attractive and who chooses to work in this male environment stands to be stigmatized as a thrill-seeker ("What she needs is a good lay"). Gail B., who did counseling in a prison while working toward a master's degree in criminology, describes how staff members directed their sexual preoccupations at her:

Although I dressed very conservatively and was not flirtatious, I still couldn't get away with the most innocent workaday joking with the men I worked with. One after another, men with whom I thought I enjoyed a light, friendly rapport started propositioning me.

Sexual extortion. What follows in Gail's account of the prison milieu is not surprising, although it still shocks:

> One day, having finished all my work, I sought permission to leave half an hour early. Before calling my supervisor, I asked *his* supervisor, who said, "Fine, just check with. . . ."
>
> So I called my supervisor, who replied, "Well, what are you going to give me for it?"
>
> Not wanting to read into that what I thought I heard, I said, "I'll do two Form 12s for you in the morning." (He hated those forms.)
>
> He laughed, and I repeated my request. "Well, can I go?"
>
> "No, not until you tell me what you're going to give me for it."
>
> "What exactly do you want?"
>
> "Well, it ain't Form 12s."
>
> "Well, then, I don't want the time that bad."
>
> I hung up and stayed the full day. I didn't report it because I wasn't sure if anyone would believe me.

This is harassment. The supervisor said what he did with impunity. He was sure he could get away with it. He will continue to get away with it until someone takes a risk and reports it.

For women in facilities such as that prison, and in varying degrees wherever women and men work together, getting through the work day can be like walking through a minefield of subtle bribes, threats, and assaults. The expression "on guard" comes up repeatedly when women relate how they negotiate this hazardous course. Friendly, outgoing women find that they must be businesslike to a fault in dress, demeanor, and speech, or else they may be misinterpreted and "caught off guard" (whether by a client or a staff member). Working women go to great lengths to avoid situations like the following, described by a case coordinator at a residential drug treatment center:

The director of the program, who had hired me in the first place, spent time talking to me in his office when I should have been monitoring groups. (He was an ex-addict, but ex-addicts aren't the only ones with lust in their hearts. I've been propositioned by attorneys and judges, too.) For a year he limited himself to hints and innuendos while I tried to fend off what was coming by playing it down, pretending I didn't understand, making a joke of it. Finally he came out with it. He did it in a nice, charming way, going through the whole line about how he was attracted to me. He took it nicely when I declined, too, but I was uncomfortable having to confront it directly. Other staff members as well as residents knew what was going on. A few of the residents thought I *was* going to bed with the director—and with five or six residents besides!

This incident, which falls well short of harassment, exemplifies the ongoing stress which many women experience as a condition of employment.

Three levels of sexual approaches. To cope better with the varieties of sexual communication that take place on the job and to clarify which ones constitute harassment, it is helpful to think in terms of three levels of overtures. Although one can best judge how to reply to these out of one's familiarity with the people involved and the setting, there are certain types of responses that are generally appropriate for each level.

Level 1 consists of the flirtatious banter, ranging from the innocuous to the insidious, that has gone on in offices and the like from time immemorial. If it is done in a good spirit, just to make the day go by more pleasantly, it need not be cause for concern. A woman with years of experience in human service agencies comments:

Two men can say the same thing (like "Come on, you don't hug me like you hug him," or "Just tell me where and when, honey"), and one of them will be playing, one of them serious. You learn to tell the difference, which boils down to a question of how much trust there is between you. A supervisor who puts his arm around everybody and calls them "honey" can be annoying but harmless. But when somebody gets persistent, you may have to tell him that you don't want to hear it anymore.

Level 2 consists of the normal sorts of invitations to begin a social relationship—invitations to go out for a drink, for dinner, and so forth. Assuming that one does not want to take up the offer, it is best to decline with as much (or as little) tact and diplomacy as is called for by the manner in which the invitation was made. Individuals vary in the weight they give to not hurting someone's feelings versus carving out their own space in the work environment. Perhaps it is an old-fashioned perspective, together with an appreciation of the politics of medical institutions, that leads this 40-year-old nurse to take as much care as she does in fielding men's overtures:

> Doctors usually come on softly with trial balloons. I know the meaning of the innuendos from the beginning, and if I don't encourage and build on them, nothing will happen. If I get an overture from a doctor I don't respect, I'll think, "He has a lot of nerve." If it's a doctor I do respect, I'll take it as a compliment. Once when a chief of service said to me directly that he wanted to see me on the outside, I thanked him for the compliment and went on my way. I wanted his respect, but I didn't want him to feel embarrassed. I saw no purpose in causing any problems.

Level 3 is harassment. It takes two major forms—uninvited intimacy up to and including physical contact (escalating to violence) and the attempt to extort sex as a quid pro quo: "You do this for me, and I'll do that for you." The "quo" may be time off (as in Gail B.'s case), a raise, a promotion, a good evaluation, a favorable assignment, exemption from a layoff, and so on. Harassment is an illegitimate exercise of power. It has nothing to do with a woman's attractiveness or other personal qualities. Women who refrain from taking action because they like to think of sexual harassment as a kind of compliment are caught up in a costly delusion.

Almost without qualification, the most effective response to sexual harassment is to do what Gail B. did not do, but Phyllis D. (in Chapter 3) did do—to document the incident and report it to one's supervisor (or if it is the supervisor doing the harassing, then to the next higher level of administration). Make it official; send a correspondence copy to the supervisor's supervisor. Document the time, place, and other relevant details as precisely as possible so as to shut off any avenue of administrative evasion. Although an administrator in whose lap the complaint falls might prefer not to do anything about it, the administrator would become vulnerable by failing to act on a documented complaint.

There is no guarantee that a woman who files a complaint will not suffer consequences, possibly extending to the loss of her job. There are places of employment where, harassment being the norm, one's choices are to accept it or to quit. On the whole, though, the sanctions feared by victims of harassment are imaginary. The consequences of doing nothing, on the other hand, are clear. Feelings of powerlessness and frustration intensify as the propositions become more lewd and more physical. One who is reluctant to act should at least talk to other women in the agency, since it is a good bet that the perpetrator is not limiting himself to one target. By enlisting a support group one can present management with a united front instead of just an individual complaint. Employees of public agencies (particularly those under civil service or military jurisdiction) should also investigate whether there are regulations prohibiting harassment and providing for redress, although there may be a disparity between regulations and practice.

There is a difference, however, between taking appropriate action and going on a crusade to save the world. On the one hand, sexual harassment is not something to be dealt with through "benign neglect." All incidents should be reported. On the other hand, understandable as the victim's anger and frustration are, it does not help anyone to carry on a personal vendetta. Redress should be pursued as dispassionately as humanly possible. Whether one files a complaint with one's supervisor or with a professional organization such as the American Psychiatric Association, one should be prepared to deal with issues rather than personalities. The accused party must have a hearing, with each case considered on its own merits. Inquiry should focus on what happened and what impact it had. Once the facts have been presented, it is up to the investigating body, not the person bringing the complaint, to decide whether or not the offender should be drummed out of the profession. A complainant who does not gain satisfaction through one such procedure has the option of initiating another (e.g., legal action).

As women move up into traditionally male positions in the management hierarchy, the social pressures as well as policies of the work environment are beginning to oppose rather than support sexual harassment. Increasingly, good management is seen to entail maintaining a tone of mutual respect among staff members. An example of the change is the assertiveness of college-educated nurses, who are not reduced to being (in the words of a nurse from the previous generation) "handmaidens of the respected, all-knowing physician." Even so, women who have left bedside nursing for administrative, educational, and other positions perceived as more "professional" report that men make more lewd remarks and sexual overtures to women of equal status than to those who clearly rank below them. The battle of the sexes will go on, albeit under different ground rules.

Finally, it may be questioned whether any sexual contact between employees of an organization, especially in superior-subordinate relationships, is free from the taint of harassment, since there can always be invisible pressures (including unspoken quid pro quos) pushing women into "voluntary" liaisons. For this reason, in addition to others considered at the beginning of this chapter, some organizations attempt to restrict intimate involvements among their staff. As workers and managers seek to resolve this dilemma, they should bear in mind that limiting the freedom of women and men to make personal choices is a high price to pay for removing any hint of coercion from the proceedings.

10
Liabilities

As we noted in Chapter 6, the concerns of the law change with the concerns of society. In recent years the feminist movement has brought issues such as family abuse to the attention of prosecutors and judges. Not surprisingly, this assertion of women's and children's rights, together with the increasing prominence of psychotherapy and the epidemic of medical malpractice claims, has aroused judicial, legislative, and public interest in the sexual exploitation of clients by therapists. Only since 1975 have the legal parameters in this area begun to be defined. Yet during these 15 years the body of relevant case law and statute law has grown dramatically. As more states enact legislation making it a felony for a therapist to have sexual contact with a client, there is both a professional and a public debate about whether criminalization is an appropriate response to the problem. There is also debate about the moral basis for both civil and criminal action against perpetrators of such abuse: exactly *why* are sanctions called for, and what kinds of sanctions best fit the offense? Meanwhile, the specter of organizational and administrative liability has arisen. In addition, therapists who treat victims of sexual abuse by previous therapists have become embroiled in questions of mandatory reporting, conflict of interest (dual agency), obtaining informed consent to traumatic legal and administrative processes, and even personal liability.

The discussion of rights, responsibilities, and liabilities that follows has been enhanced by published commentaries by attorney Paul E. Mason and by leading forensic psychiatrists such as Alan A. Stone, Seymour L. Halleck, and Thomas G. Gutheil, as well as by the work of members of the Program in Psychiatry and the Law at Massachusetts

Mental Health Center and legislative task forces in Minnesota and Massachusetts.

Malpractice and Other Civil Actions

It is by now well established that sexual contact with a client, with resultant harm to the client, constitutes malpractice on the part of a psychotherapist. In adjudicating malpractice claims, the courts rely heavily on the consensus of qualified opinion in the professional disciplines concerned. On the point in question, a number of psychotherapy professions have gone on record unambiguously. Several prominent psychiatrists were quoted in Chapter 5 to the effect that having sex with a client is an abuse of trust and a betrayal of the therapist's mission. This viewpoint found official expression in 1973 in the American Psychiatric Association's *Principles of Medical Ethics with Annotations Especially Applicable to Psychiatry.* The 1989 revision reads:

> The patient may place his/her trust in his/her psychiatrist knowing that the psychiatrist's ethics and professional responsibilities preclude him/her gratifying his/her own needs by exploiting the patient. This becomes particularly important because of the essentially private, highly personal, and sometimes intensely emotional nature of the relationship established with the psychiatrist. . . .
> . . . the necessary intensity of the therapeutic relationship may tend to activate sexual and other needs and fantasies on the part of both patient and therapist, while weakening the objectivity necessary for control. Sexual activity with a patient is unethical. (American Psychiatric Association, 1989, pp. 3,4)

In 1976 the American Psychological Association followed suit with this addition to its *Ethical Standards of Psychologists.* The 1981 revision reads:

> Psychologists are continually cognizant of their own needs and of their potentially influential position vis-à-vis persons such as clients, students, and subordinates. They avoid exploiting the trust and dependency of such persons. Psychologists make every effort to avoid dual relationships that could impair their professional

judgment or increase the risk of exploitation. Examples of such dual relationships include, but are not limited to, research with and treatment of employees, students, supervisees, close friends, or relatives. Sexual intimacies with clients are unethical. (American Psychological Association, 1981, p. 636)

The National Association of Social Workers' *Code of Ethics* (1980 edition) states, "The social worker should under no circumstances engage in sexual activity with clients." Similar pronouncements appear in the ethics codes of such organizations as the National Federation of Societies for Clinical Social Work, the American Association for Counseling and Development, the American Association for Marriage and Family Therapy, the National Association of Alcoholism and Drug Abuse Counselors, the Association of Labor-Management Administrators and Consultants on Alcoholism (employee-assistance counselors), the American Association of Sex Educators, Counselors and Therapists, and the Biofeedback Society of America (Schoener, 1989d).

Psychotherapists and counselors are thus understood to be under an even stricter ethical obligation in this regard than nonpsychiatric physicians (for whom the seduction of a patient is a violation of the Hippocratic Oath). This is because in psychotherapy the seduction both flows from and compromises the nature of the treatment itself (Halleck, 1980).

In order to win an award of damages, the plaintiff must prove to the satisfaction of the jury or judge what are called "the four Ds" of malpractice liability: *dereliction* of *duty* that *directly* causes *damage*. Once the therapist assumes the duty of care (by undertaking to treat the client professionally), the plaintiff must show that the dereliction (in this case sexual contact) did occur. This usually is a matter of one person's word versus another's, since the alleged acts are private ones, and evidence concerning the therapist's affairs with other clients (known as "Spreigl witnesses") normally is inadmissible unless it is needed to refute the defendant's testimony (say, that he or she did not have sexual contact with any other clients) (Stone, 1976).

In addition, the client must have suffered injury *directly resulting from* the therapist's breach of ethics—that is, the emotional injury must have been "proximately caused" by the therapist's wrongful act. (Although emotional injury is accepted as constituting grounds for damages, it is less easily demonstrated than physical damage or monetary loss.) In Mason's (1976, p. 40) words, "Proximate cause may be espe-cially difficult to prove in transference situations, where the injury itself is not visible or physical and where the patient's emotional state may fluctuate substantially both before and after the injury." In establishing both the injury and proximate cause, the plaintiff's task was made more difficult in early cases by the reluctance of other therapists to testify as expert witnesses against a colleague. Increasingly, however, a pool of both ethical expert witnesses and opportunistic "hired guns" is avail-able to testify for both plaintiffs and defendants.

Precedent established. Standing as an initial obstacle to lawsuits against seductive therapists were the "heart balm" acts passed by var-ious states, which barred civil liability for sexual intercourse on grounds such as seduction, breach of promise, criminal conversation, and alien-ation of affections (Mason, 1976). These statutes have been partly responsible for the generally unsuccessful outcomes of lawsuits brought by husbands against therapists who have seduced their wives. In 1972, however, a husband recovered $30,000 in hospital expenses for his wife, who had divorced him (and later committed suicide) after her psychi-atrist had promised to divorce his wife and marry her. The plaintiff ben-efited from expert testimony that the psychiatrist's acting out of countertransference feelings was conduct beneath acceptable profes-sional standards (*Anclote Manor Foundation v. Wilkinson*, 1972).

The way was opened for awards of damages to clients who consented to sexual relations with their therapists by the famous New York case (*Roy v. Hartogs*, 1975) that inspired the book *Betrayal* (Freeman & Roy, 1976). This case was tried in 1975 and heard on appeal in 1976. The defendant moved to have the suit dismissed at the outset on the strength of a previous decision in which the state's "heart balm" act (Section 80A of the New York State Civil Rights Law) was held to bar malpractice actions against physicians on the grounds of seduction. The plaintiff's attorneys argued that the fraudulent misrepresentation of sex as psychiatric treatment, with the patient deprived of informed consent by transference, differed significantly from incidental seduction by a medical doctor. The Court, in rejecting the defendant's motion for dis-missal of the suit, agreed:

> . . . there is a public policy to protect a patient from the deliberate
> and malicious abuse of power and breach of trust by a psychiatrist

when the patient entrusts to him her body and mind in the hope that he will use his best efforts to effect a cure. That right is best protected by permitting the victim to pursue civil remedies, not only to vindicate a wrong against her but to vindicate the public interest as well. (*Roy v. Hartogs*, 1975, at 301)

The plaintiff was a woman in her early thirties who, during and after a brief marriage, functioned with difficulty and in a marginal way, particularly in regard to having a lack of normal social contacts. She was diagnosed as schizophrenic by other psychotherapists both before and after her treatment by the defendant in 1969 and 1970. In the aftermath of this treatment, according to her testimony and that of the psychiatrist who took over her care, she experienced suicidal and murderous (toward the therapist/seducer) impulses, culminating in two psychotic episodes requiring hospitalization.

At the trial several expert psychiatric witnesses, including Drs. Willard Gaylin and Charles Clay Dahlberg, testified for the plaintiff that sex between psychiatrist and patient is unethical and is in itself malpractice. The statement of principle by the American Psychiatric Association was cited in support of this testimony. The defendant, along with his one expert witness, took the same position. The defense he employed was that of factual impossibility, based on the claim of impotence. To rebut this claim, the plaintiff's attorney was permitted to call as "Spreigl" witnesses several other female clients who testified that the defendant had engaged in intercourse or other sexual activity with them during therapy. Their testimony was injurious to the defendant's case.

Since no one on either side contested the ethical principle set forth by the APA, the judge instructed the jury that it was to be held binding as a matter of law. If the jury found that the defendant had in fact had sexual relations with his client, then malpractice would be proved. The jury did reach this finding.

Stone (1976) speculates about two defenses to which the psychiatrist did not resort: (1) that the client had freely consented to an affair that had been presented to her as entirely separate from the therapeutic relationship; (2) that the client had given informed consent to sex *as* therapy before transference developed. As Mason (1976) points out, the defendant might have cited Shepard's (1971) book *The Love Treatment* as evidence that one school of psychiatric thought was willing to consider the possible therapeutic benefits of sex between client and therapist. (Conceivably, he might also have argued that the APA's 1973 declaration was being applied ex post facto to his relationship with the plaintiff, which took place in 1969 and 1970.) At that time the issue still was sufficiently ill-defined that Stone (1976, p. 258) could guardedly conclude, "Both of the defenses I enumerated, though unacceptable to the mental health profession, may still be appropriate defenses in a court of law." Since then, however, the APA guideline has become so well established as a criterion for malpractice that Stone's commentary has become ancient history. In Florida in 1979, for example, a therapist who did defend his intimacy with a client as therapeutic was required to pay damages (*Keiser v. Berry*, 1979). If anything, a claim of therapeutic benefit is likely to strengthen the plaintiff's case by demonstrating a flagrant abuse of trust.

The jury in *Roy v. Hartogs* (1975) awarded the plaintiff $250,000 in compensatory damages and $100,000 in punitive damages. The trial judge, on motion by the defendant, reduced the compensatory damages to $50,000 because the evidence showed that the plaintiff's therapeutic-cum-sexual relationship with the defendant had produced only a temporary exacerbation, not a permanent worsening, of her pre-existing condition. On defendant's appeal, the New York Supreme Court, Appellate Term, further reduced the compensatory damages to $25,000 and disallowed the punitive damages altogether. Notwithstanding two concurring judges' characterization of the defendant's actions as "sex under the cloak of treatment," the Court ruled that evil or malicious intent had not been proved (Mason & Stitham, 1977). By then, however, the plaintiff had reached a separate settlement with the defendant's malpractice insuror (which had refused to support his case) for an additional $50,000 in damages (Stone, 1976).

Escalation of damages. With this precedent, it might have been anticipated that damage awards in this area of malpractice would be contained at a modest level. That has not happened. In California in 1981 a jury made, and a trial judge upheld, an award of $4.6 million. In return for an agreement by the defendant to drop his appeal, the plaintiff accepted a settlement of $2.5 million.

This case, *Walker v. Parzen* (reported in Wilkinson, 1981/82), differed from *Roy v. Hartogs* (1975) in several respects. The psychiatrist admitted having had sex with his client, while claiming that she had intimidated him with threats of suicide if he rejected her. The harm suffered by the client (from the sexual relationship as well as from the therapist's alleged promise to divorce his wife and marry her) included a broken marriage, numerous suicide attempts, and an enormous intake of sedatives prescribed by the same psychiatrist. The passage of time also appears to have been a factor in the escalation of damages. By 1981 the social forces arrayed on the side of the abused client had become all the more entrenched. Since then, six- and seven-figure jury awards and settlements have become commonplace (e.g., *Bartkus v. Molde*, 1989; *Doe v. Fanning*, 1989).

Statute of limitations. The statute of limitations for professional malpractice cases (typically three years) has been a bar to recovery of damages for many individuals who did not realize until years after the fact that they had grounds to sue their therapists. Courts sometimes have been willing to extend the statute if the client was impaired or was deceived by the therapist's assurances that the therapist had done nothing wrong. Plaintiffs' arguments that the time limit for filing suit should be extended because shame, embarrassment, intimidation, or posttraumatic stress prevented them from coming forward earlier have met with varying results. There are, after all, statues of limitations covering other shame-inducing abuses such as rape.

Recently, however, the courts have shown a greater willingness to apply the "discovery rule," by which the period specified by the statute begins to toll only from the time the plaintiff realized he or she had a cause of action. In 1989 Fredrica Carmichael was awarded $1 million in damages on the grounds that her husband, a psychologist, had committed malpractice by becoming sexually involved with her while she was his patient. The judge ruled that the District of Columbia's three-year statute of limitations did not invalidate her claim because she had not begun to realize until 1987 that the defendant's conduct had caused her emotional harm (Torry, 1989). In the same year (in a case not involving sexual misconduct) the discovery rule was extended to cover negligence by nonlicensed professionals (*Shamloo v. Lifespring, Inc.*, 1989). Such rulings, together with statutory extensions of the statute of limitations in states such as Minnesota (see below), will provide an avenue for legal redress for some victims of abuses committed before such misconduct was publicly condemned.

Liability for sexual relations with former clients. According to Halleck (1980), a properly made referral to a qualified colleague would protect the therapist from liability not only for abandonment, but also for sexual exploitation if the therapist and client initiated a sexual liaison subsequent to termination. A decade later, as discussed in Chapter 5, termination of therapy for the purpose of having a love affair with the client might well be looked upon as evidence of a conflict of interest on the part of the therapist. If the client suffered harm as a result of such an affair, might not the court rule that the therapist had betrayed the client's trust by influencing the client to exchange therapeutic for physical intimacy? According to Conte et al. (1989, p. 40), "Quite a number of therapists have used therapy termination as a defense in civil malpractice suits concerning sexual relations, but in no instance when a case has gone to appeal has a defendant been cleared on this basis."

Subject to the possible constitutional constraints noted in Chapter 5, the courts can be expected to follow the professions' own codes of ethics in this area as they have with respect to sexual relations with current clients. In 1989 the American Psychiatric Association (1989, p. 4) added this stipulation to its statement of ethical principles: "Sexual involvement with one's former patients generally exploits emotions deriving from treatment and therefore almost always is unethical." The American Association for Marriage and Family Therapy (1988, p. 1) states, "Sexual intimacy with former clients for two years following the termination of therapy is prohibited." The Feminist Therapy Institute has banned posttermination relationships outright (Gonsiorek & Brown, 1989). Other professional organizations undoubtedly will follow suit.

The effects of such pronouncements have been felt in, for example, the New York Supreme Court's denial of a psychiatrist's motion to dismiss a patient's suit for medical malpractice merely because the sexual relations alleged by the patient occurred after the patient's discharge from the hospital at which the psychiatrist was in residency. Although New York had enacted no statute defining the conditions under which sexual contact with a present or former client was actionable, the court cited statutes in Minnesota and California that established sexual exploitation of either a present or former client as a cause of action (*Noto v. St. Vincent's Hospital and Medical Center*, 1988).

Statutes governing civil actions. Ambiguities in judicial interpretations of such questions as the statute of limitations or liability for sex with former clients can be resolved by enactment of a statute explicitly making sexual contact with a client a cause of action against a therapist. States that have enacted such statutes have made it easier for clients to sue by providing that consent is not a defense against such action and that evidence about the plaintiff's sexual history is inadmissible unless the court determines it to be relevant. These laws generally allow suits to be brought for sexual contact occurring after therapy has ended, the period covered ranging from six months to two years following termination of therapy (Appelbaum, 1990).

Minnesota's civil-liability law, enacted in 1986 and used as a model by other states, establishes a cause of action if sexual contact occurred at any time or place during the period of therapy. If it occurred during the two years following therapy, there is a cause of action if the former patient was emotionally dependent on the psychotherapist or if the therapist engaged in therapeutic deception—that is, claimed that the sex was part of or consistent with the treatment. The law extends the statute of limitations for this form of malpractice to five years after the last sexual contact. It also makes the therapist's employer liable for failing to take certain precautions in hiring or monitoring the therapist (Schoener et al., 1989, pp. 709–713).

Who pays the bill? Lawsuits arising from sexual abuse by psychotherapists represent a growing proportion of all claims against such practitioners and a difficult problem for companies providing malpractice insurance. Within six months after *Roy v. Hartogs* (1975) went to trial, psychiatrists, previously not a major target of malpractice suits, faced large increases in malpractice insurance rates (Freeman & Roy, 1976). Between 1974 and 1976 the insurance company that provided malpractice protection for members of the American Psychological Association received at least five claims for sexual abuses in psychotherapy, one of which asked $2 million in damages. In response, the company dropped the APA's policy (Mason, 1976). The APA then obtained insurance that did not provide reimbursement in sexual cases (Stone, 1976). As of the late 1980s, the APA and other professional organizations have policies that set a limit of $25,000 on coverage for sexual involvement with present or former clients. This is approximately the figure for which insurers typically settle nuisance suits that cannot immediately be dismissed, even when they believe the clinician to be innocent of negligence or wrongdoing. Likewise, companies that do offer more than token coverage tend to settle plausible claims quickly to reduce their liability in return for sparing the victim the strain, exposure, and uncertain outcome of a trial.

Malpractice insurance policies generally exclude felonious acts from coverage. Ironically, then, one effect of criminalizing sexual misconduct by therapists is to give insurers a pretext for denying compensation to victims even when sexual misconduct otherwise would be included in the clinician's malpractice-liability policy. Often the plaintiff can get around this restriction by alleging other grounds for malpractice in conjunction with the felony of sexual exploitation. Nonetheless, advocates of criminalization, believing it unfair to ask victims to trade recovery of damages for deterrence, are seeking to have this common, predictable form of malpractice exempted from the exclusion of felonies from liability-insurance coverage.

When the therapist does not have insurance coverage, the value of bringing suit depends on the therapist's ability to pay damages. A client may still wish to sue for the sake of principle, but the costs of such abstract satisfaction must be considered. Clearly there is nothing to be gained monetarily from a legal judgment against, say, one of the paraprofessional drug counselors who has committed the abuses against young female addicts described in this book. One can, however, hold the public or private agency the employs the counselor liable for his acts. The indigence of the individual offender is not an issue when one can collect from a state institution or its insurer, but there may be statutory limits on an institution's liability (cf. Jorgenson, 1990).

Malpractice without sexual contact. Schoener (1989b) provides a comprehensive list of damages that may be assessed in cases of sexual misconduct by therapists. These range from failure to diagnose and treat the client's condition to using drugs or alcohol with the client to exacerbating or precipitating emotional disorder. Many of these items, of course, would constitute malpractice with or without sexual contact and should be considered as possible causes of action throughout the extensive realm of boundary violations out of which sexual misconduct may arise.

Legal liability for unprofessional conduct, breach of trust, and/or boundary violations is not limited to cases of sexual acting out. (Indeed, some insurers are beginning to exclude or set limits on coverage for liability based on financial dealings with clients as well.) A psychotherapist may be held liable for carrying on a social relationship with a client outside the office in lieu of standard professional treatment, although the unique circumstances of a particular case have been determined to justify such conduct in the interest of the client (Wilkinson, 1981/82). A case in Great Britain that helped establish this precedent was *Landau v. Werner* (1961), in which a psychiatrist unsuccessfully tried to resolve the transference with a patient who had "fallen in love" with him by carrying on social visits (without sex) to make the termination less abrupt. The court decided that the psychiatrist's departure from accepted practice had constituted malpractice.

Mason (1976) sees the significance of this case in its application of the principle of conflict of interest to the therapeutic relationship. "*Landau v. Werner,*" he concludes, "in effect has outlawed [in Britain] conduct which confuses the patient as to the therapist's motives and thus undermines the therapeutically necessary feeling of trust in the therapist" (Mason, 1976, pp. 34–35). More broadly, "the case is interesting because it holds in substance that every act which a psychiatrist employs in dealing with his patients is subject to legal stricture" (Mason, 1976, p. 33).

In view of the concern expressed throughout this book about the inadvisability of referral as a panacea when the emotional interchange between therapist and client becomes confused or uncomfortable, it is of interest that the courts have seen fit to pass upon questions of termination and referral. Halleck (1980) summarizes the psychiatrist's liability in this area:

> The physician can never unilaterally sever a professional relationship with a patient when there is still a need for continuing medical attention without giving the patient reasonable notice and assisting the patient in obtaining continued care. If a physician does this, he is liable under the doctrine of abandonment. . . .
>
> There are probably many terminations of treatment related to the patient's financial situation or to his abrasive personality traits which cannot be justified ethically. They cannot be justified legally either if the psychiatrist simply announces to the patient that treatment will be terminated and makes no effort to explain the

reasons for this decision or to give the patient ample time to deal with the consequences of termination. (p. 107)

In fact, one of the grounds for the malpractice judgment in *Roy v. Hartogs* (1975) was that, shortly after the client terminated her sexual and therapeutic relationship with the psychiatrist, he refused to see her again or recommend another therapist for her when she phoned him in distress.

Other causes of action. Aside from malpractice, other legal grounds (causes of action) for a tort suit may be available to the sexually abused therapy client, especially when the therapist/defendant is not a psychiatrist or psychologist and thus is not governed by the criteria for malpractice established in those professions. These grounds include assault, fraud, negligence, and breach of contract.

In the case of encounter and sensitivity group therapies in which practices considered outside the bounds of standard psychotherapy (including physical contact) are advertised as an essential part of the "growth experience," the causes of action listed in the previous paragraph may be more relevant than malpractice when one is proceeding against a group leader who is not a psychiatrist or psychologist. Such an action may, however, prove more difficult to sustain than a malpractice suit against a professional therapist, since the group leader can assert the defenses of consent and privilege. The fact that the client has given informed consent rules out assault as a cause of action. "Privilege" refers to a qualified right to engage in certain kinds of physical contact that individuals are accorded by virtue of their status, for example, as physicians, police officers, or prison guards. How this doctrine may apply to unorthodox humanistic therapies remains to be decided (Mason, 1976).

The use of surrogate sexual partners for single clients in sex therapy does not present the same ethical and legal issues as does physical involvement with the client on the part of the therapist. To the extent that the use of surrogates is a legitimate therapeutic technique, it cannot be said to represent an abuse of trust. However, as the code of ethics of the American Association of Sex Educators, Counselors and Therapists (1980) makes clear, the sex therapist must not act as a surrogate or otherwise engage in sex with clients; nor may the partner surrogate act as a therapist.

The Ethical Basis of Liability: Second Thoughts

Roy v. Hartogs (1975) was a major breakthrough; it established a precedent for finding that sexual contact with a client constitutes malpractice because it violates the explicit ethical standards of the profession. However, the rationale with which the plaintiff bolstered her case was a double-edged one whose ramifications continue to be felt. Julie Roy relied heavily on the notion of misuse (or mismanagement) of transference, which required that she portray herself as the equivalent of a child who, when under her therapist's power, lacked autonomous will—a passive victim incapable of meaningful consent or refusal. Indeed, in a client-therapist sexual involvement the client, consenting or not, *is* a victim of the therapist's unethical behavior. Nonetheless, feminists as well as clinicians of other theoretical orientations have expressed unease about this image of infantile regression and helplessness that *Roy* and other cases have propagated, viewing the devaluation of the client's personal wholeness, autonomy, and free choice as a high price to pay for legal redress (cf. Clements, 1987). It would seem preferable to respect the client's capacity to make choices (unless otherwise demonstrated) even while insisting that the therapist make the choice to do therapy rather than to act out the therapist's or the client's sexual feelings.

Toward this end, the Program in Psychiatry and the Law at Massachusetts Mental Health Center has worked to articulate an alternate rationale for the accepted consensus that sexual involvement with a client is always unethical on the part of a therapist and is therefore a cause of action for malpractice. Commenting on the argument that "a patient experiencing transference feelings has an impaired capacity for consent, and therefore in some ways resembles a rape victim," Gutheil (1989b) takes a different approach:

> This legal model has several deficiencies. First, it seems that professionals who belong to a school of thought that rejects the idea of transference—behaviorists, or psychiatrists who provide only drug treatment—are being held to a standard of care they do not acknowledge. Although I know of no cases on this precise point, I believe that courts would probably hold all practitioners to the same standard regardless of theoretical orientation. I also doubt

that the malpractice model [based on transference] is sufficiently respectful of victims. It often implicitly or explicitly depicts the patient, usually a woman with a male therapist, as incompetent to consent to the relationship. When the patient is an adult and not psychotic, this is misleading and contributes subtly to the stigmatization of both women and the mentally ill.

I would prefer that the courts view sexual misconduct as a breach of a fiduciary (trust-based) relationship by the exercise of undue influence to take unfair advantage. This model has often served as a basis for defining ethical deviations. . . . Mental health professionals have a fiduciary relationship with their patients in which deep confidences are shared and close ties may develop. Their professional status also creates a power asymmetry. A professional who sexually exploits a patient is taking unfair advantage of a position of power and trust. This model does not imply that the patient is impaired or incapable of consenting; competent, autonomous decision-makers can be unduly influenced. (Similar considerations, incidentally, might apply to sexual abuse in other professional relationships.) (pp. 5–6)

Even under this model it can be argued that in psychotherapy the client may be especially vulnerable, the relationship of trust especially intense, and its violation especially damaging. Still, when seen in this light, such differences between psychotherapy and other professions become differences of degree rather than of kind, and unsettling questions can begin to be asked in other quarters (cf. Coleman, 1988). One reason for the popularity of the transference model in courtrooms and legislatures may be that it sets psychotherapy safely apart from other professions. Although behaviorists and psychopharmacologists may be drawn into the net by indiscriminate application of the transference model, there is little danger that attorneys will be.

The absurd lengths to which the transference model can be taken are exemplified by a case in which a psychologist's malpractice insurer sought a declaratory judgment as to whether its policy covered the psychologist's liability for sexual involvement with a patient. The trial court ruled in favor of the insurance company, finding that the sexual involvement was not covered by the policy because it was not part of the treatment. On appeal by the patient, an appellate court remanded the case, finding that the insurer could be liable for the psychologist's failure to recognize and properly manage the transference. The court ruled:

> It is the mishandling of transference, and not the resulting sexual conduct, which gives rise to the alleged malpractice. . . . The sexual acts are an incidental outgrowth of the primary malpractice, not the proximate cause. (*St. Paul Fire & Marine Insurance Co. v. Love*, 1989)

In this reification of the transference interpretation, what began as a rationale for judging sexual involvement with a patient unethical becomes itself the cause of action, while the actual fact of the abuse is dismissed as "incidental"!

There are ample reasons to insist on proper boundaries and reject a "friendship" model of the clinician-patient relationship without resorting to the theory of transference (Illingworth, 1988). The fiduciary model assumes that the competent, adult patient may well have reasons—unsound though they may be (as discussed in Chapter 2)—for wanting to seduce or be seduced by the clinician (Gutheil, 1989c). It holds the clinician liable for dereliction of responsibility, for self-interested exploitation, for exercise of undue influence, and for actions prejudicial to the patient's developing autonomy, trust, and interdependency in therapy (Illingworth, 1989; Stone, 1989). This puts the clinical and legal focus where it belongs—on the therapeutic alliance and how it may be strengthened, undermined, or violated. The American Psychiatric Association, in the 1989 edition of its ethics code, captures the essence of the undue-influence model:

> The psychiatrist should diligently guard against exploiting information furnished by the patient and should not use the unique position of power afforded him/her by the psychotherapeutic situation to influence the patient in any way not directly relevant to the treatment goals. (American Psychiatric Association, 1989, p. 4)

Contributory negligence. Although sexual contact with a client is always unethical and always malpractice, the fiduciary model does allow the client a degree of causal, if not moral, responsibility for the involvement. Thus, it leaves open the possibility that the damage award to a victimized client might be calculated in terms of comparative negligence, with the therapist's and client's contributions to the outcome weighed against each other. Would this be fair? Whatever the justice or injustice of this approach, it is not about to be implemented in the 1990s.

In 1986 a trial court did grant summary judgment (affirmed on appeal) in favor of a psychologist and his employer, a job counseling service, who were sued by a woman with whom the psychologist had formed an intimate personal relationship while he was counseling her. The appellate court ruled that "the client condoned the breach of contract, if any, and assumed the risk of wrongdoing, if any," that the psychologist committed. The client had known that the personal relationship lay outside the definition of the psychologist's duties, and the psychologist had made no effort to convince her otherwise (*Jacobsen v. Muller*, 1986). This decision, which takes respect for the client's autonomy beyond assigning contributory negligence to denying the cause of action altogether, runs counter to most recent case law in this area. The fact that the liaison took place in the context of job counseling rather than psychotherapy may have led the court to see the client as competent to deal with the counselor on equal terms. Even so, it seems unlikely that such a decision would have been rendered even a few years later.

A few years later a defendant psychiatrist did use contributory negligence as a defense in a malpractice case brought by a woman who claimed to have suffered post-traumatic stress disorder (including suicidality and inability to work) after having had a sexual relationship with the psychiatrist while she was in treatment with him. The psychiatrist claimed that the patient, who herself had been a psychotherapist with professional credentials, knew that a sexual involvement with a therapist was unethical and harmful. The parties settled for $500,000, which suggests that the defendant's claim of contributory negligence did not get him very far—unless the severity of the plaintiff's symptoms would otherwise have won her a larger settlement or damage award (*Doe v. Roe*, 1989).

A forensic psychiatrist experienced the dilemmas of apportioning causality, responsibility, and culpability when he was asked to serve as an expert witness for the defense in a case in which the defendant psychiatrist conceded that he had been negligent by having a sexual relationship with a patient. There was, however, an unusual wrinkle in the laws of the state in which these events had occurred. As distinct from comparative negligence (which would involve a proportionate reduction of liability), the law of that state stipulated that contributory negligence on the part of the patient was an absolute bar to recovery. Since the patient was a competent, nonpsychotic adult and a licensed professional therapist, the defense sought expert testimony to the effect that she had knowingly entered into an unethical relationship.

The psychiatrist approached by the defense was reluctant to testify in favor of a colleague who had practiced unethically. Moreover, he disapproved of a law that would allow such a practitioner to avoid liability because the patient had made a conscious, competent choice. At the same time, he believed that the defendant deserved the best defense he could get under existing law. In a kind of "informed consent" procedure, he shared his misgivings with the defense attorney, explaining that although he could not condone the defendant's conduct, he could truthfully testify that the patient had acted competently. On cross-examination, however, he would have to testify that the plaintiff's knowing participation did not (according to the standards of the profession) make the defendant's conduct any less unethical. The expert was retained by the defense and testified persuasively. The jury, after listening to him respectfully, awarded the plaintiff a large sum in damages. In essence, the jurors bypassed the anomalies of the law and expressed their outrage, thereby arriving at what was, in substance, a just verdict. This outcome was consistent with Gutheil's (1989b, p. 5) view that, "in today's climate, professionals usually cannot win such cases if the accusation is true."

Criminal Prosecution

Noted sex researchers Masters and Johnson (1976) proposed that the sexual exploitation of clients by psychotherapists be treated as a criminal rather than a civil matter:

> We feel that when sexual seduction of patients can be firmly established by due legal process, regardless of whether the seduction was initiated by the patient or the therapist, the therapist should initially be sued for rape rather than for malpractice; i.e., the legal process should be criminal rather than civil.

To date, however, the courts have not accepted this interpretation, and with good reason. Rape involves force, which is not at issue in the seduction of a patient by a therapist. Conceivably, therapists who exploit their patients' trust for sexual gratification might be charged under statutes recently enacted in several states, which broaden the definition of coercion in rape or sexual battery. However, when therapists have been convicted of rape, their conduct has been such as would be regarded as criminal without reference to the therapeutic relationship (Stone, 1976). A psychiatrist was sentenced to prison for having intercourse with patients after giving them electric shock treatment or injections of hypnotic drugs. Criminal as well as civil complaints were filed against a Massachusetts physician (one of the same physicians convicted of raping a nurse, as reported in Chapter 9) accused of molesting sleeping women in their hospital beds. Psychotherapists, like schoolteachers, have been convicted of statutory rape of underaged clients. Indeed, it is under the rubric of *statutory* rape that Masters and Johnson's proposal can best be understood, its rationale being that consent has as little meaning for a client in therapy as for a child. This interpretation, however, is subject to the same objections as the transference-based model of civil liability, inasmuch as the legal definition of a therapy client as the equivalent of a helpless child might prove to be antitherapeutic and even stigmatizing.

In addition to criminal sexual misconduct (rape or coercion), Schoener (1989d) lists several categories of existing criminal statutes which, depending on their application in a given state, might be used to prosecute a therapist for having sexual contact with a client—namely, sex during medical examination, misdemeanor by a licensed practitioner, wrongful representation, consumer fraud, insurance fraud, or income-tax fraud. Wyoming allows for a charge of sexual assault if the perpetrator uses any "position of authority to cause the victim to submit" (Schoener, 1989d, p. 330). Instead of singling out psychotherapists, this statute rightly recognizes that undue influence likewise may be exercised in other professional and personal relationships.

The emerging trend, however, is to enact statutes that make a therapist's sexual exploitation of a client specifically a criminal offense. This approach bypasses the questionable association with rape and makes therapist-client sex a separate public-policy issue. As of the end of 1989, such statutes had been enacted in six states:

California, Colorado, Maine, Minnesota, North Dakota, and Wisconsin. Other states (such as Massachusetts) were actively considering similar legislation.

Although these statutes vary in the scope of their application and in other specific provisions (cf. Appelbaum, 1990; Jorgenson, Randles, & Strasburger, in press; Schoener et al., 1989), the Minnesota law is most prominently cited as a model by advocates of criminalization in other states. Enacted in 1985, this law resembles the Minnesota law governing civil actions for malpractice in that it disallows consent as a defense. It differs from the civil law, however, in that it covers a less extensive list of sexual behaviors or activities (only actual sexual contacts, not requests for sex), has a shorter statute of limitations (three years instead of five), and sets a higher standard of evidentiary proof ("beyond a reasonable doubt" instead of "preponderance of the evidence"). On the other hand, it does allow for the use of Spreigl witnesses (previous victims). Moreover, the mere fact that the act occurred is enough to establish the felony; proof of damage is not necessary in a criminal prosecution. Under this law it is always a felony for a therapist to have sexual contact with a client *during a therapy session*. However, if the contact occurs either *between sessions during the period of therapy* or *after termination of therapy*, then a felony has been committed only if the client is found to have been "emotionally dependent" on the therapist or if there was "therapeutic deception" (that is, if the therapist claimed that sex was part of the treatment).

Those who worked for passage of this legislation in Minnesota, while generally pleased with the outcome, have expressed dissatisfaction with the provision requiring proof of emotional dependency or deception in cases where sexual contact occurred between therapy sessions (Schoener, 1989f). Whatever the overall merits of criminalization, the dubious distinction between sex during a session and sex between sessions represents an uneasy political compromise. Even more serious anomalies may come to light if other states rush to enact legislation without the careful consideration and consultation that occurred in Minnesota. The California law, for example, prohibits sex with a former client only when therapy is terminated primarily for the purpose of having a sexual affair, and even this is exempted from prosecution if a legitimate referral to another therapist is made. Thus, the law legitimizes a form of expedient behavior, prejudicial to the interests of therapy, that professional ethics codes condemn (Schoener, 1989f).

As of 1989, there had been eight known prosecutions under Minnesota's criminal statute. All of the defendants were male. They included four psychologists (one of whom was involved with chemical-dependency treatment programs), two other chemical-dependency counselors, a spiritual healer, and a minister with a counseling practice. Seven were convicted (some on related charges), and five were sentenced to varying terms in prison. One appealed his conviction. Although these cases constitute a very small proportion of actual instances of abuse since 1985, advocates of the law hope that they will have an exemplary deterrent effect (Schoener, 1989f).

Some of the arguments on both sides of the criminalization debate are pragmatic and bureaucratic (Appelbaum, 1990; Strasburger & Jorgenson, unpublished). Proponents argue that criminal prosecution is the only form of accountability to which unlicensed practitioners and those without "deep pockets" to pay malpractice claims can be held. They note that declaring sexual misconduct in therapy to be a crime makes available victims' compensation funds to pay for subsequent therapy and criminal-justice grants to fund education for practicing professionals, for counselors who work with victims or perpetrators, and for the public. Opponents counter that these funds are very modest in comparison with the malpractice-insurance coverage that is lost (under some policies) when a felony is committed. Furthermore, criminal prosecution may delay civil proceedings, while the victim/plaintiff gives up control of the case to the state prosecutor, and the defendant gets the benefit of a higher standard of proof. If fear of going to prison deters commission of the offense in the first place, it may also deter the admission of guilt that would lead to restitution.

Underlying these arguments are two divergent points of view about criminalization (Strasburger, 1990; Strasburger & Jorgenson, unpublished). Those who favor it see an urgent need for society to make a clear statement that a therapist's having sex with a client is so heinous and harmful that it must be outlawed. Such a statement, it is believed, will educate the public, bolster potential victims in resisting and reporting the abuse, and put practitioners on notice that the behavior will not be tolerated. If nothing else, the threat of imprisonment may deter professionals who are unmoved by malpractice suits or disciplinary action. Criminalization also is advocated as a way to empower victims and reduce the sense of shame and helplessness they may feel.

On the other hand, therapy for victims is not an accepted function of criminal law, and the deterrent effect is unproved. Those opposed to criminalization are concerned about the arbitrariness of singling out one particular dereliction of fiduciary responsibility as criminal, while sexual abuses in other professions, not to mention other breaches of contract, are not subject to prosecution. Such selectively punitive law-making sacrifices the consistency of the law to the clamor to declare a particular abuse politically abhorrent. From this viewpoint, it would be more equitable to punish sexual abuse in therapy as other severe breaches of contract are punished—namely, by civil litigation and by removing from the professions those who violate professional ethics (cf. Bursztajn & Illingworth, unpublished). To be effective, this policy would entail bringing all psychotherapists and counselors under licensure, but with licensing options expanded to make room for the full range of legitimate therapeutic philosophies and practices.

Some breaches of fiduciary responsibility—in business relationships, for example—are subject to criminal penalties. What is needed, therefore, instead of flurries of legislation in response to particular outrages, is a systematic reexamination of the regulation of fiduciary relationships. When does a breach of contract by a person with professional responsibility warrant criminal sanctions? What underlying principles should govern our treatment of these lapses of trust? In the absence of such an overhaul of the ethical underpinnings of our legal system, we would do well to exercise caution before yielding to the impulse to criminalize even an especially flagrant abuse.

Nonetheless, as Appelbaum (1990) concludes, the trend is likely to continue:

> . . . the criminalization of patient-therapist sex is an indication of popular impatience with the seeming difficulty that professional associations have had in stemming the tide of cases. Unless newer educational efforts are markedly more successful, we are likely to see responsibility for the problem increasingly assumed by legislatures. (p. 16)

Professional Sanctions

The appeals court in *Roy v. Hartogs* (1975) recommended that the case be considered for disciplinary action by the appropriate licensing boards and professional organizations. These agencies have not proved better equipped than the courts to impose deterrent sanctions; on the contrary, their ineffectiveness has contributed to resorting to the courts. Stone (1976, p. 260) found in these regulatory bodies "an almost total lack of capacity to act." Years later, the story is much the same (Appelbaum, 1990), with one variation. In the wake of the explosion of publicity and the clamor for redress of wrongs, professional disciplinary bodies are showing a disturbing capacity to act erratically, bending with the winds of public pressure.

We can consider briefly each of the major avenues of professional discipline.

Revocation or suspension of license. Although some mental health professions (other than psychiatry) are only beginning to establish licensing procedures, physicians, psychologists, and other professionals have had their licenses to practice revoked for sexual activity with patients. The California psychiatrist who was assessed $4.6 million in damages after he admitted having had sex with his patient (and who at the time had two similar suits pending against him) was suspended for one year by the State Board of Medical Quality Assurance. In 1971 the Kansas State Board of Examiners of Psychologists revoked a psychologist's certificate to practice after two female patients separately reported to the Board that the psychologist had tried to seduce them. When the revocation (after a stay ordered by a lower court) was upheld by the state's highest court, the psychologist discontinued his private practice (*Morra v. State Board of Examiners of Psychologists*, 1973; Sinnett & Thetford, 1975).

The statutory authority granted to licensing boards varies greatly from one jurisdiction to another. An abuse that calls for revocation in one state may go unchecked in a neighboring state—or in a different year. Boards are known for blowing hot and cold, a pattern that does not inspire confidence in the justice of their proceedings. In 1989, for example, the Massachusetts Board of Registration in Medicine, after years of relative inaction, acted in what many reputable physicians considered a peremptory manner against a physician whose case was described briefly in Chapter 6, as well as against nine psychiatrists charged with sexual misconduct. These cases raised serious concerns about due process in nonjudicial proceedings.

At the same time, it is clear that a lack of professional standards and accountability among unlicensed practitioners contributes to the incidence of sexual abuse in therapy. As an initial response to this situation, Minnesota has created a Board of Unlicensed Mental Health Service Providers to regulate and study the diverse groups not presently licensed in the state (the largest of which is chemical-dependency counselors) and recommend further action.

Disciplinary action by professional associations. Professional associations, lacking even the modest and inconsistent legal authority of licensing boards, are even less capable of acting. In general, they have been easily intimidated by the threat of being sued by a therapist charged with a breach of ethics (Stone, 1976), although that climate is changing as members vocally demand reform. Theoretically, at least, sanctions imposed by professional societies can adversely affect employment opportunities and patient referrals. This occurred in the case (discussed at the end of Chapter 5) of two eminent members of the American Psychoanalytic Association.

Sanctions on the job. Except with a private practitioner, a sexually abused client may be able to gain redress (and protect others from abuse) by filing a complaint with the agency employing the therapist or counselor. One must be prepared, though, to face the inconsistent policies and procedures that different institutions have evolved for responding to such complaints. (Consider the various dispositions that might be made, on different campuses, of the accusation that a university professor had taken sexual advantage of students.) One can also expect to run up against the tendency of many administrators to suppress information in order to "protect their own," either out of personal loyalty or out of a fear of the consequences of exposure for the organization, the department, or the administrator. On the other hand, the legal sanctions discussed in the final section of this chapter are causing more and more organizations to be appropriately responsive to complaints, since the consequences of a coverup are coming to be worse than those of admitting the problem and cleaning house. In any case, a complainant who fails to obtain satisfaction at this level has the option of pursuing the complaint through higher administrative and, ultimately, legal channels.

False accusations. To date, false accusations are believed to represent only a very small percentage of all claims of sexual abuse by therapists (Gutheil, 1989a, 1989b; Schoener & Milgrom, 1989a). However, amid the public clamor for rectification of long-suppressed wrongs and the awarding of huge damage awards, the percentage of false or misleading claims may not remain so small. As Gonsiorek (1989c) cautions:

> . . . in the past, it would have been a very rare occurrence for a client to file false complaints against the therapist. The entire system was so weighted to vindicate the therapist, that such a client would have had to have severe reality-testing problems to make a false complaint. . . . As the system becomes more equitable, however, this predictable pattern *may* break down, and it is conceivable that the future may hold an increase in false or exaggerated complaints against therapists. . . . If this balance shifts as a result of the recent changes to assure accountability and equitable outcome, the process of investigating complaints by clients about therapists is likely to become significantly more difficult and complex. (p. 90)

This apt warning is especially troubling in view of the fact that some therapists are losing their malpractice insurance as well as their license to practice long before they have their day in court. While waiting years for the case to come to trial, the therapist has been involuntarily retired by the insurer's and licensing board's reflexive reaction to the mere accusation of wrongdoing. If the therapist is innocent, then this chain of events is a tragic one with numerous other innocent victims, including clients deprived of the therapist's services.

Solutions to this dilemma will not be easily reached, but they clearly involve a review of due process in administrative proceedings and some introduction of quasi-judicial safeguards. (Insurers and regulatory bodies need to take into account thresholds of plausibility and corroborating evidence.) This devastating scenario also underlines the need for clinicians to implement the principles of scrupulous practice, careful clinical management, discriminating documentation, and regular supervision and consultation (Gutheil, 1989a).

Duties and Dilemmas of the Treating Therapist

The therapist who treats a victim of admitted or alleged sexual abuse by a previous therapist has, in addition to the normal responsibilities of clinical care, special ethical and legal obligations that require sensitive handling in the interest of the client, the accused therapist, the current therapist, and society (in particular, other potential victims). These responsibilities sometimes are or appear to be in conflict. The following guidelines highlight a few of the major clinico-legal dilemmas faced by the treating therapist.

Mandatory reporting. A therapist may learn of alleged sexual abuse by another therapist when the victim speaks of it during a therapy session; the therapist may also learn about it from colleagues or while treating the abusing therapist. For the sake of public safety, as well as the resolution of individual experiences, it would be ideal if the victims or their subsequent therapists always reported the abuse to the appropriate authorities. Yet studies have shown that very small percentages of both clients and subsequent therapists report therapist-client sexual contacts (Bouhoutsos et al., 1983; Gartrell, Herman, Olarte, Feldstein, & Localio, 1987). Clients must overcome feelings of embarrassment and shame, concerns about privacy, fears of retaliation or of offending or harming the abusing therapist (about whom they may still have ambivalent feelings), mistrust of any subsequent therapist, and a realistic expectation that they may not be believed. The professional literature and case presentations are replete with horror stories of clients whose reports were ignored by complacent, insensitive regulatory boards or ethics committees (Choras, 1990; Gartrell et al., 1987). As for therapists, they have been all too ready to accept their colleagues' rationalizations, thereby devaluing and even negating clients' experiences and viewpoints (Jordan, 1990). At the same time, therapists have valid reasons for refraining from reporting—namely, a respect for the client's confidentiality and autonomy and a concern about possible negative effects of reporting on the client's well-being (Stone, 1983).

In order to hold offenders accountable and prevent further abuses, some observers (e.g., Gartrell et al., 1987) have proposed mandatory reporting of all complaints to state licensing authorities and/or professional ethics committees. Although such action might prove prejudicial to therapists against whom unsubstantiated claims were made, a therapist probably would be better off with a confidential report to a responsible authority (even with the leaks and other lapses of due process that do occur) than with gossip transmitted to the kangaroo court of the professional grapevine. If multiple complaints were filed independently about the same therapist, a regulatory board would have a good basis for proceeding. Some therapists, meanwhile, favor mandatory reporting because it would take the decision about reporting out of their hands.

Several states have enacted statutes that mandate reporting, or at least informing the abused client of the option to report (Appelbaum, 1990; Strasburger, Jorgenson, & Randles, in press). Minnesota requires that the therapist report the perpetrator irrespective of the client's wishes, although the client may choose to remain anonymous. In order to avoid a disempowering experience for the client, the therapist must forewarn the client of the reporting requirement, saying, "You can tell me everything. Just leave out the therapist's name, and I won't have to report it." This type of warning, however, does not seem conducive to the feeling of safety and to the free and open disclosure that therapy is meant to encourage.

At the opposite extreme from Minnesota's strict reporting statute is California's law, which stipulates that the therapist give any client who alleges sexual contact with a previous therapist a brochure prepared by the state (State of California, 1990) that outlines the client's rights and options for action. This is a useful step, but a limited one. It requires the therapist only to discuss the brochure with the client, not to report the alleged offense.

Wisconsin takes the middle course of requiring the therapist to seek the client's consent to making a report. The report may not identify the client unless the client consents to being identified. The licensing board and prosecutors will not investigate on the basis of one anonymous report, but will inform the therapist of further complaints against the same individual. Such confirmation can validate the client's experience and encourage the client to act. Therapists who make reports in good faith are immune from liability.

Strasburger et al. (in press) conclude that Wisconsin's approach strikes a good balance between protecting the public interest and respecting the confidentiality and decision-making autonomy of the victim. Mandatory reporting without the consent of the client may be experienced as still another violation by the abused individual. As

Levenson (1987, p. 529) cautions, the ethical obligation to report "is not an absolute one. . . ." It must be weighed against the ethical duty and clinical mission of nurturing the client's autonomy.

"Informed consent" to litigation. Political considerations, valid though they may be, should not be allowed to compromise the therapeutic role of helping the client discover what is in his or her best interest. As much as the subsequent therapist may think it healthy, assertive, or socially useful for the abused client to take action against the abuser, a therapist who urges this course on the client becomes an advocate for what may be a traumatic choice. This is true whether the action contemplated is civil, criminal, or administrative, but it is especially true for the adversarial process of litigation. Litigation, like any other procedure, has risks as well as benefits, and the client needs to be advised of these. According to Gutheil (1990), the risks include (a) stress experienced over an extended period of time; (b) reliving the trauma and victimization in a public, hostile, nontherapeutic atmosphere; (c) personal attacks by the defendant's attorney; and (d) public exposure not only of the sexual involvement, but of one's therapeutic records and life history (cf. Bates & Brodsky, 1988; Walker & Young, 1986). Calling this consciousness-raising "informed consent" is stretching the term somewhat, since litigation is an action the client undertakes independently as opposed to a therapeutic procedure to which the client must consent. But the "informing" aspect remains essential. Ideally it would be the client's attorney who would brief the client about the risks of litigation, but the attorney cannot be counted on to do so. Therefore, as with other issues in life, the therapist is left to help prepare the client for what lies ahead, irrespective of the therapist's personal or ideological preferences. As we said in Chapter 8 (in connection with "coming out" as a homosexual), it is the client who must walk the lonesome road afterward.

Avoiding dual agency. When the treating therapist actively assists a client in the legal process—for example, by testifying in court about the harmful effects of the prior therapist's abuse—both the confidentiality and objectivity of the therapist's role may be compromised. Once the therapist volunteers any information obtained in therapy (through the client's waiver of confidentiality), the entire therapeutic interchange is open to intrusion by hostile cross-examination. Moreover, the therapist's role is not necessarily compatible with that of ally in an adversarial process. Stone (1983, 1989) points a way out of this dilemma by proposing that an independent consultant be hired, as needed, to assess damages and report to the authorities. If the court or licensing board requires corroboration of the evaluator's findings by the treating therapist, the patient can give the evaluator access to the therapist's records, which the evaluator can testify are consistent with the evaluator's findings. Meanwhile, the client is assured of the therapist's continuing availability in a clinical capacity.

Personal vulnerability of the subsequent therapist. When a subsequent therapist is perceived to have instigated a client's claim against a previous therapist, the defendant's attorney may seek to discredit the treating therapist, who is then drawn into the adversarial nexus. This was exactly what happened in a 1989 Colorado case that erupted into controversy within the American Psychiatric Association (APA) and split the organization into opposing factions (Thompson, 1989). In this case psychiatrist Jason Richter was found negligent for having had a sexual affair with a woman who had recently been his patient, although the award was reduced by 18 percent by a finding of contributory negligence. As part of their defense, Richter's attorneys charged that Martha Gay, the psychiatrist who subsequently treated the patient, had prompted the lawsuit and was prolonging the patient's recovery—that is, exacerbating the damages—through improper treatment. To demonstrate therapeutic bias on Gay's part, the defense asked questions designed to reveal unresolved personal issues that might lead Gay to seek revenge against male therapists. Gay successfully fought to have the personal questions disallowed, just as the patient successfully opposed Richter's efforts to place in evidence the notes of her subsequent therapy with Gay (a precedent-setting decision). Claiming, however, that it was a conflict of interest for the APA's insurer to support both Richter's defense and her own, Gay hired her own attorney at a reported cost of $30,000.

Gay's supporters, including the Association of Women Psychiatrists and the Colorado Psychiatric Society, expressed concern that the APA's insurer was funding an intimidating assault on female psychiatrists who treated patients sexually exploited by previous therapists. Richter countered that Gay was challenging his constitutional right to an effective defense. This complicated and regrettably nasty case not only illustrates the egregious lengths to which attorneys will go to discredit an opposing witness; it also underscores the need for subsequent treating therapists to protect both themselves and their patients' therapy from such adversarial intrusion. Avoiding dual agency and obtaining a forensic consultation are two recommended steps in that direction.

Organizational Liability

Just as it was possible to sue a clinician for malpractice involving sexual contact before state statutes explicitly authorizing such suits were enacted, so one could sue the clinician's employer as well as the clinician. Medical and other professional malpractice suits typically draw in institutions (e.g., hospitals) as well as individuals, and suits brought for sexual exploitation are no exception. When a client sees a therapist or counselor at an agency, the client is not hiring this clinician independently; the clinician serves at the pleasure of the agency administrators and board of directors.

Even so, in order to clarify public policy and institutional responsibilities in this area, Minnesota has enacted a statute providing for employer liability and specifying the omissions for which employers may be held liable. According to this law, an employer of psychotherapists will not be held liable in civil actions resulting from sexual abuse of clients if the employer fulfills three requirements:

1. Check backgrounds of prospective employees.
2. Respond to background inquiries from other employers.
3. Take action when a client complains. (Sanderson, 1989b, p. 147)

Although these particular duties are not stipulated by statute in other states, they represent a good baseline for employers anywhere who seek to avoid liability by meeting their ethical responsibilities to prospective clients.

If no specific laws or regulations govern the operation of an agency in a particular jurisdiction, then the normal criterion for non-negligent performance holds—namely, reasonable and proper care according to the standards of the industry. To be safe from liability, it is best to interpret this standard on the strict side. Find out how similar agencies in your region are interpreting it and what safeguards they are employing for liability prevention.

Agencies are not liable for every peccadillo of their staff. If an incident occurs, a lawsuit may be brought with or without adequate grounds. Nonetheless, judges (especially at the appellate level) as well as investigators representing insurers, professional bodies, or state regulatory authorities usually will recognize that the administration cannot follow staff members around after work and police their lives outside the agency. Investigators will ask, on the other hand, whether reasonable steps (as defined by law or custom) have been taken to prevent or stop the abuse. In other words, know whom you are employing, and provide proper supervision and monitoring so that you will know what is going on. Specifically, the following precautions are essential:

First, the agency must have a written policy that is unambiguously clear, specific, and enforceable. The policy should be presented to and signed by every new employee upon hiring and placed in the employee's permanent file. The policy must be formulated with a view toward meeting accepted standards. For example, the agency cannot independently set an arbitrary time limit post-termination after which it is permissible for a clinician to see an ex-client socially. Increasingly, the agency's freedom of action on such questions is constrained by emerging statute law, case law, and professional ethics codes.

Second, the agency should have documented in-services at least twice a year on clinical, ethical, and policy issues pertaining to sexual contact with clients, including transference and countertransference, fiduciary responsibility, undue influence, maintenance of appropriate boundaries, ethical principles of the profession(s), documentation and consultation, professional and criminal sanctions, and civil liability for individuals and organizations.

Third, the administration must be able to intervene before or as transgressions occur. By following the guidelines for supervision in Chapter 6 and in the sources cited there, the agency will be in the best position to observe and respond to boundary violations before these reach the point of outright sexual contact. It need hardly be said that the agency must promptly follow up on any reasonable indications for suspicion.

For a more detailed checklist of administrative safeguards, see Schoener (1989a).

Although judicial decisions (especially in tort law) are never fully consistent, recent case law confirms that agencies and institutions will, on the whole, be held to reasonable standards of negligence. In *Birkner v. Salt Lake County* (1989), for example, the Supreme Court of Utah ruled that a county mental health clinic was not liable for an employed therapist's sexual misconduct because the misconduct did not fall within the time, place, nature, and purpose of the therapist's employment. However, the court found that the county could be liable for negligent supervision of the therapist if such negligence could be proved. The importance of responsible, vigilant supervision at all levels of an organization cannot be overstated (cf. Bursztajn, 1990).

11
Guidelines

Implicit and explicit in this discussion of sexual dilemmas faced by the helping professional have been the principles of Reality Therapy (Glasser, 1965) and Rational-Emotive Therapy (Ellis & Harper, 1975), augmented by Values Clarification (Simon et al., 1972). We have emphasized the ever-present possibility of choice regardless of past experiences and insistent emotional pressures, the need to understand the "givens" of a situation and to make realistic choices within them, the importance of rational thinking in enabling one to separate the real opportunities and necessities of life from the "musts," "shoulds," and "if onlys" of wishful and self-punishing fantasy, and the essential role of supportive relationships and full, open communication in helping one clarify issues and take responsibility for acting. These themes are developed and expanded upon in the sources cited.

A problem-solving exercise that combines these approaches is set forth in detail in *Burnout* (Edelwich with Brodsky, 1980, pp. 227–230) and in *Consider the Alternative* (Silverstein, 1977, pp. 81–88). It involves identifying the problem in concrete terms, brainstorming as many solutions as possible, categorizing them ("most likely," "most desirable," "more than 50/50 chance of success," "less than 50/50 chance of success," "least desirable"), weighing the costs and benefits of each solution, making value judgments, choosing a course of action, and publicly committing oneself to act within a specified time. The exercise lends itself to demonstrations in classes and workshop and therapy groups, where participants (in a model of the mutual support that can be generated among friends and co-workers) support one another in devising solutions and keeping their commitments to act. This problem-solving procedure is applicable to any seemingly irresolvable stalemate in one's daily experience. It is as useful in confronting the undercurrents of sexuality in one's relations with clients and colleagues as in coping with the discontents that contribute to job burnout.

With respect to the helping professional's work-related sexual dilemmas, the guidelines that follow summarize the ethical, therapeutic, and policy issues discussed in this book and the approaches recommended. Chapter references are included for locating the full consideration of these questions in the text. Readers who believe that the book as a whole errs on the side of prescriptiveness may find an even greater tendency toward simplification in this condensation and abstraction of what has been presented. Our intention, however, is not at all to deny the complexity of the problems considered; it is, rather, to bring them into focus so that they can be seen with some clarity. Clinicians of varying levels of training, agency staff members, supervisors, trainers, administrators, and educators welcome concreteness in the presentation of clinical and experiential issues. In providing what busy practitioners in the field are seeking, we do not mean to tempt them—and do not expect them—to leave their critical judgment behind.

This, then, is a distillation of the preceding chapters:

What are the fundamental principles to keep in mind concerning feelings of attraction and aversion to clients? (Chapters 6, 7)
  A. Personal reactions to clients are normal and inevitable and need not be repressed, denied, or explained away.
  B. Whether or not one acts on such feelings is a choice; to refrain from acting them out in an unprofessional manner is a responsibility.

What limits on involvement with clients (and former clients) should clinicians observe? (Chapter 6)
  A. Physical contact, where appropriate at all, should be limited to that which is therapeutically supportive without having erotic overtones. Nothing should be done in private that could not be done in public.
  B. Social contact should be limited to friendly greetings on occasions such as Christmas and birthdays or on chance meetings with a client. It should not extend to planned get-togethers or to extratherapeutic involvement in clients' management of their

lives (e.g., lending money). Dinners with clients should be avoided. Lunches (except where ruled out by the nature of the therapy) may be acceptable in agency settings as a matter of convenience only.

C. Therapy and counseling should be conducted only at appropriately sanctioned times and places.

D. Financial dealings with clients (including unpaid therapy, accumulation of credit, barter and employment arrangements, and the use of "inside" information obtained from a client) compromise the therapeutic relationship and should therefore be avoided.

E. Follow-up with former clients should be on a strictly professional basis and should be open to supervision. On that basis one can be accessible to follow-up calls and visits from clients even when the client does not have a specific therapeutic agenda.

F. Self-disclosure should be limited to superficial pleasantries (e.g., tastes in food, entertainment, vacation spots). It should not extend to self-revelation in sensitive areas such as one's income, social life, and sexual involvements. One who is in the employ of an agency need not justify one's credentials to clients.

Are there ever any extenuating circumstances that justify a helping professional's having sexual relations with a client? (Chapter 5)

A. No.

In what sense is it legitimate to use "seductive" techniques with a client and to manipulate the power inherent in one's presence and position as a clinician? (Chapters 2, 3)

A. Both of the following conditions must hold:
  1. That there be no sexual acting out and not the slightest hint of future sexual availability on the part of the clinician.
  2. That the "seduction" be not for the clinician's erotic or ego-gratification, but for the therapeutic benefit of the client—that is, to elicit constructive behavior and encourage openness to growth.

What ethical considerations argue for placing intimate personal relationships with former clients off limits? (Chapter 5)

A. The therapeutic exchange may be compromised by self-aggrandizing behavior (including subtle bribery and avoidance of difficult issues) motivated by the expectation or hope of a love affair after termination.

B. The client is denied future therapeutic support (if and when needed) from the therapist who becomes a lover. The client may also come to distrust therapists in general.

C. It is difficult almost to the point of impossibility to make the transition from the unreciprocated knowledge and unequal power of a therapeutic relationship to the full equality and mutuality of an intimate personal relationship.

D. A clinician who uses privileged access to vulnerable people for recruitment of personal contacts (even if only after termination) may not be able to provide the strength, safety, and supportive neutrality that are of the essence of the therapeutic role.

Are there ever any exceptions to the inadvisability of sexual relationships with former clients? (Chapter 5)

A. Whether there is much or any latitude depends on the clinician's field of practice. In general, it is more difficult for a physician than for a nurse, and virtually impossible for a psychotherapist, to shed the professional role and its responsibilities. Love affairs between teachers and ex-students are not thought to represent an ethical issue, since the student normally outgrows the inequality and vulnerability that existed with respect to the teacher.

B. In any field there are very occasional, extraordinary cases of genuine courtship between a clinician and a former client. Those who believe themselves to be involved in such a courtship must subject themselves to rigorous self-questioning and the supportive scrutiny of others as checks against rationalization. They must also be prepared to undergo the scrutiny of employers, professional ethics committees, state licensing boards, and/or civil and criminal courts.

What avenues of consultation are available to the clinician for dealing with feelings of attraction or aversion that threaten to undermine a professional relationship with a client? (Chapters 6, 7)

    A. Supervision.

    B. Peer support.

    C. Professional consultation.

What should one do—and not do—when one is attracted to a client or when a client acts seductively? (Chapter 6)

    A. DO—

      . . . acknowledge your own feelings.

      . . . separate your personal feelings from dealings with the client.

      . . . confide in your supervisor, peers, or therapist.

      . . . set limits while giving the client a safe space for self-expression.

      . . . express non-sexual caring.

      . . . confront the issue straightforwardly.

      . . . explore the client's behavior therapeutically.

    B. DON'T—

      . . . make the client's problems your own.

      . . . give your problems to the client.

      . . . be rejecting.

      . . . be drawn into answering personal questions or giving the client other "double messages."

      . . . "refer out."

When is it appropriate to share with the client one's perception of disruptive sexual undercurrents in a clinical relationship? (Chapter 6)

    A. The client's seductive manifestations may be confronted directly with the client as a therapeutic issue.

    B. One's own feelings of attraction should be worked through with supervisor, peers, therapist, or counselor rather than communicated to the client.

    C. A persistent attraction that appears in some degree mutual may need to be talked over with the client, but only after one has reestablished one's clinical bearings through supervisory or peer consultation. It may be best to speak with the client in the supervisor's presence.

On what grounds can it be considered an error to "refer out" clients who arouse one's dislike, disapproval, or discomfort? (Chapter 7)

   A. Everyone has "human feelings" of outrage and disgust, including the clinician receiving the referral.
   B. "Unconditional positive regard" is a learned therapeutic stance, not a natural, automatic personal feeling.
   C. A public agency is open to all comers.
   D. Unnecessary referrals are an abdication of responsibility. There may not be a more suitable clinician available to take the case. The client may suffer iatrogenic damage from delay, discontinuity, and feelings of rejection. Both the client and clinician are denied the experience of working out uncomfortable issues.
   E. There are no "professional experts" in such problematic areas as wife battering and child molestation, although intake screening and specialized consultation (when available) can be helpful. A professional is someone who is paid for services and is accountable for performance.
   F. One cannot anticipate all the issues that may arise in treatment. One must be prepared to deal with unsettling revelations at any stage of a therapeutic relationship.
   G. Working with a difficult client may help prevent a recurrence of the abhorrent behavior, as well as contributing to the clinician's professional growth.

How can one best work with clients whom one might otherwise be inclined to refer elsewhere? (Chapter 7)

   A. Seek support from supervisor, peers, or professional consultant.
   B. Treat the client, not the victim.
   C. Make contracts setting limits on the client's acting out in therapy.
   D. When dealing with unfamiliar problems, bring to bear specialized resources in a team approach rather than abandoning the primary therapeutic involvement.

What precautions can a clinician take to reduce the risk of assault by a client? (Chapter 3)

   A. Do not assume lightly that a client will not be assaultive. Evaluate on the basis of all relevant and available information, including history and current behavior.
   B. Do not overestimate the value of professional training in enabling

one to predict or prevent violent behavior. There is always a degree of uncertainty.

C. Where possible, structure interactions so that clients will not have reason to believe they can get away with violence. Whenever there is judged to be a significant risk of assault, it is advisable to see the client conjointly with a colleague.

What clients can legitimately be referred to another clinician or agency? (Chapter 7)

A. A client with whom the clinician is or has been personally acquainted (e.g., a friend, employee, neighbor).

B. A client who has victimized the clinician or a family member or close associate of the clinician.

C. A client who presents a threat of physical assault which, given available resources, cannot be neutralized by having conjoint sessions.

D. A client who, after all other remedies have been exhausted, is likely (in the judgment of the clinician's supervisor) to be harmed by continued involvement with the clinician.

What is the role of a supervisor in helping clinicians deal with feelings of attraction or aversion to clients? (Chapters 6, 7)

A. To legitimize the clinician's feelings while working through resistances to particular clients and categories of clients.

B. To support clinicians in their professional responsibilities without assuming the functions of a personal therapist.

C. To hold conjoint sessions where advisable to work out issues with the client and clinician together.

D. To counsel clinicians or trainees out of the field when they show a persistent inability to differentiate personal feelings from professional responsibilities.

E. To meet the needs of individual clinicians while fulfilling one's responsibilities to the agency and its clients.

What modes of supervision are used to observe the sexual dynamics of the client-clinician relationship? (Chapter 6)

A. Blind supervision.

B. One-way mirror.

C. Audiotape.
D. Videotape.

How can one best advise clients on sexual questions that commonly arise in therapy and counseling? (Chapter 8)
  A. Limit intervention to areas of clinical concern instead of imposing one's own agenda on the client.
  B. Give the client support in questioning choices rather than automatic validation. For example, with the homosexual client who must decide whether or not to "come out," explore carefully the probable consequences of both alternatives.
  C. Frame alternatives in terms of concrete choices rather than global self-identification—for example, "Do I want to act on my attraction to this individual?" rather than "Am I a homosexual?"

Why is it not useful to attempt to match client to clinician in terms of sex, race, sexual preference, clinical history, or other personal characteristics? (Chapter 8)
  A. The professional therapeutic role is different from peer support.
  B. Helping professionals can develop empathy that transcends differences between people.
  C. It is impossible to take into account all of the potentially relevant variables that set people apart (e.g., age, socioeconomic status, educational level, ethnic background).
  D. A team approach can be used when special knowledge is needed.
  E. Clients benefit from positive models of both sexes.
  F. Matching has not been shown to result in better therapeutic outcomes.

Is there any justification for discriminatory hiring of clinicians on the basis of personal characteristics such as homosexuality? (Chapter 8)
  A. No, although one who flaunts one's lifestyle (homosexual or otherwise) on the job may bring about undesirable consequences for oneself as well as for clients.

On what grounds is it good policy (and on what grounds is it not) to segregate clients from one another in group treatment settings? (Chapter 8)
  A. Coed treatment, especially in residential facilities serving adolescents and young adults, is inadvisable because clients need to

deal with survival issues before taking risks in relationships with peers (as opposed to trained clinicians) of the opposite sex.

B. It is not necessary to segregate perpetrators of abominable crimes (e.g., child murder) to spare them the verbal abuse of other residents or inmates. The institution's responsibility is limited to protecting residents from physical abuse and seeing that staff members do not engage in verbal cruelty or other antitherapeutic behavior.

C. The institution's responsibility to protect residents from coerced homosexuality does not justify *a priori* discriminatory treatment of avowed homosexuals. Homosexuals have the same rights and responsibilities as other residents. Homosexuals who manifest disruptive behavior may, like other residents, be disciplined, isolated, or removed from the facility on the basis of their actions.

How should an agency deal with intimacies between staff members? (Chapter 9)

A. Regulation of staff members' personal lives is difficult to enforce and may be resented as an invasion of privacy and an infringement of choice. However, the agency may properly concern itself with the effects of staff romances on job performance and client services, effects which may include favoritism in hiring, promotion, and evaluation; polarization around personal dynamics; and jealousies felt by clients.

What three levels of sexual approaches may occur among staff members? (Chapter 9)

A. Flirtatious banter, ranging from the innocuous to the insidious.

B. Social invitations leading to a dating relationship.

C. Harassment in the form of lewd remarks or gestures, uninvited physical contact, or attempted extortion of sex as a quid pro quo.

What course of action is open to an individual who is subjected to sexual harassment on the job? (Chapter 9)

A. Document the incident in writing as thoroughly and precisely as possible.

B. Report the incident officially to immediate supervisor.

C. If no action is taken, take the complaint to successively higher levels of administration.

Who is responsible—causally, ethically, and legally—for the occurrence of sexual contact between a clinician and a client? (Chapters 2, 10)

A. In the case of a competent adult client who consents to the sexual contact, both parties contribute to bringing about this outcome. Understanding the dynamics of their interaction can be useful in preventing future occurrences.

B. Nonetheless, the clinician is always ethically responsible for refraining from sexual contact with a client. This ethical responsibility is undiminished by the client's initiation of or consent to the contact.

C. As a rule, the clinician is held legally responsible irrespective of the client's initiation or consent, although in some jurisdictions the award of damages may be reduced by a finding of contributory negligence on the part of the client.

What does a client who has been seduced by a therapist need to prove in court to win a judgment for malpractice? (Chapter 10)

A. That the therapist had a duty to care for the client (i.e., that a professional relationship existed).

B. That the alleged sexual contact did occur.

C. That the client suffered damage directly resulting from the therapist's unethical conduct.

Are malpractice awards arising from sexual involvement with clients covered by the clinician's liability insurance? (Chapter 10)

A. Often they are not (especially in states where such misconduct is treated as a felony), or else there is a modest cap (e.g., $25,000) on coverage.

Is a clinician subject to criminal prosecution for having sexual contact with a client? (Chapter 10)

A. Yes, in a growing number of states. As of the end of 1989, six states (California, Colorado, Maine, Minnesota, North Dakota, Wisconsin) had made it a criminal offense for a clinician to have sexual contact with a client, irrespective of the client's consent. As with civil liability, depending on the state and the circumstances, a clinician may also be prosecuted for having sex with a former client.

B. Even in states where therapist-client sex has not been made specifically a felony, a therapist may be prosecuted under existing criminal law for sex during medical examination, misdemeanor by a licensed practitioner, wrongful representation, consumer fraud, insurance fraud, income-tax fraud, or (in Wyoming) taking advantage of a position of authority for the purpose of sexual coercion.

How does criminal law differ from civil law with respect to sexual exploitation of clients by clinicians? (Chapter 10)

A. As a rule, criminal law sets a higher standard of evidentiary proof ("beyond a reasonable doubt" instead of "preponderance of the evidence").

B. As a rule, criminal law does not require proof of damages. The mere commission of the act is a crime.

C. Subject to state-by-state variations, there may be other differences with respect to the statute of limitations, the scope of activities covered (solicitation of sex without actual contact may be actionable, but not prosecutable), the types of evidence allowed into testimony, and the applicability of the law to sex after termination of therapy.

What extra-judicial professional sanctions may be applied against a therapist who sexually exploits clients? (Chapter 10)

A. Revocation or suspension of license to practice.

B. Disciplinary action by professional associations.

C. Loss of employment or other sanctions by employing agency.

What are some clinico-legal dilemmas faced by a therapist who treats a victim of sexual abuse by a previous therapist? (Chapter 10)

A. The treating therapist has an ethical (and sometimes legal) duty to report any complaint of unethical conduct by another therapist. At the same time, the therapist has an ethical and clinical responsibility to respect the client's confidentiality and decision-making autonomy.

B. Although the treating therapist may want the abusing therapist to be held accountable and may think it beneficial for the client to take action, the therapist must also consider the harmful consequences the client risks by reporting, litigating, or prosecuting. As with other issues considered in therapy, the therapist's job is not to exhort, but to inform, so that the client can freely and knowledgeably choose a course of action.

C. If the treating therapist testifies in court as to the damage suffered by the client, the confidentiality of therapy is sacrificed and the therapist's role compromised. It is preferable to avoid such "dual agency" by retaining an independent evaluator to assess the client's condition.

D. A treating therapist who testifies on behalf of an abused client may also be subjected to intrusive investigation and hostile cross-examination aimed at discrediting both the testimony and the therapy.

What three steps does Minnesota's model law require an employer of psychotherapists to take to avoid being held liable for an employee's sexual abuse of a client? (Chapter 10)

A. Check backgrounds of prospective employees.

B. Respond to background inquiries from other employers.

C. Take action when a client complains.

What are the key precautions an agency must take to avoid liability for sexual misconduct by its employees? (Chapter 10)

A. Formulate a written policy that is clear, specific, enforceable, and consistent with industry standards and legal requirements. This policy should be signed by every new employee upon hiring.

B. Hold documented in-services at least twice a year on clinical, ethical, and policy issues related to sexual dynamics between clinicians and clients.

C. Implement hiring, supervision, and monitoring practices that make timely intervention possible.

D. Investigate promptly when there is any reasonable indication for suspicion.

In addition to these guidelines for clinicians and supervisors, there are several broader areas in which the "sexual dilemmas" explored here should be addressed by individuals, institutions, and society.

Training. The near-unanimous testimony of helping professionals that their training did not prepare them adequately for the stresses and challenges of a sexual nature that they would face on the job should be cause for concern among educators in fields such as psychiatry, psychology, social work, medicine, nursing, and teaching. Ethical prescriptions alone are not enough. Students need to work through their personal reactions to the sexual questions that will arise for them in practice.

Pope et al. (1986) and Borys and Pope (1989) make detailed recommendations to improve clinician training with respect to the sexual dynamics of clinical relationships. As Pope et al. (1986, p. 156) emphasize, "Education regarding this topic can be an appropriate part of almost all clinical and professional coursework and training." From the point of view of this book the following recommendations are highly salient:

> . . . the phenomenon of therapist-client sexual intimacy must be clearly differentiated from the experience of sexual attraction to clients. The latter seems to suffer from guilt by association, and the general failure to discuss the experience openly does little to clarify the situation.
> . . . educational programs must provide a safe environment in which therapists in training can acknowledge, explore, and discuss feelings of sexual attraction. If students find or suspect that their teachers are critical and rejecting of such feelings and that such feelings are treated as the sign of an impaired or erring therapist, then effective education is unlikely. (Pope et al., 1986, p. 157)

This inhibition has been found to be especially severe for female clinicians (Woolley, 1988).

In addition to training in issues related specifically to sexual attraction to and intimacy with clients, the general training of clinicians in relevant areas needs to be strengthened. Gonsiorek (1989a) addresses the vital need to shore up the ethical underpinnings of clinician education:

> The meager amount of time and effort expended in training future professionals on ethical issues is a disgrace. Many professionals go through entire training programs without any formal training in ethics. Courses that do mention ethical issues tend to do so in abstract fashion, and fail to recognize the practical issues. . . . The solution is for each profession to develop a vigorous curriculum

for teaching professional ethics and to revise it as experience is accumulated and laws are changed. (p. 570)

Practical recommendations for rectifying this situation can be found in Vasquez (1988).

The most comprehensive antidote to misconduct resulting from naivete and unexamined behavior is for the clinician to be thoroughly grounded in the legal and ethical contexts of clinical decision making. Areas to be covered include recognition and management of clinical uncertainty, the impact of legal constraints on clinical care, the necessity for intelligent documentation and consultation, and liability prevention through sound clinical and ethical practice (i.e., doing what is best for the client's well-being) as opposed to adversarial "defensive medicine." Recommended basic sources in these areas, written by leading forensic psychiatrists but applicable to issues faced by clinicians at all levels of training, are Appelbaum and Gutheil (in press), Gutheil, Bursztajn, Brodsky, and Alexander (in press), and Simon (1987). As an example of how a broad clinico-legal perspective can cut through a threatening morass of sexual undercurrents, the following passage from Gutheil (1989a) is instructive:

> From a preventive viewpoint, the clinician encountering a transference that becomes eroticized would do well to begin regularly presenting the case to a colleague, supervisor, or appropriate consultant. In addition to providing valuable input and perspective, such consultation opens the case up and avoids the dangerous insularity of the treatment dyad that often promotes boundary violations. Not only does this approach prevent the illusion that the dyad is encased in a magic bubble from forming but—through this very openness—may also offer some possible defense against false accusations of sexual misconduct. (p. 601)

Peer support for clinicians. The value of reflection and close examination of one's experience does not cease with the acquisition of a degree. Here, just as in clinical training, continuing education is essential. It is helpful for clinicians to establish communications with others in their profession or field and create networks of mutual support. In these peer-group forums individuals can confront their sexual needs in relation to their motives for becoming helping professionals and their commitment to those who come to them for help.

Public-information programs and support groups. Education and peer support should not be limited to professionals. Noting that "public education on this issue has been seriously neglected," Gutheil (1989b) recommends

> a public health approach, including radio and television announcements by mental health professional societies indicating that sexual relations with a therapist are bad for the patient's emotional health and officially censured by professional peers. Efforts might also be made to emphasize that transference feelings themselves are normal and must be clinically and ethically distinguished from sexual activity within the therapeutic context. (p. 6)

Peer-support groups, as well as groups run by professionals, for individuals who have been sexually abused by therapists are an emerging forum for public education, consciousness-raising, and empowerment. An example is Boston Associates to Stop Therapy Abuse (BASTA!). A number of self-help and consumer groups, along with publications produced by them, are listed by Schoener (1989h). He recommends Jane Rasmussen's *Couched in Silence: An Advocacy Handbook on Sexual Exploitation in Therapy* (1987), distributed by Consumers Against Sexual Exploitation (CASE) in Milwaukee, as the best guidebook to date for survivors of abuse by therapists. Also recommended, and easy to obtain, are the consumer guides and brochures produced by states that have enacted legislation on the subject (Public Education Work Group [Minnesota], 1988; State of California, 1990; Wisconsin Coalition on Sexual Misconduct, 1986).

Documentation. It is the shared responsibility of individuals and institutions to see that abuses come to light. As discussed in Chapter 10, considerations of personal well-being, autonomy, and confidentiality render it inappropriate to make reporting a moral obligation for the victim. Nonetheless, when an individual chooses to report with full awareness of the implications and possible consequences of this act, the individual as well as other potential victims and society can all benefit.

Administrators should be concerned both to give the accused a fair hearing and to prevent the expedient coverups that enable perpetrators to victimize clients or co-workers in some other agency. The self-protective suppression of information characteristic of some bureaucratic organizations impedes both research and informed policy-making. Occasionally it leads to a scandal and a large damage claim because a rapacious or incompetent individual who could have been stopped sooner was allowed to continue to practice. It also erodes public confidence in the professions involved.

Research. Further research is needed both on the incidence of sexual contact between helping professionals and their clients and on its antitherapeutic effects. In 1981 Dr. William L. Maurice, co-director of the Sexual Medicine Unit in the department of psychiatry at Shaughnessy Hospital in Vancouver, told the annual meeting of the Canadian Psychiatric Association, "In particular, there is almost no information concerning the outcome of such experiences on either the doctor or the patient. Tradition strongly suggests that it is improper and unethical. That is not the same as saying that it is damaging. Nor is any light shed on those situations which may be more damaging than others" ("MD Condemns Sex With Patients," 1981).

Now, thanks to research reviewed in Chapter 5, we know more about such harmful consequences. But there is much more to be learned about the experience of clients involved in sexual dynamics with clinicians (and that of the clinicians as well) than is revealed by subsequent therapists' assessments of the damage done. We need to understand how clients have viewed these experiences: what they found inappropriate in a therapist's (or their own) behavior, what they acquiesced to and what they refused, and why and how they were able to refuse. We need more accurate indicators of incidence rates than voluntary self-reports made by clinicians. And we need more systematic and sensitive surveys of the attitudes of various professional and lay populations toward the myriad moral dilemmas posed by client-professional relationships.

Policy-making. Too few organizations have written policies specifying disciplinary action to be taken in cases involving sexual abuse of clients and sexual harassment of employees. The disposition of cases is thus left to organizational politics, administrative expediency, and the vagaries of mass publicity. Improved documentation and research will aid in the formulation of official guidelines making clear the rights and responsibilities of all concerned.

As sexual abuses in clinical relationships gain increased attention, these recommendations are beginning to be implemented. Constructive training and peer support are exemplified by a program in the Chicago area for women in the corrections field, which has used discussion groups and role modeling to familiarize women with working conditions in the prison system. In an intervention that combines documentation, research, and education, the American Psychiatric Association undertook a two-year review of malpractice cases leading to the publication of judicial case histories for the benefit of APA members.

The same approach, applied in a less formal way, can benefit anyone involved with the issue—that is, anyone who works with people. Get support, talk things over, create a dialogue, bring the issue out into the open. Don't run away from the problem (and from the client); work it out.

References

American Association for Marriage and Family Therapy. AAMFT code of ethical principles for marriage and family therapists. Washington, DC: Author, 1988.

American Association of Sex Educators, Counselors, and Therapists. Code of ethics. Washington, DC: Author, 1980.

American Psychiatric Association. The principles of medical ethics with annotations especially applicable to psychiatry. *American Journal of Psychiatry*, 1973, *130*, 1058–1064.

American Psychiatric Association. Principles of medical ethics with annotations especially applicable to psychiatry. Washington, DC: Author, 1989.

American Psychological Association. Ethical standards of psychologists. *APA Monitor*, March 1977, pp. 22–23.

American Psychological Association. Ethical principles of psychologists. *American Psychologist*, 1981, *36*, 633–638.

Anclote Manor Foundation v. Wilkinson, 263 S 2nd 256 (Fla. App. 1972).

Appelbaum, P.S. Statutes regulating patient-therapist sex. *Hospital and Community Psychiatry*, 1990, *41*, 15–16.

Appelbaum, P.S., & Gutheil, T.G. *Clinical Handbook of Psychiatry and the Law*. Second Edition. Baltimore: Williams & Wilkins, in press.

Bartkus v. Molde, Nev., Washoe County Circuit Court, No. CV88-1034, Aug. 24, 1989.

Bates, C., & Brodsky, A.M. *Sex in the Therapy Hour*. New York: Guilford Press, 1988.

Birkner v. Salt Lake County, 771 P.2d 1053 (Utah 1989).

Borys, D.S., & Pope, K.S. Dual relationships between therapist and client: A national study of psychologists, psychiatrists, and social workers. *Professional Psychology: Research and Practice*, 1989, *20*, 283–293.

Bouhoutsos, J., Holroyd, J.C., Lerman, H., Forer, B.R., & Greenberg, M. Sexual intimacy between psychotherapists and patients. *Professional Psychology: Research and Practice*, 1983, *14*, 185–196.

Breuer, J. Fraulein Anna O. In S. Freud & J. Breuer, *Studies on Hysteria* (J. Strachey with A. Freud, Ed. and trans.). New York: Avon, 1966, 55–82.

Brodsky, A.M. Sex role issues in the supervision of psychotherapy. In A.K. Hess (Ed.), *Psychotherapy Supervision: Theory, Research, and Practice*. New York: John Wiley, 1980, 509–522.

Burgess, A.W., & Hartman, C. (Eds.). *Sexual Exploitation of Patients by Health Professionals*. New York: Praeger, 1986.

Bursztajn, H.J. Supervisory responsibility for prevention of supervisee sexual misconduct. Presentation at International Congress of Psychiatry and the Law, Toronto, Ontario, June 1990.

Bursztajn, H.J., Feinbloom, R.I., Hamm, R.M., & Brodsky, A. *Medical Choices, Medical Chances: How Patients, Families, and Physicians Can Cope with Uncertainty.* New York: Routledge, 1990.

Bursztajn, H.J., & Illingworth, P.M.L. The critogenic harms of criminalizing patient-therapist sex. Unpublished manuscript.

Butler, S. Sexual contact between therapists and patients. Unpublished doctoral dissertation, California School of Professional Psychology (Los Angeles), 1975.

Chodoff, P. The seductive patient, *Medical Aspects of Human Sexuality*, 1968, 2(2), 52–55.

Choras, P.T. Presentation at clinical case conference: Issues surrounding the accountability of therapists who are sexually involved with patients. McLean Hospital, Belmont, Massachusetts, January 23, 1990.

Clements, C.D. The transference: what's love got to do with it. *Psychiatric Annals*, 1987, *17*, 556–563.

Coleman, P. Sex in power dependency relationships: taking unfair advantage of the "fair" sex. *Albany Law Review*, 1988, *53*, 95–141.

Conroe, R.M., & Schank, J.A. Sexual intimacy in clinical supervision: unmasking the silence. In G.R. Schoener, J.H. Milgrom, J.C. Gonsiorek, E.T. Luepker, & R.M. Conroe (Eds.), *Psychotherapists' Sexual Involvement With Clients: Intervention and Prevention*. Minneapolis: Walk-In Counseling Center, 1989, 245–262.

Conroe, R.M., Schank, J.A., Brown, M.L., De Marinis, V.M., Loeffler, D.R., & Sanderson, B.E. Prohibition of sexual contact between clinical supervisors and psychotherapy students: an overview and suggested guidelines. In B.E. Sanderson (Ed.), *It's Never OK: A Handbook for Professionals on Sexual Exploitation by Counselors and Therapists*. St. Paul, MN: Minnesota Department of Corrections, 1989, 125–131.

Conte, H.R., Plutchik, R., Picard, S., & Karasu, T.B. Ethics in the practice of psychotherapy: a survey. *American Journal of Psychotherapy*, 1989, *43*, 32–42.

Dahlberg, C.C. Sexual contact between patient and therapist. *Contemporary Psychoanalysis*, 1970, *6*, 107–124.

Dietz, J. Psychotherapists, patients and sex. *Boston Globe*, January 31, 1982, pp. A1; A4.

Doe v. Fanning, Mass., Middlesex County Superior Court, No. 86-2936, July 12, 1989.

Doe v. Roe, Wis., Milwaukee County Circuit Court, No. 753–823, Sept. 11, 1989.

Edelwich, J., with Brodsky, A. *Burnout: Stages of Disillusionment in the Helping Professions*. New York: Human Sciences Press, 1980.

Ellis, A., & Harper, R.A. *A New Guide to Rational Living*. N. Hollywood, Cal.: Wilshire, 1975.

Feldman-Summers, S., & Jones, G. Psychological impacts of sexual contact between therapists or other health care practitioners and their clients. *Journal of Consulting and Clinical Psychology*, 1984, *52*, 1054–1061.

Fortune, M.M. Betrayal of the pastoral relationship: sexual contact by pastors and pastoral counselors. In G.R. Schoener, J.H. Milgrom, J.C. Gonsiorek, E.T. Luepker, & R.M. Conroe (Eds.), *Psychotherapists' Sexual Involvement With Clients: Intervention and Prevention.* Minneapolis: Walk-In Counseling Center, 1989a, 81–91.

Fortune, M.M. *Is Nothing Sacred? When Sex Invades the Pastoral Relationship.* San Francisco: Harper & Row, 1989b.

Freeman, L., & Roy, J. *Betrayal.* New York: Stein and Day, 1976.

Freud, S. Dora: *An Analysis of a Case of Hysteria.* New York: Macmillan, 1963.

Gabbard, G. (Ed.). *Sexual Exploitation in Professional Relationships.* Washington, DC: American Psychiatric Press, 1989.

Gartrell, N., Herman, J., Olarte, S., Feldstein, M., & Localio, R. Psychiatrist-patient sexual contact: results of a national survey, I: Prevalence. *American Journal of Psychiatry*, 1986, *143*, 1126–1131.

Gartrell, N., Herman, J., Olarte, S., Feldstein, M., & Localio, R. Reporting practices of psychiatrists who knew of sexual misconduct by colleagues. *American Journal of Orthopsychiatry*, 1987, *57*, 287–295.

Gartrell, N., Herman, J., Olarte, S., Localio, R., & Feldstein, M. Psychiatric residents' sexual contact with educators and patients: results of a national survey. *American Journal of Psychiatry*, 1988, *145*, 690–694.

Gechtman, L. Sexual contact between social workers and their clients. In G. Gabbard (Ed.), *Sexual Exploitation in Professional Relationships.* Washington, DC: American Psychiatric Press, 1989, 27–38.

Gechtman, L., & Bouhoutsos, J. Sexual intimacy between social workers and clients. Paper presented at the annual meeting of the Society for Clinical Social Workers, Universal City, California, October 1985.

Glaser, R.D., & Thorpe, J.S. Unethical intimacy: a survey of sexual contact and advances between psychology educators and female graduate students. *American Psychologist*, 1986, *41*, 43–51.

Glasser, W. *Reality Therapy.* New York: Harper & Row, 1965.

Glasser, W. *Positive Addiction.* New York: Harper & Row, 1976.

Gonsiorek, J.C. Responding to sexual exploitation of clients by therapists: future directions. In G.R. Schoener, J.H. Milgrom, J.C. Gonsiorek, E.T. Luepker, & R.M. Conroe (Eds.), *Psychotherapists' Sexual Involvement With Clients: Intervention and Prevention.* Minneapolis: Walk-In Counseling Center, 1989a, 567–573.

Gonsiorek, J.C. Sexual exploitation by psychotherapists: some observations on male victims and sexual orientation issues. In G.R. Schoener, J.H. Milgrom, J.C. Gonsiorek, E.T. Luepker, & R.M. Conroe (Eds.), *Psychotherapists' Sexual Involvement With Clients: Intervention and Prevention.* Minneapolis: Walk-In Counseling Center, 1989b, 113–119.

Gonsiorek, J.C. Working therapeutically with therapists who have become sexually involved with clients. In B.E. Sanderson (Ed.), *It's Never OK: A Handbook for Professionals on Sexual Exploitation by Counselors and Therapists.* St. Paul, MN: Minnesota Department of Corrections, 1989c, 81–90.

Gonsiorek, J.C., & Brown, L.S. Post therapy sexual relationships with clients. In G.R. Schoener, J.H. Milgrom, J.C. Gonsiorek, E.T. Luepker, & R.M. Conroe (Eds.),

Psychotherapists' Sexual Involvement With Clients: Intervention and Prevention. Minneapolis: Walk-In Counseling Center, 1989, 289–301.

Gutheil, T.G. Borderline personality disorder, boundary violations, and patient-therapist sex: medicolegal pitfalls. *American Journal of Psychiatry,* 1989a, *146,* 597–602.

Gutheil, T.G. Patient-therapist sexual relations. *Harvard Medical School Mental Health Letter,* 1989b, *6*(3), 4–6.

Gutheil, T.G. Scientific program: Legal and ethical aspects of therapist-patient relationships (panel). Boston Psychoanalytic Institute, Boston, Massachusetts, September 27, 1989c.

Gutheil, T.G. Presentation at clinical case conference: Issues surrounding the accountability of therapists who are sexually involved with patients. McLean Hospital, Belmont, Massachusetts, January 23, 1990.

Gutheil, T.G., Bursztajn, H.J., Brodsky, A., & Alexander, V.G. (Eds.). *Decision Making in Psychiatry and Law: Clinical and Legal Aspects.* Baltimore: Williams & Wilkins, in press.

Halleck, S.L. *Law in the Practice of Psychiatry: A Handbook for Clinicians.* New York: Plenum, 1980.

Herman, J.L., Gartrell, N., Olarte, S., Feldstein, M., & Localio, R. Psychiatrist-patient sexual contact: results of a national survey, II: Psychiatrists' attitudes. *American Journal of Psychiatry,* 1987, *144,* 164–169.

Hollender, M.H., & Shevitz, S. The seductive patient. *Southern Medical Journal,* 1978, *71,* 776–778.

Holroyd, J.C., & Bouhoutsos, J. Sources of bias in reporting effects of sexual contact with patients. *Psychotherapy: Research and Practice,* 1985, *16,* 701–709.

Holroyd, J.C., & Brodsky, A.M. Psychologists' attitudes and practices regarding erotic and nonerotic physical contact with patients. *American Psychologist,* 1977, *32,* 843–849.

Illingworth, P.M.L. The friendship model of physician/patient relationship and patient autonomy. *Bioethics,* 1988, *2,* 22–36.

Illingworth, P.M.L. Scientific program: Legal and ethical aspects of therapist-patient relationships (panel). Boston Psychoanalytic Institute, Boston, Massachusetts, September 27, 1989.

Jacobsen v. Muller, 352 S.E.2d 604 (Ga. Ct. of App., Dec. 5, 1986; rehearing denied, Dec. 19, 1986; cert. denied, Ga. Sup. Ct., Jan. 15, 1987).

Jones, E. *Sigmund Freud: Life and Work* (Vol. 1). New York: Basic Books, 1953.

Jordan, J.V. Presentation at clinical case conference: Issues surrounding the accountability of therapists who are sexually involved with patients. McLean Hospital, Belmont, Massachusetts, January 23, 1990.

Jordan, J.V., Kaplan, A., Miller, J.B., Stiver, I., & Surrey, J. More comments on patient-therapist sex (letter). *American Journal of Psychiatry,* 1990, *147,* 129–130.

Jorgenson, L.M. New developments in professional liability insurance for clinician-patient sexual misconduct: Individual, supervisor, and institutional liability. Presentation at conference: Sex Between Clinicians and Patients: Clinical, Ethical, and Medico-Legal Perspectives (Harvard Medical School, Massachusetts Mental Health Center), Waltham, Massachusetts, September 15, 1990.

Jorgenson, L. M., Randles, R., & Strasburger, L. H. The furor over patient-psychotherapist sexual contact: a survey of the law. *William and Mary Law Review*, 1991, *32*, in press.

Karasu, T. B. The ethics of psychotherapy. *American Journal of Psychiatry*, 1980, *137*, 1502–1512.

Kardener, S. H. Sex and the physician-patient relationship. *American Journal of Psychiatry*, 1974, *131*, 1134–1136.

Kardener, S. H., Fuller, M., & Mensh, I. N. A survey of physicians' attitudes and practices regarding erotic and nonerotic contact with patients. *American Journal of Psychiatry*, 1973, *130*, 1077–1081.

Kardener, S. H., Fuller, M., & Mensh, I. N. Characteristics of "erotic" practitioners. *American Journal of Psychiatry*, 1976, *133*, 1324–1325.

Kaslow, F. Some emergent forms of non traditional sexual combinations: a clinical view. *Interaction*, 1980, *3*. 1–9.

Keiser v. Berry, Cir. Ct. 78-8182 (Fla. 1979).

Kitchener, K. S. Dual role relationships: what makes them so problematic? *Journal of Counseling and Development*, 1988, *67*, 217–221.

Kuchan, A. Survey of incidence of psychotherapists' sexual contact with clients in Wisconsin. In G. R. Schoener, J. H. Milgrom, J. C. Gonsiorek, E. T. Luepker, & R. M. Conroe (Eds.), *Psychotherapists' Sexual Involvement With Clients: Intervention and Prevention*. Minneapolis: Walk-In Counseling Center, 1989, 51–64.

Landau v. Werner, 105 Sol. J. 257 [A.B. 1961], aff'd 105 Sol. J. 1008 [C.A. 1961].

Levenson, J. L. Psychiatrist-patient sexual contact (letter). *American Journal of Psychiatry*, 1987, *144*, 529–530.

Luepker, E. T. Sexual exploitation of clients by therapists: parallels with parent-child incest. In G. R. Schoener, J. H. Milgrom, J. C. Gonsiorek, E. T. Luepker, & R. M. Conroe (Eds.), *Psychotherapists' Sexual Involvement With Clients: Intervention and Prevention*. Minneapolis: Walk-In Counseling Center, 1989, 73–79.

Malcolm, J. The impossible profession (Part 1). *New Yorker.* November 24, 1980a, pp. 55–133.

Malcolm, J. The impossible profession (Part 2). *New Yorker.* December 1, 1980b, pp. 54–152.

Maltsberger, J. T., & Buie, D. H. Countertransference hate in the treatment of suicidal patients. *Archives of General Psychiatry*, 1974, *30*, 625–633.

Marmor, J. Sexual acting-out in psychotherapy. *American Journal of Psychoanalysis*, 1972, *32*, 3–8.

Marmor, J. Some psychodynamic aspects of the seduction of patients in psychotherapy. *American Journal of Psychoanalysis*, 1976, *36*, 319–323.

Maslow, A. H. *Motivation and Personality.* New York: Harper, 1954.

Mason, P. E. Malpractice of psychotherapists; the transference phenomenon. Unpublished manuscript, University of Maine School of Law, 1976.

Mason, P. E., & Stitham, M. D. The expensive dalliance: assessing the cost of patient-therapist sex. *Bulletin of the American Academy of Psychiatry and the Law*, 1977, *5*, 450–455.

Masters, W. H., & Johnson, V. E. *Human Sexual Inadequacy.* Boston: Little, Brown, 1970.

Masters, W.H., & Johnson, V.E. Principles of the new sex therapy. *American Journal of Psychiatry*, 1976, *133*, 548–554.

MD condemns sex with patients, urges widespread education. *Psychiatric News*. November 6, 1981, pp. 30; 34.

Milgrom, J.H. Secondary victims of sexual exploitation by counselors and therapists: some observations. In G.R. Schoener, J.H. Milgrom, J.C. Gonsiorek, E.T. Luepker, & R.M. Conroe (Eds.), *Psychotherapists' Sexual Involvement With Clients: Intervention and Prevention*. Minneapolis: Walk-In Counseling Center, 1989, 235–240.

Minnesota Interfaith Committee on Sexual Exploitation by Clergy. *Sexual Exploitation by Clergy: Reflections and Guidelines for Religious Leaders*. Minneapolis, MN: Author, 1989.

Mogul, K.M. Therapist-patient sexual involvement (letter). *American Journal of Psychiatry*, 1989, *146*, 1356.

Mohl, B. Mass. doctors raise funds to challenge license panel. *Boston Globe*, August 14, 1989, pp. 1, 6–7.

Morra v. State Board of Examiners of Psychologists, 212 Kan. 103, 510 P. 2d 614 (1973).

National Association of Social Workers. *NASW Policy Statements: Code of Ethics*. Washington, DC: Author, 1980.

Nelson, B. Efforts widen to curb sexual abuse in therapy. *New York Times*, November 23, 1982, pp. C1, C3.

Nielsen, L.A., Peterson, M.R., Shapiro, M.G., & Thompson, P. Supervision approaches in cases of boundary violations and sexual victimization by therapists. In B.E. Sanderson (Ed.), *It's Never OK: A Handbook for Professionals on Sexual Exploitation by Counselors and Therapists*. St. Paul, MN: Minnesota Department of Corrections, 1989, 55–68.

Noto v. St. Vincent's Hosp. & Med. Ctr., 537 N.Y.S.2d 446 (1988).

Peele, S. *Diseasing of America: Addiction Treatment Out of Control*. Lexington, MA: Lexington Books, 1989.

Peele, S., with Brodsky, A. *Love and Addiction*. New York: New American Library, 1976.

Perry, J.A. Physicians' erotic and nonerotic physical involvement with patients. *American Journal of Psychiatry*, 1976, *133*, 838–840.

Plasil, E. *Therapist*. New York: St. Martin's Press, 1985.

Pope, K.S. How clients are harmed by sexual contact with mental health professionals: the syndrome and its prevalence. *Journal of Counseling and Development*, 1988, *67*, 222–226.

Pope, K.S., & Bouhoutsos, J. *Sexual Intimacy Between Therapists and Patients*. New York: Praeger, 1986.

Pope, K.S., Keith-Spiegel, P., & Tabachnick, B.G. Sexual attraction to clients: the human therapist and the (sometimes) inhuman training system. *American Psychologist*, 1986, *41*, 147–158.

Pope, K.S., Levenson, H., & Schover. L.R. Sexual intimacy in psychology training: results and implications of a national survey. *American Psychologist*, 1979, *34*, 682–689.

Pope, K.S., Schover, L.R., & Levenson, H. Sexual behavior between clinical supervisors and trainees: implications for professional standards. *Professional Psychology,* 1980, *11,* 157–162.

Pope, K.S., Tabachnick, B.G., & Keith-Spiegel, P. Ethics of practice: the beliefs and behaviors of psychologists as therapists. *American Psychologist,* 1987, *42,* 993–1006.

Public Education Work Group. *It's Never O.K.: A Handbook for Victims and Victim Advocates on Sexual Exploitation by Counselors and Therapists.* St. Paul, MN: Minnesota Department of Corrections, 1988.

Rasmussen, J. *Couched in Silence: An Advocacy Handbook on Sexual Exploitation in Therapy.* Milwaukee, WI: Author, 1987.

Rice-Smith, E. Sex in G-d's name: Violations in traditional and new age religious practices. Presentation at conference: Sex Between Clinicians and Patients: Clinical, Ethical, and Medico-Legal Perspectives (Harvard Medical School, Massachusetts Mental Health Center), Waltham, Massachusetts, September 15, 1990.

Rice-Smith, E. *Holy Seductions: Unspoken Taboos of Sexual Desire, Attachment, and Abuse in American Religious Life.* Book in preparation.

Rieker, P.P., & Carmen, E.H. Teaching value clarification: the example of gender and psychotherapy. *American Journal of Psychiatry,* 1983, *140,* 410–415.

Rigby-Weinberg, D.N. Sexual involvement of women therapists with their women clients. Paper presented at the eleventh national conference of the Association for Women in Psychology, 1986.

Roy v. Hartogs, 366 N.Y.S. 2d 297, 81 Misc. 2d 350 (1975).

Rutter, P. *Sex in the Forbidden Zone: When Men in Power—Therapists, Doctors, Clergy, Teachers, and Others—Betray Women's Trust.* New York: Jeremy P. Tarcher, 1989.

St. Paul Fire & Marine Insurance Co. v. Love, 447 N.W.2d 5 (Minn. Ct. App. 1989).

Sanderson, B.E. (Ed.). *It's Never OK: A Handbook for Professionals on Sexual Exploitation by Counselors and Therapists.* St. Paul, MN: Minnesota Department of Corrections, 1989a.

Sanderson, B.E. Employer liability for sexual exploitation of clients. In B.E. Sanderson (Ed.), *It's Never OK: A Handbook for Professionals on Sexual Exploitation by Counselors and Therapists.* St. Paul, MN: Minnesota Department of Corrections, 1989b, 147–152.

Sanderson, B.E. Similarities between counselor/client sexual contact and professor/student sexual contact in counselor training programs. In B.E. Sanderson (Ed.), *It's Never OK: A Handbook for Professionals on Sexual Exploitation by Counselors and Therapists.* St. Paul, MN: Minnesota Department of Corrections, 1989c, 115–123.

Scheflen, A.E. Quasi-courtship behavior in psychotherapy. *Psychiatry,* 1965, *28,* 245–257.

Schoener, G.R. Administrative safeguards. In G.R. Schoener, J.H. Milgrom, J.C. Gonsiorek, E.T. Luepker, & R.M. Conroe (Eds.), *Psychotherapists' Sexual Involvement With Clients: Intervention and Prevention.* Minneapolis: Walk-In Counseling Center, 1989a, 453–467.

Schoener, G.R. The assessment of damages. In G.R. Schoener, J.H. Milgrom, J.C. Gonsiorek, E.T. Luepker, & R.M. Conroe (Eds.), *Psychotherapists' Sexual Involvement*

With Clients: Intervention and Prevention. Minneapolis: Walk-In Counseling Center, 1989b, 133–145.

Schoener, G.R. The child or adolescent victim. In G.R. Schoener, J.H. Milgrom, J.C. Gonsiorek, E.T. Luepker, & R.M. Conroe (Eds.), *Psychotherapists' Sexual Involvement With Clients: Intervention and Prevention*. Minneapolis: Walk-In Counseling Center, 1989c, 121–131.

Schoener, G.R. Filing complaints against therapists who sexually exploit clients. In G.R. Schoener, J.H. Milgrom, J.C. Gonsiorek, E.T. Luepker, & R.M. Conroe (Eds.), *Psychotherapists' Sexual Involvement With Clients: Intervention and Prevention*. Minneapolis: Walk-In Counseling Center, 1989d, 313–343.

Schoener, G.R. A look at the literature. In G.R. Schoener, J.H. Milgrom, J.C. Gonsiorek, E.T. Luepker, & R.M. Conroe (Eds.), *Psychotherapists' Sexual Involvement With Clients: Intervention and Prevention*. Minneapolis: Walk-In Counseling Center, 1989e, 11–50.

Schoener, G.R. The new laws. In G.R. Schoener, J.H. Milgrom, J.C. Gonsiorek, E.T. Luepker, & R.M. Conroe (Eds.), *Psychotherapists' Sexual Involvement With Clients: Intervention and Prevention*. Minneapolis: Walk-In Counseling Center, 1989f, 537–565.

Schoener, G.R. The role of supervision and case consultation: some notes on sexual feelings in therapy. In G.R. Schoener, J.H. Milgrom, J.C. Gonsiorek, E.T. Luepker, & R.M. Conroe (Eds.), *Psychotherapists' Sexual Involvement With Clients: Intervention and Prevention*. Minneapolis: Walk-In Counseling Center, 1989g, 495–502.

Schoener, G.R. Self-help and consumer groups. In G.R. Schoener, J.H. Milgrom, J.C. Gonsiorek, E.T. Luepker, & R.M. Conroe (Eds.), *Psychotherapists' Sexual Involvement With Clients: Intervention and Prevention*. Minneapolis: Walk-In Counseling Center, 1989h, 375–398.

Schoener, G.R. Sexual involvement of therapists with clients after therapy ends: some observations. In G.R. Schoener, J.H. Milgrom, J.C. Gonsiorek, E.T. Luepker, & R.M. Conroe (Eds.), *Psychotherapists' Sexual Involvement With Clients: Intervention and Prevention*. Minneapolis: Walk-In Counseling Center, 1989i, 265–287.

Schoener, G.R., & Conroe, R.M. The role of supervision and case consultation in primary prevention. In G.R. Schoener, J.H. Milgrom, J.C. Gonsiorek, E.T. Luepker, & R.M. Conroe (Eds.), *Psychotherapists' Sexual Involvement With Clients: Intervention and Prevention*. Minneapolis: Walk-In Counseling Center, 1989, 477–493.

Schoener, G.R., & Gonsiorek, J.C. Assessment and development of rehabilitation plans for the therapist. In G.R. Schoener, J.H. Milgrom, J.C. Gonsiorek, E.T. Luepker, & R.M. Conroe (Eds.), *Psychotherapists' Sexual Involvement With Clients: Intervention and Prevention*. Minneapolis: Walk-In Counseling Center, 1989, 401–420.

Schoener, G.R., & Milgrom, J.H. False or misleading complaints. In G.R. Schoener, J.H. Milgrom, J.C. Gonsiorek, E.T. Luepker, & R.M. Conroe (Eds.), *Psychotherapists' Sexual Involvement With Clients: Intervention and Prevention*. Minneapolis: Walk-In Counseling Center, 1989a, 147–155.

Schoener, G.R., & Milgrom, J.H. Psychotherapy cults. In G.R. Schoener, J.H. Milgrom, J.C. Gonsiorek, E.T. Luepker, & R.M. Conroe (Eds.), *Psychotherapists'*

Sexual Involvement With Clients: Intervention and Prevention. Minneapolis: Walk-In Counseling Center, 1989b, 217–223.

Schoener, G.R., & Milgrom, J.H. Sexual exploitation by clergy and pastoral counselors. In G.R. Schoener, J.H. Milgrom, J.C. Gonsiorek, E.T. Luepker, & R.M. Conroe (Eds.), *Psychotherapists' Sexual Involvement With Clients: Intervention and Prevention.* Minneapolis: Walk-In Counseling Center, 1989c, 225–234.

Schoener, G.R., Milgrom, J.H., Gonsiorek, J.C., Luepker, E.T., & Conroe, R.M. (Eds.). *Psychotherapists' Sexual Involvement With Clients: Intervention and Prevention.* Minneapolis: Walk-In Counseling Center, 1989.

Seligman, M.E.P. *Helplessness: On Depression, Development, and Death.* San Francisco: W.H. Freeman, 1975.

Sell, J.M., Gottlieb, M.C., & Schoenfeld, L. Ethical considerations of social/romantic relationships with present and former clients. *Professional Psychology: Research and Practice.* 1986, *17*, 504–508.

Shamloo v. Lifespring, Inc., 713 F. Supp. 14 (D.D.C. 1989).

Shapiro, C.H. Creative supervision: an underutilized antidote. In W.S. Paine (Ed.), *Job Stress and Burnout: Research, Theory, and Intervention.* Beverly Hills, Cal.: Sage, 1982.

Shepard, M. *The Love Treatment: Sexual Intimacy Between Patients and Psychotherapists.* New York: Peter H. Wyden, 1971.

Shepard, M., & Lee, M. *Games Analysts Play.* New York: G.P. Putnam's Sons, 1970.

Shochet, B.R., Levin, L., Lowen, M., & Lisansky, E.T. Roundtable: dealing with the seductive patient. *Medical Aspects of Human Sexuality,* 1976, *10*(12), 90–104.

Silverstein, L.M. *Consider the Alternative.* Minneapolis: CompCare Publications, 1977.

Simon, R.I. *Clinical Psychiatry and the Law.* Washington, D.C.: American Psychiatric Press, 1987.

Simon, S.B., Howe, L.W., & Kirschenbaum, H. *Values Clarification.* New York: Hart, 1972.

Sinnett, E.R., & Thetford, P.E. Protecting clients and assessing malpractice. *Professional Psychology,* 1975, *6*, 117–128.

Smith, J.T., & Bisbing, S.B. *Sexual Exploitation by Health Care and Other Professionals.* Second Edition. Potomac, MD: Legal Medicine Press, 1988.

State of California, Department of Consumer Affairs. *Professional Therapy Never Includes Sex!* Sacramento: Medical Board of California, 1990.

Stefanson, A.D. Countertransference issues for therapists working with sexually exploitative therapists. In B.E. Sanderson (Ed.), *It's Never OK: A Handbook for Professionals on Sexual Exploitation by Counselors and Therapists.* St. Paul, MN: Minnesota Department of Corrections, 1989, 91–93.

Stone, A.A. *Mental Health and Law: A System in Transition.* New York: Jason Aronson, 1976.

Stone, A.A. Sexual misconduct by psychiatrists: the ethical and clinical dilemma of confidentiality. *American Journal of Psychiatry,* 1983, *140*, 195–197.

Stone, A.A. Scientific program: Legal and ethical aspects of therapist-patient relationships (panel). Boston Psychoanalytic Institute, Boston, Massachusetts, September 27, 1989.

Strasburger, L. H. Criminalization of sexual abuse in therapy. Presentation at McLean Hospital, Belmont, Massachusetts, January 16, 1990.

Strasburger, L.H., & Jorgenson, L.M. Criminalization of psychotherapist-patient sex: pros and cons. Unpublished manuscript.

Strasburger, L.H., Jorgenson, L.M., & Randles R. Mandatory reporting of sexually exploitative psychotherapists. *Bulletin of the American Academy of Psychiatry and the Law*, 1990, *18*, in press.

Taylor, B.J., & Wagner, N.N. Sex between therapists and clients: a review and analysis. *Professional Psychology*, 1976, *7*, 593–601.

Thompson, P., Benoist, I.R., Percy, W.H., & Stefanson, A.D. Therapeutic approaches for clients who have been sexually abused by therapists. In B.E. Sanderson (Ed.), *It's Never OK: A Handbook for Professionals on Sexual Exploitation by Counselors and Therapists*. St. Paul, MN: Minnesota Department of Corrections, 1989, 45–52.

Thompson, T.L. Bias and conflict of interest alleged in handling of malpractice suit. *Psychiatric Times*, October 1989, pp. 1, 26.

Torry, S. Divorce-malpractice suit won by heiress: judgment against psychologist is $1 million. *Washington Post*, October 22, 1989, pp. B1, B9.

Vasquez, M.J.T. Counselor-client sexual contact: implications for ethics training. *Journal of Counseling and Development*, 1988, *67*, 238–241.

Walker, E., & Young, T.D. *A Killing Cure*. New York: Henry Holt, 1986.

White, W.L. *Incest in the Organizational Family: The Unspoken Issue in Staff and Program Burnout*. Rockville, MD: HCS, Inc., 1986.

Wilkinson, A.P. Psychiatric malpractice. *American Journal of Forensic Psychiatry*, 1981/82, *2*(3), 3–8.

Winnicott, D.W. Countertransference. *British Journal of Medical Psychology*, 1960, *33*, 17–21.

Wisconsin Coalition on Sexual Misconduct. *Making Therapy Work For You*. Madison, WI: Author, 1986.

Wolf, S. Counseling—for better or worse. *Alcohol Health and Research World*, Winter 1974–75, pp. 27–29.

Woodward, K.L., & King, P. When a pastor turns seducer: churches confront sexual predators. *Newsweek*, August 28, 1989, pp. 48–49.

Woolley, S.T. Transference, countertransference, erotic issues, and the female therapist. Unpublished Ed.D. thesis, Harvard University, School of Education, Dept. of Counseling and Consulting Psychology, 1988.

Index

About the Authors

JERRY EDELWICH, M.S.W., C.I.S.W., is Assistant Professor of Drug and Alcohol Rehabilitation Counseling at Manchester Community College, Manchester, Connecticut. He pioneered both in studying the formerly taboo area of client-clinician sexual dynamics and in developing practical guidelines for clinician training in this area. Edelwich is Director of the New England Association of Reality Therapy, which conducts training on a regional, national, and international scale. Together with Archie Brodsky, he has co-authored *Burnout: Stages of Disillusionment in the Helping Professions* (1980), *High on Life: A Story of Addiction and Recovery* (1981), *Diabetes: Caring For Your Emotions As Well As Your Health* (1986), and *Group Counseling for the Resistant Client* (1991).

Edelwich, who received his M.S.W. degree from the University of Connecticut, has served as a clinical supervisor or consultant for the U.S. Navy, the Connecticut Department of Corrections and Department of Children's and Youth Services, the Connecticut Superior Court, skilled-nursing facilities, and state and regional training agencies. He travels extensively throughout the United States, Canada, and Europe conducting workshops and training sessions in individual and group counseling skills, staff burnout, human sexuality, professional ethics, and drug and alcohol rehabilitation. He has presented introductory and advanced workshops on clinical supervision for the National Association of Alcoholism and Drug Abuse Counselors (NAADAC).

ARCHIE BRODSKY, a professional writer, is senior research associate at the Program in Psychiatry and the Law, Massachusetts Mental

Health Center, Harvard Medical School. In addition to the books he has written with Jerry Edelwich, he is co-author of *Love and Addiction* (1975), *Medical Choices, Medical Chances* (1981, 1990), *If This Is Love, Why Do I Feel So Insecure?* (1989), and *The Truth About Addiction and Recovery* (1991). He has also co-authored articles in such journals as *Psychology Today, The New England Journal of Medicine, American Journal of Psychiatry, Psychiatric Quarterly, Addictions, Alcoholism Treatment Quarterly,* and *Medical Decision Making.*